YO-EHY-521

Mexican Screen Fiction

To Mexican friends

PN
1993·5
·M4
S65
2014

95538

Mexican Screen Fiction

Between Cinema
and Television

Paul Julian Smith

CONCORDIA COLLEGE LIBRARY
BRONXVILLE, NY 10708

polity

Copyright © Paul Julian Smith 2014

The right of Paul Julian Smith to be identified as Author of this Work has been asserted in accordance with the UK Copyright, Designs and Patents Act 1988.

First published in 2014 by Polity Press

Polity Press
65 Bridge Street
Cambridge CB2 1UR, UK

Polity Press
350 Main Street
Malden, MA 02148, USA

All rights reserved. Except for the quotation of short passages for the purpose of criticism and review, no part of this publication may be reproduced, stored in a retrieval system, or transmitted, in any form or by any means, electronic, mechanical, photocopying, recording or otherwise, without the prior permission of the publisher.

ISBN-13: 978-0-7456-8078-1
ISBN-13: 978-0-7456-8079-8(pb)

A catalogue record for this book is available from the British Library.

Typeset in 10.5 on 12 pt Sabon
by Toppan Best-set Premedia Limited
Printed and bound in Great Britain by Clays Ltd, St Ives

The publisher has used its best endeavours to ensure that the URLs for external websites referred to in this book are correct and active at the time of going to press. However, the publisher has no responsibility for the websites and can make no guarantee that a site will remain live or that the content is or will remain appropriate.

Every effort has been made to trace all copyright holders, but if any have been inadvertently overlooked the publisher will be pleased to include any necessary credits in any subsequent reprint or edition.

For further information on Polity, visit our website: www.politybooks.com

Contents

Figures

Preface

I would like to thank, above all, the five audiovisual professionals who kindly and generously responded to my questions and whose answers are reproduced as an Appendix to this book: Jesús Mario Lozano, Daniela Michel, Alejandro Ramírez, Roberto Fiesco and Leticia López Margalli. Their contribution is invaluable.

Thanks are also due to my editors at *Film Quarterly* (Rob White) and *Sight & Sound* (Nick James, James Bell and Kieron Corless); to Raúl Miranda López and his staff at the Cineteca library; and to John Thompson at Polity for his kindness and impressive efficiency. Much of the material included here has been presented at conferences and lectures in Mexico, the US and Europe, and I am grateful for audience responses there, especially at 'Mexican Itineraries' organized by Oswaldo Zavala at the Graduate Center in 2012.

Julia Tuñón and Guillermo Orozco have been great inspirations in film and TV studies, respectively. Patricia Torres' work on cinema reception has also proved invaluable. My students and colleagues at CUNY Graduate Center, especially in the Hispanic and Luso-Brazilian Program (José del Valle, Isaías Lerner and Lía Schwartz) have created the precious and productive environment within which this book was so happily written.

All of the 'Jump Cut' texts were first published in *Sight & Sound*, with the exception of the last, which was first published in *Film Quarterly*. Part of chapter 1 was published in Spanish as 'Revisiones del cine mexicano', *Casa del Tiempo* [Mexico], 29 (March 2010), 46–9; and parts of chapter 2 in *Film Quarterly* and as 'Report on

Guadalajara: art and industry', *Studies in Hispanic Cinemas* 8.1 (2011), 101–108.

This book is dedicated with affection and respect to the Mexican friends who have opened up a new world to me over the last ten years.

New York City, November 2012

Introduction:
Mexican Screen Fiction

This book is the first to examine audiovisual fiction in Mexico since 2000, examining film and television together. Most of the material it treats remains very recent and has thus not yet received critical attention.

As is well known, cinema in Mexico was revived at the start of the millennium with the critical and popular successes, at home and abroad, of *Amores perros* (Alejandro González Iñárritu, 2000) and *Y tu mamá también* (Alfonso Cuarón, 2002). Since that date production has increased to a healthy seventy features a year and Mexico's films now encompass a wider range than any comparable country: from austere art films, generally shown at international festivals and little seen in Mexico itself, to popular genre movies, localist in theme and audience, via the works of transnational auteurs such as Alfonso Cuarón, Alejandro González Iñárritu and Guillermo del Toro. It is striking that as I write these words (May 2012) the three films chosen for the Best Mexican Feature competition at the Ariel Awards 2011 are remarkably diverse: art movie *Miss Bala* (Gerardo Naranjo) (which I treat at some length in this book), riotous comedy *Nativity Play* (*Pastorela*, Emilio Portes) and a mid-market network narrative highly reminiscent of González Iñárritu, *Days of Grace* (*Días de gracia*, Everardo Valerio Gout).

Meanwhile television, although still largely subjected to the exhibition duopoly of Televisa and Azteca, has nonetheless broadened its offer, going beyond traditional telenovelas to produce for the first time higher value series and mini-series, especially in the criminal and historical genres, and staking a claim to being the most vibrant, as well as the most pervasive, national narrative. While film-makers complain that, unlike in Spain, there is no Cinema Law obliging TV companies to cross-subsidize feature films, there has in fact been a convergence between the two media in the industrial, aesthetic and thematic fields, and one that has generally gone unnoticed. It remains the case, however, that the worlds of cinema and television (both for practitioners and academics) remain separate. My intention, which may well prove polemical, is thus to bring them together, calling attention to their commonalities.

Paying close attention to the text of these rich screen fictions (for the first time in the case of television, whose researchers, in Mexico as elsewhere, rarely focus on content), this book draws on multiple sources. These include media theory, recent Mexican scholarship on cinema and TV audiences (especially the pioneering work of Patricia Torres San Martín and Guillermo Orozco Gómez), internet fan forums, and the trade and general presses. Scholarly debates in Mexico on violence by scholars such as Rossana Reguillo are also addressed in detail. In addition to this academic focus, the book provides some of my own journalistic reportage from the Mexican media scene. It also pays proper attention to the film critics of the Mexican newspapers and magazines, who often give the most incisive and far-sighted commentary on their country's cinema: Carlos Bonfil (above all), Leonardo García Tsao, Fernanda Solórzano and (also a distinguished historical researcher) Jorge Ayala Blanco.

The book begins by charting the audiovisual territory. The first chapter argues for a revision of contemporary Mexican cinema in the light of a new relation to the visual heritage of the 'Golden Age' of the 1940s, new attention to gender and the role of women, and a re-reading of the 'national' in national cinema. It also examines three features by young directors which blur the barrier between art cinema and popular film. The second chapter gives an account of the two most important festivals in Mexico (the very different Morelia and Guadalajara) in the years 2009 and 2011. Festivals are now the most important venues for the screening of many local films, which often fail to make it to theatres at home. My chapter offers a panorama of recent cinema and gives an industrial account of conditions of production, distribution and exhibition for the new decade, including the fraught relationship with television.

The second pair of chapters (chapters 3 and 4) is more textualist and compares and contrasts single films by two very different auteurs. Julián Hernández is an openly gay art director who now has three small budget features to his credit, films which have received wide festival acclaim. Funded, surprisingly perhaps, by the cultural institu-

tions of the Mexican government, Hernández appeals to the transnational register of European art cinema even as he engages with
highly local elements of *mise-en-scène* and narration. Here I examine
his first, distinctive feature, *A Thousand Clouds of Peace* (*Mil nubes
de paz*, 2003). Guillermo del Toro, on the other hand, is of course a
celebrated transnational film-maker who has worked widely in
Mexico, Europe and the US. Chapter 4 examines *Pan's Labyrinth* (*El
laberinto del fauno*, 2006), a film shot in Spain (arguing that it is a
Mexican who has made the most original contribution to the cinema
of the Spanish Civil War) and which, in spite of its wager on cultural
distinction, relies on a horror genre that has a distinct history in both
countries.

The third pair of chapters (chapters 5 and 6) makes the transition
to television via genre once more and the (still) marginal subjects of
the young and women. In the first, *Rebel* (*Rebelde*, Televisa, 2004–6),
a notoriously successful teen telenovela, is contrasted with *I'm Gonna
Explode* (*Voy a explotar*, Gerardo Naranjo, 2008), an accomplished
art movie also with adolescent protagonists. I argue that the feature
film coincides thematically and even formally with the TV series, even
as it seeks to distance itself from the critically reviled medium of
television. Chapter 6 in this pair deals with two innovative TV shows
on the rare theme of female killers. In *Women Murderers* (*Mujeres
asesinas*, Televisa, 2008–10), the dominant broadcaster adapted an
Argentine police format of one-off dramas to a Mexican setting to
great effect (when exported to the US this series beat the English-
language networks in the ratings). In the second, *The Aparicio Women*
(*Las Aparicio*, Argos, 2010–11), independent Channel 3 breached the
broadcasting duopoly with an innovative telenovela that featured an
all-female cast and an explicitly feminist and lesbian agenda. Both
fictions boasted expert cinema-style production values, casts and
scripts.

The final pair of chapters compares perhaps the most important
theme in contemporary Mexico, namely violence and insecurity, in
the twin media of film and television. Chapter 7 addresses three films
in distinct genres in order to investigate their specificity: a mordant
political satire, *Hell* (*El infierno*, Luis Estrada, 2010), a popular farce,
Saving Private Pérez (*Salvando al soldado Pérez*, Beto Gómez, 2011),
and the ambivalent art movie, *Miss Bala* (Gerardo Naranjo, 2011).
The final chapter traces the histories of violence in two big-budget
mini-series shown in 2010: *In the Sewers* (*Drenaje profundo*, Azteca,
2010) is an expert genre piece (between police and horror), which,
it is argued, obliquely addresses Mexico's violent past as well as its
bloody present; *Cries of Death and Freedom* (*Gritos de muerte y*

libertad, Televisa, 2010) is a prestige production made for the Bicentennial year of Independence, which, beyond celebration, suggests that violence is at the very origin of the state. The Conclusion highlights the links between cinema and television in the current decade.

These formally written chapters are supplemented by what are called 'Jump Cuts', interpolated reviews of ten feature films released between 2001 and 2012 originally written for *Sight & Sound* and (in the final case) *Film Quarterly*. While these texts, which were composed on the occasion of each film's initial release, lack the academic apparatus of referencing to be found in the main chapters, they supplement scholarly reflection with a sense of journalistic zeitgeist, which I believe is essential when treating contemporary material. Moreover, they widen the scope of the book to include a number of directors who are both established (Alfonso Cuarón, Alejandro González Iñárritu, Maryse Sistach, Carlos Reygadas) and new and little known (Jorge Michel Grau, Michael Rowe, Paula Markovitch). Both the main chapters and the Jump Cuts are presented in broadly chronological order, thus giving a sense of how Mexican screen fiction has developed over the course of the first decade of the millennium.

My own text is supplemented and complemented by an Appendix made up of extended interviews carried out in 2012 with five audiovisual professionals, whose work I address at different points in this book: a feature director, a festival director, an exhibitor, a producer and a TV screenwriter. What is striking in the responses of my interviewees (which I have limited myself to translating from their original Spanish) is how much, from their distinct professional perspectives, these distinguished figures both coincide with and diverge from one another, thus offering invaluable evidence for the richness and complexity of the current Mexican audiovisual scene.

As will be evident, the first chapters focus mainly on institutional questions (production, distribution and exhibition in theatres and at festivals). But I have attempted to integrate such quantitative material into the close qualitative readings of texts that follow. Thus the opening chapter on 'revisions' of Mexican cinema includes an initial account of the current situation in Monterrey (taken from Lucila Hinojosa Córdova), which it juxtaposes with Julia Tuñón's feminist reading of Golden Age cinema, and case studies of three low-budget fiction films. The festival chapter includes a detailed account of a Forum on the Future of Mexican Film that I was privileged to attend in Guadalajara. The case studies of film-makers that follow take the conditions of genre and nationality (and gender and sexuality) as necessary and perhaps productive material constraints on unfettered auteurship, even as they provide close readings of individual features.

In the second half of the book, youth culture is framed within Gabriel Orozco's analysis of 'televidencia' (the particular mode of TV consumption), while femme fatale drama is read in the light of strains in the hegemony of both the telenovela and Televisa, the still-dominant genre and broadcaster. And in the last pair of chapters, film fictions of violence are contextualized by two contrasting accounts of the cinematic scene in 2010, while TV histories of violence are placed within the framework of twin surveys of the televisual year.

By using a wide range of sources for this quantitative material, I hope to give a nuanced account of the field (indeed, some of these sources contradict each other). And by offering close readings of all my chosen texts I am suggesting that even those that are wholly deprived of cultural distinction (most blatantly, teen telenovelas) are more complex and significant than they may at first appear. Certainly my aim is to contest the consensus of foreign film scholars and critics, who tend to focus on the small number of art movies that gain international distribution and are barely screened at home.

Such rare and little-seen features, whatever their artistic virtues, can hardly be called representative of their home nation and need to be supplemented by an awareness of TV series (like *Rebel*) and popular movies (like *Saving Private Pérez*) that have audiences in the millions. Moreover actors and, increasingly, directors migrate freely between the two media of film and television. It thus makes little analytical sense to separate the two vehicles of Mexican screen fiction that go to make up what is now de facto a single audiovisual sector. While, as I mentioned earlier, many Mexican film practitioners and scholars display an intense hostility to television, there exists one important scholarly precedent for my transmedia study, albeit for a slightly earlier period and on a more specialized topic: Raúl Miranda López's expert monograph on Televisa's neglected feature film production (2006).

Over the last decade of visits to Mexico, since I conducted the research for my book on *Amores perros* (Smith, 2003), I have been struck by two things: how an apocalyptic view of the (nonetheless very real) scourges of violence and corruption has made some citizens forgetful of their growing economic success and democratic gains since the turn of the millennium; and how a similarly negative attitude towards Mexican feature films and (on the rare occasions that they are treated seriously) television series have made critics and viewers blind to the increasing wealth of offer in both media. Curiously this instinctive hostility towards local production and continuing reluctance to think of cinema and television together occurs not just in Mexico, but also in Spain, a territory with which Mexico would otherwise seem to have little in common. I have published an earlier book on that country with similar intent and title (Smith, 2009b).

This book is, then, like its predecessor, the fruit of the pleasure I have felt in discovering and exploring screen fictions of the current decade, aided in this case by the invaluable guidance of Mexican scholars and friends. It is offered to readers in the hope that others may find that same pleasure in some of those texts (fragments of which are readily available on the internet), even if my accounts of them may prove polemical. Certainly my writing could hardly match the richness and diversity of Mexican screen fictions themselves, so self-evident to any knowledgeable and sympathetic observer.

Jump Cut 1

Y tu mamá también (Alfonso Cuarón, 2001)

Mexican cinema is on a roll. Despite the political turmoil and crisis that plague the government-funded film institute IMCINE, it has produced a string of local hits. These have most recently been crowd-pleasing comedies that couldn't be more different from earnest art movies by the likes of Arturo Ripstein that are usually distributed abroad. Domestic cinema may even survive proposals, condemned by Ripstein and others, to increase the market for US imports – now shown only with subtitles – by dubbing them into Spanish. Nostalgic for the Golden Age of the 1940s, when the Mexican industry was one of the world's largest, boasting stars like Dolores del Río and directors like Emilio Fernández (not to mention Buñuel), local producers hope this latest revival may be here to stay.

Alfonso Cuarón's smart and sexy road movie *Y tu mamá también* broke the all-time domestic box-office record for a Mexican film, taking $2.2 million in its opening week, despite a widely ignored 'X' rating that should have excluded much of its target audience. A reprise of the oldest story in the book, *Y tu mamá también* tells the tale of two teenage hedonists, wealthy Tenoch (Diego Luna) and poor Julio (Gael García Bernal), who take off from the city with unhappily married Spaniard Luisa (Maribel Verdú) in search of a mythical beach called Boca del Cielo (Heaven's Mouth). *Y tu mamá también* is both a love-triangle and a coming-of-age movie in which, in the familiar cliché, 'none of them would be the same after that summer'.

Writing in *Variety*, Mexican film scholar Leonardo García Tsao dismisses the film as a 'south-of-the-border *Beavis & Butthead*', its protagonists 'oversexed and underdeveloped'. He also describes the theme of a boy's sexual education by an older woman as a fantasy 'straight out of *Penthouse*'. There's no doubt many viewers read the film in this way: a glance at the messages posted on the film's official website confirms this salacious response. But most of the film's frequent and graphic nudity is male, for example when the two boys are shown desperately servicing their girlfriends before the latter leave on holiday in the opening sequences. In a later shower scene, Luna gamely wears a prosthetic glans (unlike the actor, his character Tenoch is circumcised). To accuse the film of crudeness is not only to misread its grungy technique but to confuse the characters' viewpoints with the film's own. Apparently a slight comedy, packed with the lewdness for which Mexican speech is famous, *Y tu mamá también* subtly revises models of gender and national identity for a new Mexico and a new international audience.

Cuarón himself is eager to disassociate himself from what he calls a 'cinema of denunciation': the explicitly political output of an earlier generation of engaged auteurs who explored poverty and exploitation among the underclass, or attacked US imperialism. Cuarón is willing to risk being branded as superficial because his film is entertaining, treacherous because it draws on US culture, and reactionary because it deals with bourgeois characters. Yet his attack on what he calls 'ideology' could itself be read as ideological. Julio's sister, a leftist student who supports the Zapatista rebels, is given short shrift: she exists only to loan the boys the battered car in which they make their trip. The opening sequences in Mexico City include such high-end locations as Tenoch's palatial home and a plush country club, and the official website unashamedly plays for pleasure: surfers are invited to tour the characters' station wagon, dress the boys in their favoured grungy garments and shoot down flying phalluses that flit across the screen.

Nevertheless, there's no doubt that, like Alejandro González Iñárritu's *Amores perros* (2000), which also starred the charismatic García Bernal, *Y tu mamá también* marks a new cinematic moment that coincides with a new political order. Indeed, its sober closing sequence refers explicitly to the defeat in July 2000 of the oddly named Institutional Revolutionary Party (PRI) which had ruled Mexico with the dead hand of corruption for seventy-one years. With the election of new president Vicente Fox of the rightist National Action Party (PAN), Mexicans were more than ready for political and cultural change. The first film to herald the end of the *ancien régime* was Luis Estrada's political satire *Herod's Law* (*La ley de Herodes* [1999]), a cause célèbre after the PRI-controlled IMCINE tried in vain to prevent its distribution. But while *La ley de Herodes* is too local to appeal to foreigners, *Y tu mamá también*'s coming-of-age story has hit a universal nerve, winning film awards for Best Screenplay and Best Newcomer at 2001's Venice festival.

Rejecting the glossy professionalism of his Hollywood features *A Little Princess* (1995) and *Great Expectations* (1997), Cuarón employs a loose and supple technique. The plot develops, in true road-movie fashion, with apparent spontaneity, helped by the fact that the film was shot in sequence with the actors seeming to change and mature over the 105 minutes of its running time. The camera work is seemingly artless: Cuarón's account of his collaboration with director of photography Emmanuel Lubezki recalls Buñuel's relationship with Gabriel Figueroa in that both seek to avoid prettiness, refusing to film if the light or landscape is too beautiful. Cuarón and Lubezki also favour sequence shots – when Luisa goes off with the boys, the camera watches her linger in her apartment and go out of the door before simply wandering to the window to see her exit into the street below. Performances appear improvised. García Bernal and Luna are real-life long-time friends, first having worked together at the age of twelve. Their intimacy and awkwardness in the sex scenes seem quite unforced, while their expert *chilango* (Mexico City dialect) will prove as opaque to outsiders as it is to the Spanish Luisa.

But just as the seeming absence of ideology is itself ideological, so the apparently artless form relies on artistry. Though the actors contributed to the script during the rehearsal process, the screenplay (by Cuarón and his brother Carlos) is deceptively well made. When they set out on their journey, the two boys recite a Rabelaisian manifesto to Luisa – it comes down to 'do what you want' (but don't screw another guy's girlfriend). Towards the end of what is now an exhausting trek, Luisa lays down the law herself, improvising an alternative, woman-centred manifesto. Dramatic irony ensures the audience knows more than the characters: we have seen Luisa split up with her philandering husband, but the boys have not.

The casual-looking cinematography is also smarter than it appears. When the camera strays from the table where the main characters are enjoying a meal, it is to enter the kitchen where Indian women cook. As the trio crudely discusses sexual techniques in the car, they pass roadblocks where we glimpse soldiers interrogating peasants. In long shot, the car, suddenly diminished, vanishes in the vast landscape or appears behind women washing clothes in a river. If framing unobtrusively makes a political point, then so does editing. Cuarón cuts for contrast: from the sunny swimming pool where the boys jerk off together to the fantasized image of 'Salmita' Hayek to the dark bedroom where a solitary Luisa confronts her husband's infidelity on the phone. A student demonstration in the city is juxtaposed with the teenagers' trip to a vast supermarket in the suburbs – a temple to consumerism.

Favouring long shots and lengthy takes as the film does, its principals need all their professional technique to keep control. Cuarón has said that initially he intended to cast amateurs, but they couldn't give the performances he required. The experience of Maribel Verdú, veteran of some thirty films in Spain, anchors the relative newcomers García Bernal and Luna. From a prim, melancholy wife (dressed in ivory satin), she is transformed into a denim-clad sexual predator who takes on the boys in a seedy motel and on the back seat of a car. Her voyage of discovery thus complements the teenagers' more familiar quest for identity. All three are at their best in a final drunken dinner scene, a tour de force that lasts for an unbroken take of seven minutes.

But the strongest indication of the unforced seriousness of this sexy, funny film lies in its use of voice-over. Throughout, dead-pan, third-person narration informs us of what the characters can never know or choose not to reveal. Speeding heedlessly through the city, the young lovers are ignorant of the fact that a migrant worker has been killed on the same road. Later Tenoch doesn't tell his companions they are passing the village of his Indian nanny, whom he called 'mother' until he was four. The fisherman the characters meet on the magical beach will, we are told, be displaced by a luxury hotel. Cuarón cites Godard as an inspiration for the voice-over and *Y tu mamá también* can be re-read as a Mexican *nouvelle vague*, deftly skewering the Latin American *cinéma de papa* even as it shares aspects of its predecessors' social critique.

The notorious Oedipal Mexican profanity to which the title refers is also incorporated and ironized. Luisa may be a mother-whore or *Penthouse* fantasy, but she has hidden motives for her sexual abandon. Moreover, she loudly exposes the homoeroticism underlying Mexican machismo, claiming the boys only fight like dogs because they want to fuck each other. Gender stereotypes are revised, culminating in a final twist that has disconcerted some fans, just as national identity is re-evaluated. The only sign of fetishistic folklore is at a glamorous wedding where *charros* (cowboys) and *mariachis* perform in a muddy arena. But Cuarón's camera pointedly abandons the wealthy masters to follow a maid taking food to the chauffeurs outside. Or again the camera tracks after Tenoch's nanny as she treks through the huge family house to deliver a sandwich and answer the phone ringing unheeded at his side. The 'cinema of denunciation' Cuarón critiques is not so much abandoned in *Y tu mamá también* as fully and unself-consciously integrated into the film's narrative and form.

Important here is a new aspect of cultural nationalism: Mexican-ness need no longer be defined in opposition to the US. Cultural commentator Carlos Monsiváis has recently noted Mexico's natural-ization of Hallowe'en, a holiday hitherto unknown. Likewise, Cuarón Mexicanizes the US genre of the road movie and is confident enough to employ a gloriously hybrid soundtrack. While the script was written to the sound of Frank Zappa's melancholy instrumental 'Watermelon in Easter Hay', the songs booming from the boys' cas-sette player stray from Eno and Natalie Imbruglia to Latin dance numbers. Most telling is the fact that the term *charolastra*, which the boys use to describe themselves (an invented word said to mean 'space cowboy'), is derived from misunderstood English-language lyrics overheard on the radio. This is significant because the idiosyn-cratic speech is the most local element in the film: the Castilian-speaking Luisa repeatedly asks the boys to translate their *chilango*, and while *Y tu mamá también* has been shown around the world, most Spanish speakers are partly excluded from its dialogue. As sociologist Manuel Castells has written, globalization is combined with a resurgence of intense localism. The website is intriguing here – surfers from Montevideo to Madrid lament their failure to under-stand *chilango* but an equal number post their fan mail in versions of that same idiolect. Like a Mexican *A Clockwork Orange*, *Y tu mamá también* schools its consumers in a rich and strange idiom.

If the language remains irredeemably local, the same goes for the landscape. Heading south and east of the capital through the impov-erished states of Puebla and Oaxaca to the Pacific coast, *Y tu mamá también* reveals unselfconsciously and unobtrusively a Mexico rarely seen on screen. The travellers chance on popular traditions: a local carnival queen being used to extract money from cars stopped on the highway; an ancient woman standing guard over an indigenous altar where saints and candles mingle with fluffy toys. And when we finally, miraculously, reach the longed-for beach, we are not allowed to forget the ravages of tourism on this unspoilt environment as the voice-over informs us that the fisherman the friends encounter will end up as a hotel caretaker. The 'magical, musical Mexico' toasted by the drunken trio is both ironically celebrated and ruefully mourned.

In a final, downbeat sequence the two boys meet up by accident back in the city. This is the only time the voice-over is explicitly political – the PRI has, we are told, just lost the presidential elections.

Cuarón has described Mexico as an 'adolescent' country, struggling to grow up and acknowledge aspects of itself for which it was not prepared. The sombre dialogue here (filmed in shot/reverse shot as opposed to the wide shots and long takes favoured in the rest of the film) suggests the boys' quest for identity is equally unsettling: there are some things about ourselves we would prefer not to know.

While the decline of state funding for film is disturbing in a country where the government was for so long a major participant in production, *Y tu mamá también* (like *Amores perros* before it) is testimony to a sector newly invigorated in part by private money. Like the equally surprising Argentine renaissance, the revival of Mexican film will lead to destinations that cannot be predicted. This is the final moral of Cuarón's artfully artless road movie.

Sight & Sound (April 2002)

Part I

Setting Scenes

1

Revising Mexican Cinema

Repeating and Renewing

In October 2008 a special issue of the cultural magazine *Letras Libres* put an evocative image on its cover, reworked from a nineteenth-century engraving of the Zócalo or main square of Mexico City: on the left is the Cathedral, looking as it always has, but to the right, perfectly preserved, is the long-destroyed Aztec temple, which had originally stood in that place, complete with Mexican flag hoisted proudly at its summit. Within this issue are collected essays offering alternative versions (or 'revisions') of Mexican history, imagining (as in the cover image) that the Spanish and Aztec cultures had reached an accommodation, or even that the indigenous civilizations had conquered the conquistadors and survived to our time. According to the editor of the magazine, 'Mexico is, for better and for worse, what it is. But it could have been otherwise.' ('México es, para bien y para mal, lo que es. Pero pudo haber sido de otro modo.') These 'imagined pasts' or 'invisible Mexicos' are 'ghosts' used to 'combat historical determinism and intellectual resignation' ('combatir el determinismo histórico y la resignación intelectual', 2008: 7).

This first chapter explores some recent revisions of the national narrative of Mexican cinema, which are perhaps similar to those suggested by *Letras Libres* in the case of the Mexican nation and which offer radically different perspectives on the development of this cinema. These revisions are: the special issue of *Artes de México* entitled precisely 'Revisión del cine mexicano', focused on the

so-called 'Golden Age'; Julia Tuñón's reinterpretation of that Golden
Age from the perspective of gender and women's studies (a feminist
approach much less familiar in Mexico than in the USA or UK); and
two recent case studies of Mexican cinema from the UK and Mexico,
by Andrea Noble and Lucila Hinojosa Córdova respectively. The
chapter concludes with a discussion of three feature films of the millennium that exemplify this process of revision (of repetition and
re-creation) which I have proposed as central to current Mexican film
and its relation to the past. It is no coincidence that all three address
the theme of adolescence, emblematic of a cinema that, despite a long
and rich history, still regards itself as somewhat immature and
underdeveloped.

But first, a few comments on the concept of 'revision' that I am
proposing. In a historiographical context, the term 'revisionism' has
nuances in English that are contradictory and even disturbing. On
the one hand, it is used in cases of transparent and ideologically
motivated mendacity, as in the denial of the Holocaust; but it is also
used, like its Spanish cognate, to name a continuous and necessary
process under which canonical ideas are put to the test, citing new
materials and new hypotheses.

Likewise, according to the dictionary of the Spanish Royal
Academy, 'revisionismo' is the 'tendency to submit established doc-
trines, interpretations or practices to methodical revision with the
aim of updating them' ('tendencia a someter a revisión metódica
doctrinas, interpretaciones o prácticas establecidas con la pretensión
de actualizarlas', *DRAE*, 2012: s.v. revisionismo). This is how I
understand 'revision' in the context of Mexican cinema, irrespective
of how different the successive versions of this phenomenon may be.
In the words of *Letras Libres* once more, such revisions are fighting
against historical determinism and intellectual resignation. Secondly,
if I may return to a theoretical model that is now somewhat outdated,
revision as it is presented here is a 'supplement' in both senses of
Jacques Derrida's use of the term: it is both the insertion of an addi-
tional element that serves to fill a gap or absence and the replacement
of an existing element with a new one (1998: 141). I suggest that the
logic of the revision, then, as in the case of the supplement, is both
cumulative and substitutive.

This process is seen even in the least ambitious of my materials,
the special issue of *Artes de México*, which originated in an exhibition
of photographs on the legends of Mexican cinema held in the capital's
Palace of Fine Arts (Palacio de Bellas Artes) in 1990 (the issue was
re-published in 2001). The magazine, beautifully produced, is presented in general terms as an encyclopedia of cultures in Mexico,

resurrected (it was first founded in 1951) to give a new perspective on visual culture and using a method that 'ranges between history of mentalities and cultural studies' ('oscila entre la historia de las mentalidades y los estudios culturales', 2001: no page number). The issue itself is presented in a wilfully paradoxical way as a 'visual narrative' and 'an image essay' ('narrativa visual . . . ensayo de imágenes', 2001: 25), both of which are carried out by means of the glamorous photos that occupy the vast majority of its pages. The texts, on the other hand, are rather brief and based on interviews with well-known figures in their respective fields (cultural commentator Carlos Monsiváis, historical scholar Emilio García Riera and director Arturo Ripstein). According to the editors, they constitute 'images that are in a sense written' ('de alguna manera imágenes escritas', 2001: 25), documenting the emotional and aesthetic relationships of the contributors with Mexican cinema, and based on 'favourite moments' or 'elements . . . that could be taken up to develop a new aesthetic for the end of the century' ('momentos favoritos . . . elementos . . . que se podrían retomar para formular una nueva estética de final del siglo', 2001: 25).

Although the editors are aware that the magazine, halfway between image and text, is only 'one of many possible itineraries' and 'routes of memory' for Mexican cinema ('uno de los múltiples recorridos posibles . . . rutas de la memoria', 2001: 22, 23), and claim that this issue is a tool against a falsely totalizing 'overall account' ('recuento global', 2001: 23), it is clear that this self-proclaimed revision includes some perspectives even as it excludes others.

For example, in historiographical terms, the emphasis on the Golden Age is overwhelming, beginning with the many faces on the cover: here we first see Dolores del Río and Pedro Armendáriz, luminous in *María Candelaria* (Emilio Fernández, 1943), and once the cover is unfolded, María Félix in a gorgeous gown in *May God Forgive Me* (*Que Dios me perdone*, Tito Davison, 1948) and Jorge Negrete as a handsome rancher in *Rapture* (*El rapto*, Emilio Fernández, 1954). Even a critic as wilfully iconoclastic as Jorge Ayala Blanco examines in his essay a Golden-Age film of love and deadly passions, *Sensuality* (*Sensualidad*, Alberto Gout, 1951) with Ninón Sevilla (albeit under the tendentious title 'Necrophilia is Culture' ['La necrofilia es cultura']). Only the young Guillermo del Toro dares to invoke another history of Mexican cinema. In an essay entitled 'Retomar el cine de géneros' ('Retaking Genre Cinema'), the last of the collection, he deals, uniquely in the volume, with neglected or scorned genres such as wrestling movies, horror and popular comedy (2001: 79).

In a somewhat predictable way, then, the extravagant visuality of the Golden Age blends with the hegemony of the image in a magazine that here serves the function of a museum. But there is some irony nonetheless: the fetishistic scopophilia so gloriously displayed in *Artes de México* is based not on the films themselves but on still photos that were taken in studios for publicity purposes. Such promotional shots, 'supplementary' in nature, serve here as both substitutes for and additions to the movies of the Golden Age. It is perhaps with good reason that the editors write (2001: 22) that mental images of Mexican cinema fail to come together to make continuous sequences, such is the power of these stills, frozen as they are into immobility.

Just as the editors of *Artes de México* propose the hybrid terms 'visual narrative' and 'image writing' to address Mexican film heritage in a new way, so the distinguished historian Julia Tuñón incorporates within her minute study of the Golden Age her own terminology, which is at once visual and textual. *Mujeres de luz y sombra en el cine mexicano: la construcción de una imagen (1939–1952)* (*Women of light and shade in Mexican cinema: the construction of an image*, 1998) starts with what the author calls an 'establishing shot', and proceeds with a 'travelling', a 'sequence-shot', and even a 'high angle', all of them, of course, written and not filmed.

For Tuñón, in the introduction to her study (characteristically entitled 'Trailers'), the films themselves are not enough, acquiring their full meaning only in the context that creates them and which they in turn address (1998: 13). According to the author, such movies are deeply involved in the construction of sex and, revealing as they do the dominant ideology of the period, serve as invaluable sources for the historian (1998: 13). However, this historiographical imperative is not limited by positivism. Tuñón develops a new mode of looking (in my terms, a 'revision') that incorporates its own subjectivity and affectivity: 'My reading does not break down the images shot by shot, but appeals rather to a mode of attention, that is floating, careful, annotated by the movies' ('mi lectura no desarma las imágenes toma por toma, sino que acude más bien a la atención flotante, cuidadosa, anotada de las cintas', 1998: 14). On the same page she proposes her intention of 'working on the film as one browses a book . . . with the reflection, leisurely pace, and analysis that is elicited by the printed word' ('trabajar la película así como se hojea un libro . . . con esa reflexión, detención, análisis que provoca la letra impresa'). Tuñón even suggests that 'working on a film when one has been touched or irritated . . . is important in order to penetrate its unique meaning' ('trabajar una película cuando una ha sido conmovida o irritada . . . es importante para penetrar en su sentido propio', 1998: 15).

Moreover, reading 'between the lines or, rather, between the images' ('entre líneas, o más bien, entre imágenes', 1998: 18), Tuñón discounts the criterion of quality as a basis for scholarly insight, claiming rather that 'it is the crude or bad films that show . . . the hidden face [of gender ideology]' ('las [películas] burdas y malas son las que . . . muestran esa cara oculta', 1998: 18). And if she identifies some recurring elements and fetish figures in her large sample of films (love, family, motherhood and sexuality; the bride, wife, daughter, lover, mother and prostitute [1998: 20]), even these elements are not stable or easily accessible: 'films are not a window to the world but a construction of that world' ('los filmes no son una ventana al mundo sino una construcción del mundo', 1998: 21).

Besides the evocative analyses of the Golden Age films themselves (many of which coincide with those appearing in the 'visual essay' of *Artes de México*) and the innovative methodological approach of the study, Tuñón explicitly proposes a revision (or 'recycling') of the Mexican film canon which engages author and reader alike in a process of renewed analytical and emotional interpretation: 'I trust . . . that the reader will share . . . the code that allows me to recycle movies without freezing them [and] I seek [his or her] complicity' ('Confío . . . en que el lector comparta . . . ese código que permita mi intención de reciclar las cintas pero sin congelarlas . . . solicito una complicidad', 1998: 21). Freed from the voyeuristic burden to which they are subject in the glossy pages of *Artes de México*, these 'women of light and shadow' may have 'caged bodies' like the nineteenth-century women Tuñón studied in another book of that name (2008), but under her close inspection, at once critical and complicit, they yield meanings that may be latent or patent, but are always moving, in both senses of the word.

Although it is not her priority, Tuñón also offers some well-judged comments on the transnational aspect of her revision of Mexican cinema, insisting on the latter's distinct 'personality' even as she acknowledges the 'obvious' influence of Hollywood (1998: 17) and concluding at the end of her study that the 'originality' of Mexican cinema lies in the fact that 'unlike in that of the United States, love between a man and a woman does not bring happiness' ('a diferencia [del estadounidense] el amor hombre-mujer no da la felicidad', 1998: 289). As we shall see, the interplay of gender and the national project are also central to the argument of British scholar Andrea Noble in her monograph *Mexican National Cinema* of 2005.

As with other contributions to Routledge's collection (such as the excellent *Spanish National Cinema* by Nuria Triana Toribio, 2003), the author's aim here is not to celebrate but to question the concept cited in her title, thus combating historical determinism. With this in mind, Noble's very first chapter is called, somewhat surprisingly, 'Remaking Mexican Cinema' and focuses on a feature produced in 1991: Arturo Ripstein's *Woman of the Port* (*La mujer del puerto*), which was a new version of the classic of the same name made by Soviet exile Arcady Boytler in 1934. Noble begins her chapter, again surprisingly, by examining the conclusions of these two films: in the original, the prostitute-protagonist, having performed an unknowing act of incest with her sailor-brother, commits suicide in a highly melodramatic way; in the remake, there is by contrast a disturbingly happy ending: the two siblings have formed a couple and now have one daughter and another child on the way.

In a rather complex argument and alluding both to Mexican scholarship and to the issues typical of what Noble calls 'Euro-American movie studies', the author proposes that 'the relationship between the two films becomes a vehicle through which we can tell a history of the development of Mexican cinema . . . linked to the geopolitics of the Mexican nation and the pursuit of cultural modernity' (2005: 24). These are all key themes of her book.

Noble further suggests that the first *Woman of the Port*, celebrated today as a classic of national cinema by critics as different as Emilio García Riera and Jorge Ayala Blanco, sought in its time to go 'beyond the national, with the intention of articulating themes and forms with international resonance' (2005: 32). The director himself, Noble writes, explicitly rejected films that were too 'vernacular' in subject and tone (2005: 33). In its attempt to place Mexico at the international forefront of modern culture, *Woman of the Port* employs that modernity both as a theme (the story narrates the vicissitudes of a modern life in which the old certainties about social and sexual relationships no longer hold) and as a technological achievement (the film's unusually high production values rival those of Hollywood and it very consciously creates a local star, Andrea Palma, who is modelled on the cosmopolitan Marlene Dietrich) (2005: 33). Moreover, the film's theme of family breakdown is fused with that of the 'modern form of social organization experienced as dispossession and dislocation' (2005: 34), both of which are conveyed in 'a sophisticated film language' (2005: 35). In a rather Derridean way, one might say that the 'original' term is here itself a repetition; and the classic film, the property of a presumed national cinema, is contaminated from the start by cosmopolitan alienation.

For Noble, Ripstein's remake of *The Woman of the Port*, with its iconoclastic ending and overtly postmodern self-reflexivity, irony and pastiche, 'contests the myth of progress articulated by the first film'

(2005: 44). The 'cosmopolitan nationalism' of Boytler and of the 1930s has long failed and for Ripstein local, folk and popular elements have triumphed, ironically for a Mexican film of the 1990s which was aimed primarily at the international circuit of arthouse cinemas (2005: 46). Hence the importance of the unusual theme of incest here, reminiscent perhaps of the 'necrophilia' so ironically invoked by Ayala Blanco in *Artes de México*. The endogamous relationship par excellence is rejected by Boytler as superseded by modernity (the main character has no choice but suicide), but it is reborn by a Ripstein who delights in the supposed continuing underdevelopment of an inbred Mexico.

But there is for Noble another element here linking geopolitics with (failed) modernity: psychoanalysis and national adolescence. She cites Samuel Ramos who, in his famous *El perfil del hombre y la cultura en México* (*Profile of Man and Culture in Mexico*) of 1934, posits the continuing existence of a national childhood trauma historically based on the experience of the Conquest (2005: 38). According to Ramos, the Mexican male, still maimed by an inferiority complex towards his European 'parents', requires re-education in order to be integrated into Western civilization. It goes without saying that for Noble (as for Tuñón in the case of gender) such a hypothesis is evidence for the construction of nationality in a certain historical moment and cannot be taken as an essential or timeless truth. Yet, as we will see in my approach to the three films on the theme of adolescence, psychology merges, still, with geopolitics in both national cinema and the nation-state.

To conclude this overview of the *status quaestionis*, I would like to contrast Noble's geopolitical and psychoanalytic revision with another very different monograph on the national film project: *El cine mexicano: de lo global a lo local* (*Mexican Cinema: From Global to Local*) by Lucila Hinojosa Córdova, published in 2003. Essentially quantitative rather than qualitative, unlike the studies by Tuñón and Noble, and focused not on film texts themselves but on government and industrial institutions, Hinojosa's book (like Tuñón's) uses a film term to visualize its methodology: the latter is defined as a 'cognitive zoom, an approach that attempts to create a horizon of meaning on how globalization, with its uncertain and complex dynamics, is changing the production process of Mexican cinema, not to mention its exhibition and consumption' ('*zoom* cognoscitivo, una aproximación que intenta crear un horizonte de sentido acerca de cómo la globalidad, en su dinámica incierta y compleja, está modificando el proceso productivo del cine mexicano, así como su exhibición y consumo', 2003: 5–6). For my own purposes, the 'revisionist' contribution of Hinojosa's study to the narrative of national cinema lies in the fact that, perhaps in spite of its author's intentions, the familiar history of Mexico's underdevelopment and failed modernity is supplemented here by another more positive, albeit contradictory, evolution in which increased globalization and market liberalization have facilitated the emergence of new and fragile forms of production and consumption.

In her first chapter, Hinojosa, reviewing theories of the new global order, sketches out the conflicting positions of the 'apocalyptic' scholars who predict a future of cosmopolitan cultural homogenization and the 'integrated' theorists who are supporters of 'glocalization'. According to the latter, 'the global and local are mutually constitutive rather than exclusive' ('lo global y lo local constituyen, no excluyen, el uno al otro', 2003: 30). It is a debate that, as we have seen, Noble traces back to the 1930s. Hinojosa's second chapter deals with Mexican cinema's recent battle with market forces (2003: 44), outlining the familiar story of the gradual abandonment by the government of industrial protectionism, which resulted in the sudden collapse of production (from fifty-six features in 1994 to just fourteen in 1995) (2003: 46). Meanwhile, market concentration was increasing in the exhibition sector, with the closing down of old facilities and the opening of new theatres by national exhibition chains dedicated, with the rising cost of entry, to a more educated and affluent audience (2003: 47).

However (and this is where I discern the 'revisionist' element in Hinojosa's study), despite such devastating conditions for national cinema, from the turn of the millennium domestic production began to grow once more. And viewers returned to theatres that were no longer decrepit and even went on to surpass their previous total (there were 1,434 screens in 1994 and 2,200 in 2001) (2003: 48). As for distribution, US films experienced some decline (if not as much as the Mexican movies) from 219 in 1990 to 145 in 2001 (2003: 47). Unlike Canada, Mexico had not negotiated a 'cultural exception' when it came to its signing of NAFTA with the US. However, the Mexican public returned to the cinema to see national blockbusters, which were small in number but big at the box office, such as *Amores perros* and *Y tu mamá también*. These titles were produced with private capital outside the old system of protectionism and cronyism. Such films, although very few, managed to achieve a global impact that far exceeded any Canadian feature of the period.

Putting supply to one side to address audience and demand, Hinojosa outlines once more the dominant theories in the field of Mexican cultural consumption. She notes that already in 1995 Néstor García

Canclini had shown that there was a Mexican audience, especially a young and educated one, eager for a cinema that offered not just the light entertainment typical of Hollywood but rather a 'problematic treatment of contemporary issues concerning everyday life' in their own country ('tratamiento problemático de cuestiones actuales, cercanas a la vida cotidiana', 2003: 74). This diversification of tastes may well be derived, as García Canclini himself suggests, from a new 'fashioning of domestic citizenship' ('la formación de una ciudadanía doméstica', 2003: 74). But clearly it also corresponds to a certain revision of the preferences of those attending theatres in Mexico, one which is closely related to the industrial changes in production and exhibition so often denounced by scholars and practitioners of Mexican cinema alike.

Hinojosa ends with an empirical analysis of audiences in the northern industrial city of Monterrey in 2001, a valuable contribution to the study of the local. The results confirm that it is young people and the better educated who frequent the theatres in the metropolitan area (51 per cent are between twenty and twenty-nine years old; 55 per cent of them are professionals [2003: 91]); and that, while favouring US movies, such spectators are not averse to domestic product. While there is some standardization of offer (most theatres exhibit fewer films than they did in the 1990s [2003: 89]), of those spectators who recall seeing any Mexican film (56 per cent of the sample), 79 per cent said they enjoyed it (2003: 100). Interestingly, in third position after two highly transnational titles (*Y tu mamá también* and *The Devil's Backbone* [*El espinazo del diablo*], Guillermo del Toro, 2001), the film most remembered by the Monterrey audience is an unsung teen romantic comedy, *Inspiration* (*Inspiración*, Angel Mario Huerta, 2001). It may be no accident that this film was one of the few features shot in the same city in which the young audience saw it (2003: 101).

In her epilogue, Hinojosa regrets the increasing convergence of cultural industries and the unequal access to their enjoyment, trends harmful to the public interest and quality of life (2003: 111). And the difficulty of making and showing movies in Mexico should not be minimized. But when the author argues for a more regulatory role by the state in order to promote the film industry, she seems to discount the 'revisionist' data that she herself has provided: the fact that there is already a young audience willing to consume national or local films with serious themes, if only they could succeed in being produced and distributed. In the second section of this first chapter, then, I will discuss three films of this type, placing them within the context of the multiple revisions (textual, sexual and industrial) that we have outlined above.

Three 'Third-Way' Features

What caught my attention in these fiction features (two of which are from first-time directors) is not just the privileged role of the theme of adolescence, but rather their revision (recycling and renewal), in a local context, of a genre usually associated with Hollywood: the youth film (I return to youth film and television at greater length in chapter 5 of this book).

Given that their budgets are reduced, if not negligible even by Mexican standards, my three films do not seek the high status of what I have called elsewhere 'prestige pictures' (by transnational auteurs Alejandro González Iñárritu, Alfonso Cuarón and Guillermo del Toro); but nor do they conform to the more austere and minimalist parameters of the purist 'festival films' (by art directors Carlos Reygadas, Nicolás Pereda and the relatively accessible Fernando Eimbcke) (Smith, 2012: 68). They could thus be considered a 'third way' within national production. And within a global context, my youthful trio adopts and adapts some stylistic techniques considered to be typically 'European' without wholly abandoning the narrative drive and visual pleasure held to be characteristic of much US cinema. In this they attempt to circumvent the dilemma facing Mexican filmmakers whose works, according to Jesús Mario Lozano (latterly an established film-maker himself), are judged and legitimized by foreign standards: compelled in a Catch-22 situation to choose between what he calls 'cinéma mexicain' (French-style auteur films) and (in English) 'Mexican cinema' (American-style commercial movies) (Lozano, 2011: 265).

The features are *Así* by the aforementioned Jesús Mario Lozano (2005), *Año uña* by Jonas Cuarón, son of Alfonso (2007), and *I'm Gonna Explode* (*Voy a explotar*, 2008), by Gerardo Naranjo. In the first, a solitary young man from Monterrey, who has only one friend, who is blind, is progressively involved or entangled with a couple of practitioners of street performance; in the second, a teenager from Mexico City undertakes an uncertain and inconclusive affair with a somewhat older American girl; and in the third, which is more clearly melodramatic, two kids from Guanajuato, the girl as charismatic and rebellious as the boy, attempt to escape their monotonous provincial lives (I treat this film at greater length in chapter 5).

Despite this common theme of youth, what we do not find here is the familiar tenets of social realism, in which the teen condition is presented as one of the problems of contemporary life; and, although the three plots all have a romantic or erotic element, nor do we find

Figure 1 *Así* (Jesús Mario Lozano, 2005)

the explicit scenes of sexual acts as in the case of the first two films of Carlos Reygadas. Likewise, avant-garde film techniques (which one might call 'French', in contrast with the more transparent style of commercial cinema from the US) are refurbished or recycled so as not to interfere too much with the enjoyment of narratives that are somewhat elliptical but by no means at odds with entertainment.

With *Así*, Lozano sets himself a radical formal test, limiting the vast majority of the takes of his movie to an arbitrary length of thirty-two seconds and inserting sober fades to black between them. But the viewer is seduced (entangled like the protagonist) in a plot that is fragmented and delayed but linear and consistent, by the freshness of the performances and by the transparent visual pleasure of the colour palette and frame composition. Likewise the sets and exteriors shot in Monterrey, a location that is branded 'ugly' within the film itself, do not fail to offer certain elements that are exotic (for example, the young man's pet turtles) even as they are presented as everyday. And though some sequences are completely static and silent (a striking high angle observes the protagonist lying semi-naked in bed [Figure 1]), Lozano also offers moments of convulsive movement, both for the actors and the camera (the violent and ambiguous rehearsals of the two dancers, an apparent robbery and shooting that interrupts the climactic street performance). Even intermittent examples of *temps morts* typical of Ozu (a sudden rain hits the deserted roofs and trees of Monterrey) are shot in such a way as to provide us with a generous dose of visual pleasure.

In *Año uña*, technique is yet more voluntarily limited, since the film is composed entirely of still photos, mostly in black and white. The previous best-known example of this case is Chris Marker's *La Jetée* (1962). However (and unlike the glacial alienation of Marker), the impossible, but endearing, love affair between the New Yorker and the Chilango (Mexico City native) evolves in such a way that it connects very well with the spectator, who even manages to forget at times that this is not a film shot in the conventional manner. In a similar way, the script is clearly structured around parallels between the two locations associated with the main characters (the family home in Mexico City, an equally localist New York embodied by the seedy but much-loved amusement park in Coney Island). The sequences, too, are composed in fairly traditional style, using still photo equivalents of the well-known resources of continuity editing: establishing shots followed by medium shots and close-ups, shot/reverse shot, cross cutting, and point-of-view shooting.

Finally, *I'm Gonna Explode* borrows from Jean-Luc Godard the discontinuity editing and jump cuts of *Breathless* (*À bout de souffle*, 1960). At first somewhat disorienting, this technique does not fail to surprise and seduce the viewer, not least because of the film's swift and vertiginous pace, so different to the extended takes typical of Mexican film-makers who are the favourites of the festival circuit. Also, although in this case (as in my previous films) the young actors have little experience, they are not required to adopt that style of performance that is devoid of any affect and is characteristic of the non-professionals directed by Reygadas and his followers. Moreover, rejecting the unaesthetic casting of Reygadas once more, the comely physical attributes of the protagonists of the three films form a welcome and essential part of their undeniable attraction to the public.

These actors (whose names, with the exception of perhaps *Año uña*'s Diego Cataño, are still little known) may not have the legendary status of the stars of the Golden Age celebrated in *Artes de Mexico*. But they are still subject to a certain extent to that fetishistic scopophilia that is inherited from the classic films. In *Así*, Lozano provides us with a handsome visual story that is not reliant on the dialogue and a voice-over that is sometimes laconic, or on the disturbing persistence of a fixed moment in time (11.32 p.m.) that is shown on a digital clock in each scene. In *Año uña*, as we have seen, the image is frozen by Cuarón into immobility, but only so that we can appreciate all the more its aesthetic qualities, so carefully crafted. Naranjo himself points to his film's diverse wealth of resources, describing *I'm Gonna Explode* as 'an essay or journal of ideas with music, written word, and internal dialogue' (*I'm Gonna Explode*, 2009: 5). Reclaiming the fragment, like the texts baptized 'written images' in *Artes de México*, these films also take a route or path of memory, implicitly invoking the rich historical legacy of Mexican cinema and rejecting the rigorous visual unpleasure to which a large proportion of current production aimed at international festivals holds so fast. In supplementary style, they thus both add to and substitute for the existing exhibits in the museum of memory that is the legacy of Mexican cinema.

Walking the fine line between innovation and tradition, my sample of three revisionist features (films that repeat and renew the visual and romantic pleasures of the past) deserves that floating, careful and annotated attention, analogous to that provoked by the written word, which Tuñón dedicates to Golden Age cinema. But of course, created and directed as they are in a very different context, my films show signs of an entirely renewed construction of sex. The camera focuses as much or even more on faces and bodies that are male rather than female; and women, no longer made of mere light and shadow, are the protagonists of the action. In *Así* the male teenager falls for a beautiful female dancer, but the erotic charge of the film is focused more on him than her, whether he is alone on his bed, horsing around somewhat ambiguously with his male blind friend, or even anally penetrated by the handsome dancer at the orders of his girlfriend. The Yankee star of *Año uña* may fantasize about the young Mexican, transforming a simple horny teen into the perfect Latin lover, but it is she who controls (and ultimately abandons) the incipient love affair between the two. And the somewhat androgynous heroine of *I'm Gonna Explode* shows herself to be more committed than her male companion, willing as she is to die for their rebellion without a cause. These female figures can hardly be reduced to the typical daughters, girlfriends and prostitutes of yore. It seems that it is rather the males who are caught or trapped, their bodies (and minds) caged by new narratives and cinemas that present them as erotic objects that are passive or unaware of their situation. It remains the case, however, that as in Tuñón's Golden Age melodramas (and unlike in the Hollywood tradition), love between a man and a woman does not bring happiness.

Although the pleasurable aesthetics shared by these three films do not coincide with the more austere school of 'festival films', *Así*, *Año uña* and *I'm Gonna Explode* nonetheless achieved some projection outside of Mexico: in fact, all premiered in Venice, the second festival in terms of worldwide prestige. And just as they revise the construction of sex, so they renew the national film scene; or, in Noble's terms, they replay the geopolitics of the Mexican nation (from Guanajuato to Monterrey, via Mexico City) and the pursuit of cultural modernity.

Both the 'prestige pictures' and the 'festival films' target a transnational public. Although the first exhibit a mastery of those showy resources (of cinematography and editing, script and performance) which the latter, more ascetic and minimalist, prefer to reject, the two trends represent a new form of the 'cosmopolitan nationalism' identified by Noble in Boytler. Testimony to this phenomenon are the voluntarily abstruse titles, which are either portentously abstract (*Battle in Heaven* [*Batalla en el cielo*], Carlos Reygadas, 2005) or misleadingly precise (*Lake Tahoe* [Fernando Eimbcke, 2008] is set in the Yucatán). As suggested by Pierre Bourdieu, the enigmatic and disturbing title is the usual sign of the artistic work that has pretensions of cultural distinction (1996: 137).

My three revisionist films, on the other hand, lay claim to some extent to the local and the vernacular. Set in the everyday life of recognizable locations, *Así* and *I'm Gonna Explode* offer unpretentious images of urban Monterrey and Guanajuato respectively which are very different from each other but equally boring for the young characters. And although *Año uña* begins with the recitation of the names of Mexico City metro stations by an American who is somewhat dazzled by the exoticism of her environment, the most characteristic image of the capital offered by Cuarón's film is of the family home with its little pleasures (food, dogs) and its inevitable tragedies (the death of the grandfather). Here the contemporary life of Mexico is presented neither (as in the case of Boytler) as the dispossession and dislocation that has disintegrated social relations nor (as in the case of Ripstein) as the failed modernity that can be represented only by self-reflection, irony and pastiche.

And if the focus of the three plots is on an adolescence that could be read as an allegory of the state of the nation, the first two films show little childhood trauma or inferiority complex. Even in *I'm Gonna Explode*, the trauma experienced by the two protagonists (the loss of a mother and father, respectively) has little representative value, although the boy's father is a politician. The couple's rebellion has no motive or objective and becomes a parody of the bourgeois adulthood from which they are trying to escape (the kids build a temporary home complete with TV and barbecue on the roof of the boy's family home). It might perhaps be said that these three young Mexican directors have borrowed some cinematic techniques from their European 'fathers' but, needless to say, they neither seek nor need to integrate into Western civilization as prescribed by the psychoanalytic-historical schemas of yesteryear. Nonetheless they need to negotiate Lozano's twin perils of 'cinéma mexicain' and 'Mexican cinema'.

It thus follows that although these three films are localist, they remain relatively accessible to a transnational public through their revisions of a Hollywood genre (the youth film) and a European aesthetic (a moderately experimental shooting and cutting style). They contradict the 'apocalyptic' critics cited by Hinojosa Córdova who predicted cultural homogenization, and identify rather with the 'integrated' scholars for whom the global and the local are mutually constituting.

Hence, while the international distribution of these three films has been uneven, they are all plausibly directed to a new domestic citizenship, thus reflecting the diversification of tastes that has transformed the national public in tandem with changing conditions of exhibition and consumption. Sticking close as they do to everyday life, they display, unlike the radically engaged cinema of the past, no clear political commitment. But they do reveal some interest in the treatment of current issues (even *Así*, whose protagonist seems so isolated from the world around him, recycles a television report on an indigenous Zapatista demonstration). Moreover, although the director of *Así* complained of the lack of interest in Mexican cinema in his city, besieged as it is by Hollywood (Luna, 2006), the theme of the three films clearly seems to coincide with the demographics of the new national audience: young, educated and well-disposed towards an intelligent Mexican offer, and, even in the case of Monterrey, towards the few films made in their own metropolitan area.

In conclusion, Mexican public interest and quality of life, as defined in the broadest of terms, are enriched by the kinds of cinematic revision I have outlined here. These offer alternative versions of Mexican cinema that put to the test the existing paradigms of 'genre movie', 'prestige picture' and 'festival film'. Fighting determinism and defeatist resignation, they constitute valuable examples that not only revise (repeat and renew) the past, but also suggest imagined futures for a Mexican cinema that, like Mexico itself, could be otherwise.

2

Following Festivals

Morelia, 2009: The Legacy of the Past, the Problematics of the Present, and the Retreat from the City

The Morelia International Film Festival, which celebrated its seventh edition 3–11 October 2009, is unique for a number of reasons. For one thing, it takes place in an exquisite Mexican colonial town, all pink stone and baroque curlicues. Even the press office is housed in an eighteenth-century building. And while most press and commercial screenings take place in the enviably modern Cinépolis Centro theatres, complete with stadium seating and digital projection, free shows are also held for the general public in such historic sites as the small square in the shadow of the majestic twin-towered cathedral.

Keeping close to its origins as a showcase for shorts and documentaries, the festival has now expanded to include Mexican features, both in competition (for which I served as a juror) and out, as well as foreign premieres. Stellar international guests (Todd Haynes last year, Quentin Tarantino this) are combined with a continuing commitment to home-grown production. The latter includes a strand for films made in Morelia's home state of Michoacán and, this year, homage to a local star: Fanny Cano, the 1960s siren of sex comedies with names like *How to Hook a Husband* (*Como pescar marido*, Alfredo B. Crevenna, 1967).

Focused on the present (the feature competition is restricted to first or second films by young directors), still the festival investigates the past. Another special strand, sponsored by the Mexican association of Women in Film and Television, celebrated pioneering female directors with Dorothy Arzner from the US playing alongside Adela Sequeyro from Mexico. And it is rare for any film festival to have such a strong academic focus. The Mexican Society of Film Theory and Analysis (whose Spanish acronym is SEPANCINE or 'Know Film') and the Autonomous Metropolitan University at Cuajimalpa mounted a large congress just before the festival, while a further scholarly round table studied films of the Mexican Revolution, whose centennial would take place the following year. Add to this a long-standing and invaluable forum for Mexican indigenous or 'First Nation' film-making and this makes for a rich and strong brew.

Nonetheless, tensions ran high at the lavish opening ceremony, sponsored by *InStyle* magazine. As telenovela starlets twirled for the TV cameras on the red carpet outside, Tarantino, presenting his latest feature, roared to the auditorium audience 'Are you ready for some *bastardos?*' The ecstatic response suggested they were. Even the digni-fied Romanian ambassador, whose country was honoured as the first 'invited nation' at the festival, was caught up in the excitement, con-fessing on stage that she felt like a movie star. But beyond celebrity there was serious business here. It was the Governor of Michoacán who recalled the unprecedented terror attack on the city by drug cartels just one year ago, a trauma from which (he said) the film community had helped Morelia to recover.

A speech by Consuelo Sáizar, the feisty director of CONACULTA (the National Council for Culture and Arts), proved surprisingly controversial. Catcalls greeted her claim that the current (rightist PAN) federal government respected the film profession and consid-ered cinema to be the most important medium for making Mexico a world cultural power. Facing down a hostile audience, she claimed that the budget for IMCINE, the National Film Institute, had recently been doubled and that production had increased. In spite of the eco-nomic crisis (which has hit Mexico harder than most, dependent as it remains on remittances from the US), she promised that next year would see no cuts in the level of public subsidy or in the number of features produced per year, which she gave as seventy. This is clearly a matter of national pride, as the *annus mirabilis* of 2010 would mark not only the centennial of the Revolution but also the bicentennial of Independence.

Sceptical film folk questioned the minister's statistics and pledge on production, arguing that the problem is rather one of distribution, which remains dominated by US companies and product. A case in point is the fate of the excellent winner of Best Documentary last year at Morelia. Eugenio Polgovsky's *The Inheritors* (*Los herederos*, 2008), which deals with child labour in the Mexican countryside, achieved the rare privilege of theatrical distribution in Mexico City where it was playing during the course of the current festival. In spite of its unprecedented success at the box office, however, by the second week major exhibitor Cinemex had scheduled it only for 11 a.m. screenings, reserving better slots for US imports. Ironically also, the recent and welcome upgrading of Mexico's once derelict theatres, by chains such as Cinépolis and Cinemex, has once more transformed movie-going into a mainly middle-class activity: the price of a single ticket now outstrips the minimum wage.

But whether you are bullish about Mexican cinema's prospects like its government paymasters at CONACULTA and IMCINE, or bearish like the perennially pessimistic industry, there remains little doubt that Morelia, with its unique emphasis on first-time film-makers, serves (as one of its organizers claimed) as a kind of 'crystal ball', predicting the future of Mexico's cinema. And if we take this year's Morelia selection as a litmus test for current film-making it is striking that favoured genres range so widely: from the purely commercial (such as Miguel Necoechea's *The Kid* [*Chamaco*], a proficient boxing movie that tells a familiar tale of triumph over adversity) to the resolutely arthouse (Matías Meyer's *The Cramp* [*El calambre*], an austere parable about a morose Frenchman taught life lessons by a Caribbean fisherman). One player is, however, especially influential: Mantarraya ('Stingray'), which last year celebrated its tenth anniversary at Morelia, is a producer-distributor devoted to a new generation of Mexican film-makers. It is associated with controversial auteur Carlos Reygadas (*Japón* [2002], *Battle in Heaven* [*Batalla en el cielo*, 2005], *Stellet Licht* [*Silent Light*, 2007]), who now has a cluster of young protégés working alongside him. As we shall see, this year once more Mantarraya became one of the success stories of the festival.

As different as the Mexican features shown at the festival were, they displayed three recurring themes or leitmotifs that crossed the boundaries between genres, including the dividing line between fiction and documentary. The first is the murderous legacy of the past, including machismo, small-town repression and perennially corrupt powers that be, such as politicians and the police. The second is the anxious problematics of the present, such as the inescapable presence of the US border and the pervasive fear of insecurity, revealed in violent crime such as drug trafficking and kidnapping. And the third is the retreat from Mexico's contemporary urban reality into an Edenic ruralism, where the twin territories of the sea and desert offer respite, however circumscribed and problematic, from the megalopolis of Mexico City, which now boasts some twenty-two million inhabitants. A fantasized rural past and a stylized urban present come together in the boldest film of the festival, Julián Hernández's three-hour homoerotic epic *Enraged Sun, Enraged Sky* (*Rabioso sol, rabioso cielo*), which I examine at at the end of this survey.

First, then, the wounds of the past. Jaime Ruiz Ibáñez's *The Half of the World* (*La mitad del mundo*) traces the sexual awakening of a young man with special needs who lives with his over-protective mother in a small town in rural Mexico. Developing as a sex comedy (the young man is eagerly seduced by frustrated local wives who in one scene feast off his naked body), it stages a daring tonal shift in its final act. Accused of rape, the vulnerable protagonist is hunted down by the corrupt mayor and denied protection by the local priest.

Alejandro Gerber Bicecci's *Becloud* (*Vaho*, which received a Special Mention from the jury) is very different in genre and ambitions. An example of the now familiar multi-narrative strand of Mexican film-making, influenced by the prize-winning collaborations of director Alejandro González Iñárritu and Guillermo Arriaga (*Amores perros* [2000], *21 Grams* [2003], *Babel* [2006]), *Vaho* flashes backwards and forwards in time, cutting between the linked stories of three youths in Iztapalapa, an impoverished and drought-ridden borough in the east of Mexico City. The extravagant visuals and operatic tone climax with a lengthy sequence shot on the streets at Iztapalapa's annual and hugely popular *Passion Play*. The Crucifixion of Christ here restages the innocent sacrifice of a victimized character within the film, a tragedy that has scarred the three boys' lives. It is telling that *The Half of the World* and *Becloud*, which could hardly be more different in register or scale, both end with a lynching, that most primal act of savage violence.

If Mexico's bloody past is inescapable, then its problematic present is also unavoidable. The US border, evoking an uneasy mix of mortal danger and seductive promise, quite literally looms large in Rigoberto Perezcano's accomplished *Northless* (*Norteado*), which offers frequent telling shots of the fortified fence between the two nations, marching defiantly across the barren desert landscape or dwarfing the modest Mexican houses on its southern side. Like *The Half of the World*, *Northless* stages an unexpected tonal shift. The first fifteen minutes seem to fall well within the familiar aesthetic of austere festival favourites pioneered in Mexico by Reygadas. In lengthy takes with no music or dialogue we observe as protagonist Andrés, a migrant from southern Mexico, fails in his attempt to cross the border, betrayed by the guide whom he has paid to help him. There are frequent shots of his small pathetic figure lost in the vast landscape. Sent back to Tijuana, Andrés offers to help out in a small store. There, slowly and shyly, he becomes involved with two lonely, loveless women working there. What began, then, as observational pseudo-documentary evolves into a delicate and touching romance, with humorous touches. At the film's end Andrés makes a final attempt at the crossing, this time lovingly sewn into a sofa (*sic*) by his new-found friends. While the story remains open (the last shot is of the sofa on a truck stuck in endless lines of traffic), director Per-ezcano lends a generously human face to the ongoing tragedy of the border with his strikingly original approach to an oft-told tale.

Michel Franco's *Daniel & Ana* (*Daniel y Ana*, shown out of com-petition) offers a much frostier take on a contemporary problem. The titular couple, the teenage son and daughter of a wealthy bourgeois family, are kidnapped from their car. In extended and brutal takes reminiscent of Michael Haneke (whose *White Ribbon* [*Das weisse Band*] received its Mexican premiere at the festival), the pair are stripped, brutalized and forced to have sex with one another as they are videotaped. While the director insisted on the veracity of his tale (supposedly told to him by the psychotherapist to whom the real-life sister turned), his film develops as a chilly chamber piece as the brother (played in his debut by Dario Yazbek Bernal, half-brother of Gael García Bernal) retreats into traumatized catatonia and, finally, spectacular aggression. While some viewers questioned the plausibil-ity of the film's premise (the criminals' motive is not blackmail, but an illicit trade in the rare specialism of incest pornography), it remains the case that the film treats in its stylized and abstracted way the sadly pervasive problem of kidnapping, which affects not only the middle classes in Mexico and contributes to that sense of a general-ized 'insecurity' which is the country's most disturbing current characteristic.

Still, some Mexicans have it worse than others. *Presumed Guilty* (*Presunto culpable*), the deserving winner of the Feature Documen-tary competition, tells the shocking tale of Toño, a young man picked up by the police in Mexico City for a murder he could not have com-mitted and locked up for two years in a hell-hole of a prison. Jointly directed by Roberto Hernández, a lawyer now studying public policy at Berkeley, and Geoffrey Smith, a distinguished director for British television, the film is shamelessly exciting. Borrowing from the best US crime series, it is dynamically shot and cut and finds in its subject a compellingly attractive protagonist: Toño even recorded a rap song and video (included in the film) about his case. Granted unprece-dented access to the Mexican inquisitorial justice system, so different to the Anglo-Saxon adversarial mode, *Presumed Guilty* includes unlikely footage of an 'Alice in Wonderland' world in which the defence lawyer is forbidden by the judge to ask whether the arresting officers recognize the defendant and where the smirking prosecutor refuses even to speak at the retrial, claiming she will just provide the judge with a disk with her argument on it. The brave hero of the film, who, now finally released, must surely fear reprisals from the same authorities he has so publicly humiliated, received a Tarantino-size welcome at the screening I attended. Later, a large general audience of Mexican families, including many children, sat mesmerized at a public showing in the Cathedral plaza. The film's producers (who include Martha Sosa of *Amores perros*) hoped to use *Presumed Innocent* as a tool in the then current campaign to make the presence of cameras standard in Mexican criminal trials.

Given such urban narratives, small wonder, then, that a trip out of the city to the wilderness, whether sea or desert, might prove appealing. The winner of both the Best Feature competition and the Audience Prize, Pedro González-Rubio's *Alamar* (literally 'Tothesea'), a Mantarraya production, charts a winning and deceptively simple voyage into the ocean. Playing themselves are Jorge, a charismatic Caribbean fisherman with a strong resemblance to Johnny Depp in pirate mode, and Natan, the impossibly photogenic blond child Jorge has fathered with the Italian mother from whom he is now separated (Figure 2). Gently but firmly Jorge initiates his young son, just arrived from urban Italy, into the rich mysteries of Mexican nature: recognizing flora and fauna, fishing with a line or a snorkel, living in a small shack built on fragile poles sunk in the sea. A garrulous grandfather serves as a humorous counterpoint to the romantically reserved

Figure 2   *Alamar* (Pedro González-Rubio, 2009)

father, while a glamorous white crane (christened 'Blanquita' – 'Whitey') also drops in for a self-assured cameo. At one memorable point crocodiles lurk in the water just feet away from where the child plays happily on the shore.

González-Rubio, who also served as director of photography in *Alamar*'s two-man crew, might appear at first sight to be making an observational documentary. But his non-professional actors are indeed acting, as their real personal circumstances are quite different to those shown in the film: the father and mother have not split up, the 'grandfather' is unrelated to the principals, the floating house (devoid of women) serves in reality only as a temporary home for the fishermen who are habitually based on shore with their families. Fictional elements are combined with exquisite filmic craftwork. Glorious wide shots of the ocean shining in the sunset or dappled by a sudden rainstorm are combined with extreme close-ups, carefully chosen, of, say, the father's and son's feet inching perilously down a rough tree trunk. And, a deliberate world away from stereotypes of Mexican machismo, the film focuses movingly on masculine tenderness and nurturing.

Called 'Nanook of the South' by local wits for its apparent ethnographic focus, *Alamar* has something in common with José Álvarez's *Flowers in the Desert* (*Flores en el desierto*), which was also produced by Mantarraya and photographed by González-Rubio. *Flowers*, which won the Special Mention in the Best Documentary section, takes place wholly amongst the Huicholes, a large indigenous nation spread over several modern Mexican states. Flagrantly picturesque in their embroidered costumes and feathered hats, they are shown undertaking traditional pilgrimages to three sacred sites: the woods where they hunt deer, the coast where they sacrifice cattle to a sea deity, and the desert where they seek out and consume formidable quantities of peyote.

Although the subjects sporadically comment on the process of film-making, in an indigenous language with which they no doubt assume the crew to be unfamiliar (the whole film is subtitled) and occasionally pick up the camera themselves, Flowers is rigorously observational in technique: the crew refuses to question their subjects, much less intervene in their world, circumscribed as it is by millennial and apparently unquestionable tradition. This leaves many questions unanswered. Indeed, one incident serves as a black hole, menacing the whole movie: one of the young wives (the Huicholes are polygamous) is taken to the sea to be 'purified'. Later we learn that she has hanged herself from a tree. Celebrating uncritically, as it does, the indigenes' supposed communion with nature, the film is unable to critique those aspects of their culture (such as machismo) that might prove more problematic, much less to examine the place of such traditions within a rapidly modernizing Mexico.

It takes a film-maker as daring and original as Julián Hernández to bring together these two alien worlds of sublime pre-Columbian myth-making and all-too-real gritty urbanism. After *Enraged Sun, Enraged Sky* was shown in Morelia at its full 191 minutes' length, I attended its theatrical premiere on 12 October at Cinépolis Diana on Paseo de la Reforma, Mexico City's most glamorous avenue, in a version shorn of an hour of footage. Hernández's third feature, and already the winner of the Teddy Award in Berlin, it begins with a dazzling evocation of the city. Shot in luscious black and white, a 'goddess' returns to the graffiti-scarred megalopolis, seeking true lovers who (according to the synopsis) will transcend the limits of space and time. The exotically named Kieri and Ryo will traverse many and varied gay cruising locations (most spectacularly the dilapidated porno theatre of the Cine Tacuba) in a wordless, but urgent, desire-fuelled quest. Driven quite literally by *nostalgie de la boue* (at one point an unfortunate actor drags himself through what seems to be an urban bog), Hernández takes care to compose a glorious sound collage that matches his meticulously grungy *mise-en-scène*. Deprived almost entirely of dialogue (with the characters' motives and actions left uncommonly obscure), still we are given at points a cacophony of urban voices, an acoustic counterpoint to the infinite flow of people and places in the city.

Sadly, the excised hour contains the main body of the film's other strand: a mythic narrative of (once more) amorous pursuit amongst mainly naked youths, but this time shot in bleached-out colour and in the spectacular rural locations of desert plains, caves and pre-Columbian archeological sites. Hernández's erotic myth-making may not prove to be the taste of every art movie fan. But it remains the case that, on the basis of this year's Morelia Festival, a national cinema that in a single year can produce three such varied and distinguished films as *Alamar*, *Presumed Guilty* and *Enraged Sun, Enraged Sky* would seem, in spite of critical and industrial claims to the contrary, to be in unusually good health.

Guadalajara, 2011: Art and Industry

The Festival Internacional de Cine en Guadalajara (FICG), to give it its full title, is generally held to be the most important in Latin America. Beginning as a simple 'Muestra' or showcase for Mexican cinema in 1986, it expanded into a fully-fledged festival in 1995, now embracing the whole of what it calls 'Iberoamerica', including Spain and Portugal. The FICG coincides to some extent with the newer and smaller Mexican festival of Morelia, offering as it does strands for documentaries and first features. But unlike the more intimate Morelia, it is also the main market for Latin American film, with an industrial as well as a cultural focus.

The twenty-sixth edition of the Festival, which took place from 25 March to 1 April 2011, was something of a new departure. Beyond 'Iberoamerica', it boasted Israel as 'guest country' and a retrospective of Werner Herzog, who gave a master class (the Basque Country was also invited and respected local actress Diana Bracho honoured). To this transnational end, celebrity visitors included both glamorous international stars (Eva Longoria came as co-producer of *The Harvest* [*La cosecha*], a documentary on child labour) and beloved Mexican veterans (Angélica María, former child star, promoted two unusual co-productions: the Israeli *Tel Aviv Salsa* [*Salsa en Tel Aviv*] and the Galician *Years Later* [*Años después*]).

An enterprising new director, Iván Trujillo, had moved the Festival's main site to the huge Expo conference centre on the edge of Mexico's second city, a location big enough to host simultaneously the 'Mangatron' comics' convention with its many festively dressed attendees. For the first time the new venue allowed adequate space for the large market section and for press screenings of the Mexican fiction features, followed by Q&As with their directors, also on-site. As in previous years, however, general screenings were scattered over a number of locations throughout the city, including such public spaces as the Plaza de la Liberación, outside the handsome Teatro Degollado in the picturesque historic centre.

While the Expo itself is hardly picturesque and the atmosphere can feel like a trade fair (complete with girls handing out drinks and flyers), the new setting also allowed for open-air events on-site, such as musical concerts. For example there was a flute and piano recital in memory of Mexican cinema's best-known composer, *maestro* Manuel Esperón, writer of standards such as the romantic 'Amorcito corazón' and the localist '¡Ay, Jalisco, no te rajes!' Taking advantage of the pleasant spring temperatures, free evening screenings were also held outside the Expo, notably a programme of vampire films curated by Guillermo del Toro. Murnau's original *Nosferatu* (1922) was shown with expert piano accompaniment; and Fernando Méndez's Mexican revision *The Vampire* (*El vampiro*, 1957) proved a revelation: expertly designed and powerfully performed, reminiscent of Val Lewton in its exemplary use of limited sound stages.

One screening, however, proved surprisingly controversial. Although the Festival had paid for the restoration of a rare feature from 1968 starring the silver-masked wrestler known as Santo (called, alternately, *The Vampire and Sex* [*El vampiro y el sexo*] and *Santo and the Treasure of Dracula* [*Santo y el tesoro de Drácula*]), it was cancelled at the last minute, as the deceased star's son claimed that the film, which was said to feature copious nudity, was damaging to his father's reputation (Solís, 2011). As we shall see, in line with this controversy over the value of a popular film, it is perhaps the opportunity to experience Mexican genre cinema at Guadalajara that is most valuable to foreign visitors, who are more likely to have access to auteur fare at festivals and arthouses in their own countries.

Parallel events to the Festival proper included a two-day academic conference on the theme of documentaries by first-time directors; and the launch of a hefty book of collected articles, *Tendencias del cine iberoamericano en el nuevo milenio* (*Trends in Iberoamerican Cinema in the New Millennium*, 2011), edited by Juan Carlos Vargas, from the local university. Elsewhere the Ninth Market of Iberoamerican Film (for completed films seeking distribution) was complemented by the Seventh Encounter of Film Co-production (for new projects seeking financing). And the third edition of Talent Campus Guadalajara lured established professionals (including screenwriter Guillermo Arriaga) into workshops with young hopefuls. But most valuable to the film scholar was perhaps a day-long Forum, the fifth in an annual series, on 'The Present and Future of Mexican Cinema', featuring speakers from the industry (mainly producers) and government (the head of IMCINE and even a local senator).

As Mauricio Durán, Vice-President of Marketing and Distribution at Universal Pictures Latin America, noted in the first session of the Forum, the current position of Mexican cinema is paradoxical. As new screens have opened, local production has boomed to match exhibition, reaching fifty-two features in 2010. Yet while Mexican films made up 17 per cent of the total titles screened in that year they gained only 5.6 per cent of the box office. Market share has thus fallen, even as production has risen, putting Mexico in a lowly tenth position in the main global markets when its percentage of market share is compared to that of other large countries whose local films are more popular with their own audiences. Moreover, just one film (Alejandro Springall's popular comedy *It's Not You, It's Me* [*No eres tú, soy yo*], 2010) was responsible for one quarter of the domestic share, while the top three made up fully half. This tiny number of successful features, on which the national industry is overly reliant, remains itself dependent on state support: González Iñárritu's

Biutiful, the most successful feature to be wholly funded from private sources, was only the fifth most popular local film in the year, in spite of its celebrity director and star, Javier Bardem.

Jorge Sánchez, former director of the Festival and founder of the new Casa del Cine ('House of Cinema') in the historic centre of Mexico City, continued the theme. There were now more films, more genres and more prizes at international festivals for Mexican titles. And, as he spoke, Roberto Hernández and Geoffrey Smith's *Presumed Guilty* (*Presunto culpable*, premiered a full two years earlier in Morelia) had become on its delayed theatrical release the most successful Mexican documentary of all time, achieving wide exhibition and plentiful press coverage and even provoking a national debate on legal reform. Yet none of this had seemed to help the Mexican industry to consolidate itself. Sánchez went on to raise two topics repeated throughout the day: the decisive role of distributors affiliated to the Motion Picture Association of America in discriminating against local films in favour of Hollywood fare and the necessity for audiovisual education to train audiences – supposedly 'deformed' by television – to accept more challenging Mexican (and other) cinema.

This second idea of 'audience development' ('creación de públicos') recurred in different contexts and was examined from different angles. Although one speaker claimed that film-makers should think more in terms of the audience when crafting their narratives, another suggested they go into schools to promote the appreciation of quality cinema. A third noted that 2,000 towns in Mexico no longer even have a cinema, while greedy exhibitors are building out multiplexes in the upmarket Mexico City *colonia* of Polanco.

While complaints of the lack of interest, or indeed frank hostility, of local audiences towards local films are as common in Spain as they are in Mexico, it was telling to hear Spain being cited as a model in a panel on the relationship between cinema and television. Producer Inna Payán noted that Spanish TV stations were obliged by law to fund films, with Televisión Española alone supporting ninety-three features in the last year. Two Mexican public TV officials (the directors of university channels) lamented the stranglehold of the duopoly of Televisa and Azteca, who seemed indifferent to the fate of film, and were comparable to the twin exhibitors Cinemex and Cinépolis, who also dominated their sector. Journalist Javier Solórzano was, however, more sceptical of such arguments for cinema as a cultural exception. Citing the programming of innovative channel 11, he noted that not all television was trash and claimed that there was a 'clear divorce' between the contents of local feature films and Mexican society.

The final panel was on the possibility of a new Cinema Law for Mexico, perhaps along similar lines to that in Spain. One producer suggested US-biased exhibitors be sued for violation of anti-competition law, while another proposed a new public regulatory entity for what was held to be a 'strategic sector' for Mexico. Marina Stavenhagen, warmly received by the audience, stated that she believed IMCINE (the Mexican Film Institute), of which she is director, *is* that public entity, aiming as it does to serve both the film industry and the wider community. She stressed that the government had indeed passed measures to support the sector (the ubiquitous fiscal stimulus known as 'Article 226' received an entire panel to itself). Rather, she said, there were failures in the chain of production that harmed the interests of creators and producers alike, especially the lack of proper promotion for features on their release. She also called on the film community to 'citizenize participation in cinema' by (once more) 'constructing audiences'. Cinema could also, she claimed, be 'strength-ened' by the participation of television companies in the production process. (It was telling that no representative of the TV medium took part in the Forum.)

While all speakers seemed to agree that Mexico had made great strides in democratization since 2000, when the PRI (the Institutional Revolutionary Party) was finally ejected from power, and that there was now little or no effective media censorship, it was felt that this transition had become 'frozen' in the audiovisual sector as at the macro-political level, with further renovation stalled indefinitely. Characteristically, we heard, a proposed new law for the audiovisual sector had no hope of passing the Senate.

Let us now examine more closely the current crop of Mexican fiction features shown at Guadalajara in 2011 to see how they emerge from or engage with this industrial and legislative context. No fewer than fourteen films were shown in competition. And, reconfirming the theme of innovation at the Festival if not in the Forum, a full eight of them were from first-time directors and five from women. Yet, as the *Hollywood Reporter* wrote, 'relatively few [of them] gen-erated significant buzz' (Hecht, 2011), and indeed, after one dismal day of press screenings, a well-known critic told me it would be 'heroic' if I continued to research Mexican film in the face of such evidence. Moreover, there was a marked divide between the tastes of juries and the public. There were complaints of low attendance at commercial screenings and by the end of the Festival even gala tickets were being offered at two for the price of one.

Best Mexican Fiction Feature went to *The Prize* (*El Premio*) by Paula Markovitch, an Argentine resident in Mexico, hitherto best known as the screenwriter for Fernando Eimbcke's *Duck Season* (*Temporada de patos*, 2004). This much-praised drama of the Dirty War was shot on the wintry Argentine coast with an Argentine cast and crew. Stretching the definition of 'Mexican film' to the limits, it was funded by IMCINE and FOPROCINE (Fondo para la Producción Cinematográfica de Calidad) but clearly made little connection with the local audience.

The festival audience gave its prize, awarded by popular acclaim, to a film openly despised by critics. *The Misfits* (*Los inadaptados*) is an ensemble comedy that retreads the multi-strand narratives that have become something of a cliché in Mexican film since the influential example of *Amores perros*, but this time in a humorous vein. Here, a young techie makes a date with an internet friend, who turns out to be his mother; a suicidal misanthrope hooks up with a kooky waitress who tells her straight-laced family that he is a porn star; and an arrogant Don Juan is trapped in a lift with a dignified maid, impregnated by her mistress's son. In the least likely narrative, a group of senior citizens, comfortably well off, plan to rob a bank, just for the hell of it.

As my synopsis suggests, the film encompasses some abrupt tonal shifts that it fails to negotiate with any grace. But here the production context is of interest. At the press screening it was revealed that the project was initiated by young actors and telenovela veterans Luis Arrieta and Luis Ernesto Franco (taking the producing name of 'Los Güeros' ['The Blonds'], from their fair hair), who had for the first time taken responsibility for one of their own features. And, although the film is credited in the festival programme to Jorge Ramírez Suárez, each of the four plot strands had been helmed by a different director. It was thus unsurprising that it failed to coalesce into a satisfying whole.

A second attempt to revitalize a familiar genre, in this case the thriller, was León Serment's *The Tequila Effect* (*El efecto tequila*) of 2010. Set before and after the Mexican financial crash of 1994 (which is clearly intended to be reminiscent of more recent global economic crises), this film replays *Wall Street* in a Mexican mode, with Eduardo Victoria in the role of the emblematically named José Fierro, the young thrusting trader who gets in over his head. Abundant in transnational cliché (José punches the air in his steel and glass office building one too many times), still *The Tequila Effect* offers a mordant commentary on its home country's recent history. One publicity shot shows just a bald pate from behind, recognizable only to those in the know as that of then president Carlos Salinas de Gortari. José's diabolical boss tempts him with easy money ('Mexico is getting rich.

Why aren't you?'); and explains, using talismanic English words, the distinctive nature of Mexican capitalism ('This is the country not of "know-how" but of "know-who"'). Even a subplot seemingly transplanted from a telenovela comes with a sting in its tail. José's neglected wife takes up with a handsomely bearded hippy-style lover, the polar opposite of her materialist husband. But the lover swiftly dumps her on seeing that she intends to take her young daughter with her when they elope.

If *The Misfits* shows that an audience-friendly comedy can be studiously non-specific in its context, *The Tequila Effect* places an equally abstracted and predictable narrative (the glossy thriller) in a much more precise setting. Indeed, the film's website promises to remind local viewers of the 'real names and deeds of those who made us believe that credit cards were blank checks' (*El efecto tequila*, 2011). And as financial scandal morphs into a melodrama of political corruption and assassination, *The Tequila Effect* swerves definitively from its *Wall Street* model. It remains to be seen whether the content of such commercial features, uncharacteristic of those normally funded by IMCINE, will indeed connect with the Mexican society whose specific ills the film claims to chronicle.

The Tequila Effect's office setting coincides with that of a much more ambitious and frankly bizarre critique of capitalism, David Michán's *Adverse Effects* (*Reacciones adversas*). Starring the ubiquitous Héctor Kotsifakis (who also had supporting roles in both *The Misfits* and *The Tequila Effect*), this existential drama begins with repeated shots of blurry lights, glowing red, green and gold on the sodden streets of what will prove to be a satanic Mexico City. Kotsifakis' Daniel is a depressed salaryman (the title refers to the side effects of his medication). Apparently fired from his job in a nameless corporation, he returns to attempt suicide in his solitary flat where his only phone messages are from credit-card debt-collecting agencies.

While this initial premise seems realistic (and indeed reminiscent in its sterile setting of *The Tequila Effect*), Michán's script, mirroring the disorientation of its subject's drugged state, soon veers into fantasy. Daniel's boss nonchalantly vomits onto a report he hands back to his subordinate and his office colleagues are literally cardboard cut-outs. Daniel is later given advice on taking vengeance on a hostile world by a talking dog and a mysterious American, who cites both Carl Perkins and William Blake.

The script appears at first to take a more conventional turn in its second and third acts when Daniel, having shaved his hair *Taxi Driver*-style, meets a mysterious chanteuse in a nightclub reminiscent of David Lynch's films (although here the fetish fabric is red, not blue, velvet); and engages in a bloody battle with the criminals who stole the money and cellphone with which he planned to start a new life with his femme fatale. The sex and violence, however – the staples of much current Mexican cinema – are reframed within a subjective perspective and called into question by unreliable narration: the love affair and shoot-out, the film suggests, may simply be chemically induced fantasies, adverse reactions to Daniel's prescription drugs.

Some critics were themselves averse to Michán's slick style and glossy cinematography (a first-time director of features, he is known for his work in commercials). But his exploration of male subjectivity was matched in a feminine mode by the competition's most established auteur: Maryse Sistach with her *Moon Rain* (*Lluvia de luna*). Foreign audiences who know Sistach mainly from *Perfume de violetas* (2001), a realist tale of the rape and bullying of poor schoolgirls in Mexico City, will be shocked by her latest feature, which, like Michán's, is decidedly non-naturalistic. Beginning with three girls on a moon-white beach in Quintana Roo and a fourth luxuriating in the warm sea water, *Moon Rain* cuts to a middle-aged singer and her daughter (Angela – María Filipini – and Lisa – Naian González) squabbling in Mexico City.

Slowly the narrative fragments coalesce. When Lisa dies in an accidental fall, Angela drives south to scatter her ashes at the Mayan site of Tulum, pausing to pick up a hitchhiker: Pablo (Alan Estrada), the boy on whom her daughter had a crush and whom the girls we saw in the prologue are also awaiting. Such implausible coincidences are matched by much New Age posturing, set to the plaintiff flute played by the youth or the mother's mournful vocalizing on the shore. By the end of the film, which features frequent allusions to *Alice in Wonderland* (a resurrected Lisa falls down a hole once more, this time a *cenote* or water-filled underground cave), it would appear that all three main characters are dead, revived only for a brief chance at love, whether maternal or romantic.

Like *Adverse Reactions*, then, *Moon Rain* essays a difficult tone, in this case more fey than nightmarish, but one which is equally hard to sustain across a full ninety minutes. Yet, in spite of *Variety*'s hostile review (which claimed that 'international prospects look DOA': Koehler, 2011), foreign audiences may well respond to the film's cultural feminism, with its exotic evocation of the moon, ocean and Mayan magic. And, as in the case of *Adverse Reactions* once more, the cinematography (here much of it underwater) is unusually handsome. Rejecting the film's exploration of fantasy, however, critics at the Q&A following the press screening quizzed the director on a factual point: the relationship between the accidental death of her own daughter in real life and that of the young woman in the film.

How do the four films on which I have focused match up with the debate on the present and future of Mexican film also featured at the FICG? Initially, at least, they confirm the breadth of genre and register currently subsidized by the public funds of IMCINE and FOPROCINE, ranging as they do from crowd-friendly comedies and thrillers to more minority auteurist projects, both male and female oriented (all these films received government money). Whether they find local distributors is yet to be seen (as the Festival began, only *The Misfits*, the winner of Guadalajara's audience prize, had been sold); and yet more difficult will be the competition with US blockbusters when the local films come to seek slots with exhibitors biased against Mexican product.

Interestingly, however, the implied audience for each feature is somewhat different. While *The Misfits* is a contemporary comedy, *The Tequila Effect* must be targeted at an older demographic, as it will have little resonance with spectators who fail to remember the historic crash invoked. And although *Adverse Reactions'* experiment with subjectivity and unreliability may seem arthouse-friendly, its slick visuals make it relatively accessible to all, especially with its graphic and stylized violence directed to the mainstream male market. Even Sistach's unapologetically personal myth-making is packaged in an attractive format, with motherly grief accompanied by turquoise waves and buff teenage bodies. Clearly more film-makers are thinking in terms of their existing audience when crafting their narratives, rather than seeking to create new spectators who will be more accepting of uncommercial forms and themes. Moreover, the bourgeois settings of all four films coincide with the new constitution of cinema audiences in Mexico, where the increase in ticket price means that only the wealthy can afford regular attendance in multiplexes in places like Polanco. And arguably it is the most commercial film (the one whose form most closely approximates to that of Hollywood) that engages most closely with a locally specific context: *The Tequila Effect* presents itself from the start as a national narrative couched in readily accessible terms.

And here (as in the Forum) the role of television is central. Although mainstream Mexican TV channels may not fund feature films as they do in Spain, clearly televisual narrative patterns and aesthetics are converging with film. Even an ensemble comedy such as *The Misfits* (which I traced back in form to *Amores perros*) might be read rather in the context of telenovela, with its proliferating casts and storylines. Most of the actors mentioned here will be well known to local audiences from television. And there is one case in point: Alan Estrada, the dream boy flautist of *Moon Rain*, came to fame as a singer on Televisa's reality competition called, appropriately enough, *El show de los sueños* (*Dream Show*). In this case, at least, the culturalist understanding of film as a vehicle of national identity – Mayan ruins included – would seem to coincide with the commercial imperative of corralling young, TV-trained viewers into theatres.

Ironically, perhaps, a more potent example of feminism than Sistach's is to be found in one of those innovative TV series briefly mentioned at the Forum. As we shall see in chapter 6 of this book, *The Aparicio Women* (*Las Aparicio*, made by independent producer Argos, outside the Televisa/Azteca duopoly, and aired in 2010) features an all-female family without men who would have added a little steel to *Moon Rain*'s whimsy. Certainly the tagline of *The Aparicio* ('A whole woman doesn't need another half' ['Una mujer entera no necesita media naranja', Argos, 2011]) is an antidote to the strand of teenage, heterosexual romance in Sistach's fantasy of love after death.

While film-makers may indeed be adjusting the content of their films to be more closely aligned with Mexican society, Marina Stavenhagen's ideal of 'citizenizing' participation in cinema would appear to remain distant. But the great virtue of the FICG, as the major festival in Latin America as well as the main market for Iberoamerican film, is that, uniquely, it allows and indeed encourages critical analysis of the field with an industrial as well as a cultural focus.

I was invited to Morelia as a juror in the Mexican Feature Competition and as a journalist for Film Quarterly. *My thanks are due to Daniela Michel, General and Artistic Director of the Morelia International Film Festival; James Ramey, Academic and Strategic Consultant; Montserrat Guiu, Jury Services; and my editor, Rob White. I attended Guadalajara as a panelist at an academic conference organized by Nancy Berthier of the Sorbonne and Álvaro Fernández of the Universidad de Guadalajara, who kindly provided a press pass for screenings and special events at the Festival.*

Jump Cut 2

Perfume de violetas (Maryse Sistach, 2001)

Mexico City, the present. Yessica, a poor teenager who lives with her abused mother, violent stepfather and sexist stepbrother Jorge, has her first day at a new school. She was expelled from her previous school for hitting a teacher. In class she meets the more reserved Miriam, who becomes her best friend. The two girls hang out together at Miriam's apartment, while Miriam's single mother is working at a shoe shop. Jorge, angered by Yessica's rebelliousness, arranges to have her raped by a colleague. Pocketing his fee, he buys shoes at Miriam's mother's shop. The traumatized Yessica confesses what has happened to Miriam but is ashamed to tell anyone else. Yessica is repeatedly punished at school by hostile teachers, who fail to appreciate what she is going through. Meanwhile two benevolent boys become interested in the girls and they start to go out together. Miriam's mother is increasingly disturbed by her daughter's friendship with the erratic Yessica, who has stolen a bottle of perfume from a market. Yessica then steals money from Miriam's mother and gives it to her own mother to pay the rent. Even when Miriam tells how she saw Yessica abducted for a second time by the rapists, Miriam's mother denounces Yessica as a slut who was asking for it. When Yessica turns up at school dirty and bruised, the authorities finally seem to take notice. Arranging to meet Miriam in the school toilet, Yessica accidentally pushes her friend who cracks her head against the floor and is apparently killed. In the final scene Miriam's mother returns home to find Yessica curled up in her friend's bed.

Perfume de violetas is the anti-*Y tu mamá también*. While Alfonso Cuarón's sunny road movie sent two schoolboys out of the city on an erotic adventure, Maryse Sistach's dark drama confines two schoolgirls to an urban setting where there is no escape from sexual harassment. And while the dignified *Perfume* was chosen as Mexico's entry for the Academy Awards, the scandalous *Mamá* (the biggest grossing Spanish-language film ever in the US) was pointedly passed over.

Sistach is now an established director, trained at the National Film School and with five features under her belt. It is no surprise, then, that *Perfume* is reminiscent of old-school Latin American neo-realism. But there are still surprises in store. The varied authentic locations are well chosen: poor Yessica lives in a ruinous bungalow without running water; wealthier Miriam in a neat apartment complete with bathtub. One of the most touching scenes of intimacy between the two girls is when they take a bath together. For once, Mexico City, the notoriously polluted and impoverished megalopolis, is not depicted as hell on earth. The kids make excursions to surprisingly rural parkland and the shops and markets are inviting. Compared to its counterparts in the UK or US, this is hardly Girlz 'N' the Hood.

On the other hand, the plot is starkly Manichaean. Yessica, neglected at home by her downtrodden mother (the distinguished actor-director-politician María Rojo), is relentlessly chastised by her teachers, even when evidence of abuse becomes obvious. A sympathetic school nurse who appears towards the end mysteriously disappears. When Yessica's hostile stepbrother Jorge sells her to a thuggish rapist, the camera lingers on his expensively shod feet, the reward for his horrible deal. The credit sequence superimposes photos of the two friends over newspaper headlines of violent crime in the capital. But although *Perfume* is based on a true story, the odds are stacked too heavily against its innocent protagonists. It is typical of the film that, of all the shoe shops in the city, Jorge should go to the one run by Miriam's mother to get his ill-gotten designer trainers.

It is not difficult to imagine what a British director like Ken Loach would make of such miserable material. Sistach, however, focuses winningly on female friendship. The principals are first-time actors trained at a local theatre school. Both make their characters convincingly addicted to the teenage pleasures that are symbolized by the heady perfume of the title. These girls just want to have fun and there is an unforced eroticism that surrounds their friendship as they bathe together and smell each other's hair. Thankfully, the rape scene is also sensitively handled. The camera shows us only Yessica's girlish cosmetics and school supplies spilled pathetically on the ground. And although Yessica's fate spirals ever downwards, Sistach leaves us with an impressively open and evocative ending: Yessica shelters beneath the blankets of her friend's bed, briefly enjoying that sense of belonging she has sought in vain throughout the film. *Perfume de violetas*, then, is no radical breakthrough in the context of recent Mexican cinema. But it remains a worthy achievement and a refreshingly female-centred film.

Sight & Sound (February 2003)

Frida (Julie Taymor, 2002)

Mexico City, 1954. Artist Frida Kahlo, gravely ill and forbidden by her doctors to attend an exhibition of her work, is carried on her bed to the gallery. We flash back to the 1920s when, as a spirited young girl, she first met the womanizing muralist Diego Rivera. After a devastating trolley accident in 1925, Frida is crippled and bedridden. Her middle-class parents provide her with art materials to keep her busy. Gradually she regains her mobility and discovers her artistic gift. After showing her paintings to Rivera, she is introduced into the vibrant Mexico City avant-garde, meeting such figures as photographer Tina Modotti and painter David Alfaro Siqueiros. Although Diego's ex-wife Lupe remains close to him, Frida becomes Diego's mistress and then wife. Diego's constant infidelities make their life stormy, although Frida herself takes lovers, both men and women. Diego is invited to New York where he begins his murals in the Empire State Building. When he refuses to remove a portrait of Lenin, the murals are destroyed before completion by patron Nelson Rockefeller. Later Frida is invited to Paris where she is lionized by the Surrealists. Back in Mexico, Frida discovers Diego is having an affair with her own sister. Frida breaks off the marriage and they divorce. Diego persuades her, however, to give shelter to the exiled Trotsky and his wife. Frida begins an affair with Trotsky, who later moves out and is murdered. Frida's health continues to deteriorate but Diego, chastened, suggests they remarry. On her deathbed, Frida gives him an antique ring as an anniversary present.

By all accounts, Salma Hayek has worked long and hard to bring her biopic of Mexican icon Frida Kahlo to the big screen, fighting off such heavyweight rivals as Jennifer Lopez. Taking co-producer credit with her own company Ventanarosa, Hayek is barely off the screen.

She is even credited for tango choreography with dance partner Ashley Judd (as photographer Tina Modotti). Clearly Kahlo's work is increasingly relevant to a modern artistic sensibility. Modern audiences may well be reminded of more recent women artists who use their private lives and bodies as directly and vividly as Frida did in her work. It is sad to report, then, that *Frida* is, to use the name of a dish loved by the artist's husband Diego Rivera, a *pozole*: a Mexican stew of varied ingredients, some more appetizing than others.

Things begin well with the notorious trolley accident, which was to cripple Frida, shown as a gorgeous riot of flying glass, gold dust and blue birds. An all-too-brief animation from the Brothers Quay turns Frida's convalescence into a nightmare of gurning medical skeletons. The New York and Paris scenes are suggestively shot in sepia again with constructivist animation: echoing one of Frida's paintings, the Empire State Building dissolves magically in her bath. Stylish cantina sequences showcase gravelly voiced chanteuse Chavela Vargas, who gives authentically cadaverous versions of folk songs. Shot almost entirely on location (only Frida's famous blue house was reconstructed in the studio), the film features some astonishing locations including the huge pyramids of Teotihuacan, north of Mexico City. Hayek pleaded with the President himself to gain access to this ancient and fragile site. In the rich cinematography of Rodrigo Prieto (*Amores perros*), the abundant food and frocks look fabulous. Such is the continuing love of Frida, elderly Mexicans queued up to offer antique shawls for use in the lavish production design. Salma Hayek tells us in the press book that when she tried on one of Frida's real-life dresses she discovered she was exactly the same size as her heroine.

Director Julie Taymor, best known for her acclaimed adaptation of *The Lion King* for the stage, is happiest with the fantasy sequences, such as the three-dimensional reproductions of some well-known paintings. She is constrained, however, by the limits of the biopic genre and historical realism. The script, based on Hayden Herrera's book and credited to no fewer than four screenwriters, contains some crass dialogue. Characters seem to speak to each other in headlines: 'The marriage of an elephant and a dove' (Frida's mother on her daughter's wedding); 'I paint what I see, you paint from inside' (Diego to the young Frida); and this memorable exchange near the end: Frida: 'You've lost weight.' Diego: 'You've lost your toes.' As the narrative flags, the film turns into a historical pageant. Walk-ons by stars like Antonio Banderas as Diego's rival muralist Siqueiros come off as (barely) animated waxworks. Geoffrey Rush's Trotsky is particularly excruciating. The film seems to assume we will care for these characters because they are historically significant, but it does not take the trouble to integrate them into its plot. When Trotsky's murder is cross-cut with Frida's double self-portrait, both awash with blood, the effect is unearned. We do not feel there is truly a connection between life, history and art.

Frida is strangled, then, by an overdose of reverence. Not only were Diego's grandchildren present on the set to ensure historical accuracy, even the dogs used in the film are direct descendants of Frida's pets. There is a clear contradiction in the film's two aims: to honour a great national figure and to further her imaginative legacy. The final result is stranded somewhere between heritage movie and surrealist manifesto. The philandering but loving Diego asks Frida the woman to understand the difference between fidelity and loyalty: it is a fine distinction that *Frida* the film does not manage to make.

Sight & Sound (March 2003)

Part II

Auteurs and Genres

3

A Case Study in Transnational Gay Auteurism: Julián Hernández's *A Thousand Clouds of Peace Encircle the Sky, Love, Your Being Love Will Never End* (*Mil nubes de paz cercan el cielo, amor, jamás acabarás de ser amor*, 2003)

Straying Further

Much research on globalizing cinema has focused on commercial genres (Miller et al., 2001). And, in the case of Mexican cinema, particular attention has been paid to the three directors of 'prestige pictures' held, outside their home country at least, to have kick-started a 'New Wave' of feature films that aspire to artistic quality while still achieving some box office success around the world: Alfonso Cuarón, Guillermo del Toro and Alejandro González Iñárritu. As is well known, these three film-makers have also combined rare locally made features with international projects, shot in the US or Europe, thus rendering their status within the 'imaginary coherence' of an assumed 'national cinema' problematic indeed (Arroyo Quiroz, Ramey and Schussler, 2011: 18). One scholar has gone so far as to link Iñárritu to a 'global Hollywood gaze' which is complicit with cultural tourism (Shaw, 2011).

It is somewhat ironic that this perceived renaissance took place (as several commentators have noted) after changes in the state-funding regime that many predicted would destroy, rather than revitalize, Mexican cinema. Industry sources such as Rosa Bosch (of Tequila Gang, the production company associated with del Toro) claim that is precisely because the new big three directors, profiting from global distribution and promotion, were free from financial and artistic dependence on state-controlled IMCINE that they could stage a 'take-over' of the industry from an older generation identified with the once canonized and now sidelined masters Arturo Ripstein and Paul Leduc (Wood, 2006: 168).

This third chapter focuses rather on the phenomenon of low-budget transnational auteurist film, in which the achievement of distribution depends on a fine balance between artistic elements held to be local or indigenous and those that stake a claim to an international cinematic tradition. Like the better-known case of Carlos Reygadas, Julián Hernández is a transnationally distributed young film-maker from Mexico with three features to date (*A Thousand Clouds of Peace* [*Mil nubes de paz*, 2004], *Broken Sky* [*El cielo dividido*, 2006], and *Enraged Sun, Enraged Sky* (*Rabioso sol, rabioso cielo*, 2009, this last film examined in chapter 2 of this book) which are unapologetically arthouse in narrative structure and film form. Unlike Reygadas, however, who has appealed to graphic, but notably unerotic, scenes of heterosexual activity, Hernández seeks to inscribe himself within a gay or homoerotic tradition that includes European old masters (Fassbinder, Pasolini) and gestures perhaps towards contemporary Asian auteurs (most especially Wong Kar-wai and Tsai Ming-liang).

As we shall see, the theme of homosexuality is central, but contested and contradictory, here. The film-maker and his critics both defend the specificity of a homoeroticism that is often held to be hitherto absent from Mexican cinema (although Hernández has himself cited the example of the prolific and durable gay auteur Jaime Humberto Hermosillo [*Cinencuentro*, 2009]) and insist that Hernández's films are universal in both thematics and audience address: they are said to treat an erotic and psychic experience that is relevant, if not accessible, to all. Hence, although the director insists, auteur-like, that 'all of my films are about me and what happens to me every day' ('Todas mis películas hablan de mí y de lo que me ocurre todos los días'), *A Thousand Clouds*' novice star, more diplomatic or cautious, claims that the film 'goes beyond homosexuality: it's a love story and love has no limits' ('va más allá de la homosexualidad; se trata de una historia de amor y el amor no tiene parámetros') (*Cómo Hacer Cine*, 2004). Hernández himself says elsewhere that the origin of his script lay in an episode not from his own life but from that of Fassbinder (Golem, no date [2004]).

I will suggest that, in spite of such disavowals, homosexuality is inextricable from auteurism here. Only when an overtly gay thematics (the common preoccupation of Hernández's *oeuvre*) is couched within the rarefied aesthetic of the art movie is it acceptable to

Figure 3   *A Thousand Clouds of Peace* (Julián Hernández, 2004)

Mexican critics and audience alike, even as they take care to decry the 'homophobia' of their own cinematic tradition. The conspicuous and very specific pleasures of young male bodies are thus bought at the cost of a transnational arthouse technique, much of which is, ironically, shared by the very heterosexual Carlos Reygadas: an overtly aestheticized cinematography, an editing strategy that is (over-)reliant on the punishingly long take, and a style of narrative and characterization whose premises remain wilfully obscure. Even the impassivity and affectlessness of the central performance in *A Thousand Clouds* (attributed by unsympathetic critics to its young protagonist's inexperience) is as reminiscent of grand European auteurs such as Bresson, as it is of Reygadas (Figure 3). The cultural distinction that such cinema seeks, potentially threatened by the all-too-obvious pleasures of the naked ephebe, is thus assured by a self-conscious distancing from commercial aesthetics.

   The unfeasibly long titles that are Hernández's trademark (*A Thousand Clouds* . . . is said to be taken from a poem by Pasolini [*Cómo Hacer Cine*, 2004]) are perhaps the most self-evident of these strategies. Indeed, as I mentioned in my first chapter, in *The Rules of Art*, his study of the perilous balances and trade-offs between culture and commerce, Pierre Bourdieu cites 'the obscure and disconcerting title' (1996: 137) as one of the essential characteristics of the artwork that aspires to distinction by offering consecrated critics the chance to display the ingenuity of their interpretative skills.

It is perhaps no accident that Mexico's most acerbic critic (Jorge Ayala Blanco), the scourge of both the official state cinema of Ripstein and the new transnational independent films of González Iñárritu, has been unusually supportive of Hernández, even naming *A Thousand Clouds* as one of the top twenty films in the history of Mexican cinema (*La Jornada*, 2004). And if authoritative Mexican critics are eager to display their critical ingenuity when confronted by disconcerting obscurity, then those on the left at least (in *La Jornada*, 2004, again) are equally anxious to show that, unlike their fellow Mexicans, they are unafraid of the rather different challenge of relatively graphic gay content that includes male frontal nudity.

It is worth looking a little closer at the discourse used in support of Hernández by the licensed heretic, Jorge Ayala Blanco, the distinguished film historian and notoriously vituperative critic for financial paper *El Economista*. Writing in his collection *La fugacidad del cine mexicano* (*The Fleetingness of Mexican Film*, 2001) even before the first feature has been released, Ayala Blanco has no qualms in calling Hernández's informally distributed short *Long Nights of Insomnia* (*Largas noches de insomnio*, 2000), a rare 'cult film of the precarious national [i.e. Mexican] gay cinema' ('una película de culto del precario cine nacional gay', 2001: 444). But he takes care to distance it from global gay film, which, he claims, tends to aim for the 'shocking' gesture (the word is given in English) or a flamboyantly camp avant-gardism that he calls 'post-[Derek] Jarman'. Praising Hernández for the subtlety of his 'textures' and tones (white, grey and black), Ayala Blanco also celebrates the narrative 'reticence' ('pudor') whereby he carefully erases his own 'footsteps' or 'traces' ('huellas') from the script he has himself written (2001: 446). These 'slippages of pleasure' ('deslices del placer'), we are told, go beyond a simple statement of the social exclusion of homosexuals in contemporary Mexico to address the 'enigmatic splendour' ('esplendor enigmático') of young men (or 'young people' ['jóvenes']) in general (2001: 447). According to Ayala Blanco, Hernández thus re-stages Pasolini's *Una vita violenta* (*A Violent Life*), transferring the exotic *ragazzi* of Rome to prosaic Mexico City.

Like Hernández himself, then, Ayala Blanco attempts to balance local reference with global resonance and to trump social testimony with an aesthetic ambivalence as fleeting and formless as the slippages of desire. The critic thus eases the way for the budding auteur to adopt a perilous and provisional, but potentially prestigious, position in the contested Mexican cultural field. It is thus no surprise that, in a book subsidized by the government bodies devoted to culture and cinema (CONACULTA and IMCINE), an apparently marginal film such as *A Thousand Clouds* could be chosen as the first of just four Mexican features representing 2004, the year of its release (González Vargas, 2006: 242–5).

But to propose such institutional motives for Hernández's unlikely and qualified success is not to minimize the sheer difficulty of his achievement, which may not have been helped by his brave and open self-identification with Mexico's gay community. Although he was a graduate of one of the two official film schools, the CUEC at UNAM (National Autonomous University of Mexico), sources (including Ayala Blanco, who has taught a course on film aesthetics at that same school [2001: 444]) claim that Hernández was unpopular and unappreciated there. After numerous shorts, his first feature, *A Thousand Clouds*, was shot on a micro-budget and temporarily abandoned midway through lack of resources. Hernández has thus been forced to embrace flexible accumulation in the low-budget production of features with high-end production values (seen especially in his business partner Diego Arizmendi's luminous black and white cinematography), making highly uncommercial features against all the odds (see Vázquez, 2004).

But Hernández has attempted to offset production difficulties at home with distribution possibilities abroad. Like other independent Mexican directors (including, ironically, González Iñárritu), he has managed to exploit a potent reverse cultural flow. His debut feature was consecrated at numerous foreign festivals before it received, a full year after screenings abroad, a limited theatrical release in Mexico that led to nominations for eight Ariel awards, including those for Best Director, which Hernández had won at Guadalajara, and Best Original Screenplay (the film finally won in three minor categories). Once more, gay interest (far from harming prospects of distribution) may have actively helped: *A Thousand Clouds* won the Teddy award at Berlin, a dedicated LBGT prize. In Madrid, the film's only screenings have been at the dedicated Lesbian and Gay Festival and, subsequently, at an officially sponsored round-up of Mexican cinema, a nice pairing of queer and nationalist showcases that points to a confluence of two brands of identity politics. In *Cómo Hacer Cine*, Hernández balances respectful nods to Pasolini (that immoderately long title again) with admiring references to that most Mexican of Golden Age directors, Emilio 'El Indio' Fernández.

While Hernández has insisted in interview that his first picture achieved its foreign success because it refused to recycle clichés of both homosexuality and *mexicanidad*, in fact his films appeal to a mediascape of fluid and irregular representations that are difficult to place. His features are at once materially embedded in the authentic shooting locations of Mexico City (*A Thousand Clouds* offers – like

Amores perros – an early brief glimpse of the central skyscraper Torre Latinoamericana, a highly recognizable landmark; *Broken Sky* was filmed on the distinctive UNAM campus and in the gay-friendly Zona Rosa) and aesthetically abstracted from that very particular context in ways that render the films accessible to international audiences. Tellingly, Hernández, in spite of his preference for his native Distrito Federal and unlike other current directors, does not rely on such quintessentially national locations as the Zócalo, which was juxtaposed with an explicit scene of fellatio in Reygadas' *Battle in Heaven* (*Batalla en el cielo*, 2005) and was, ten years earlier, the scene of a more genteel gay assignation in Jorge Fons's *Midaq Alley* (*El callejón de los milagros*, 1994) (see Noble, 2005: 119–21).

Rather than exploiting, and subverting, such symbolically charged territories, Hernández's national production processes are rooted in the Morelos Film Cooperative that he set up as part of a triumvirate with cinematographer Arizmendi and producer Roberto Fiesco (their production company remains named after this first film, 'Mil Nubes'). Yet his first feature, which asserts its artistic and commercial independence, was still subsidized in part by the national film body IMCINE, while receiving development funding from the Rockefeller and MacArthur Foundations. Sundance, a crucial international source of both finance and legitimation, has also supported his work.

I would argue that Hernández's transnational reception is based on a hybridized revision of the homoerotic motifs that no doubt contributed to this sympathetic funding from abroad. On its limited release in the US, critics in New York, Los Angeles and San Francisco (where I myself attended a near empty screening at the Castro Theatre) were variably resistant to *A Thousand Clouds*' exacting tempo and opaque narrative (Holden, 2004; Dargis, 2004; Johnson, 2004). But they had no trouble placing it within a dissident auteurist tradition that was as much literary as it was cinematic (Jean Genet is the emblematic name that recurs here). Hernández thus emerged in his first feature with that prerequisite of auteurism, a signature style and subject, already fully fledged, even as he strayed from the existing templates of Mexican cinema, whether classic or iconoclastic.

Looking Closer

Let us look now in more detail at the textual composition of Hernández's film, which stakes its claim to distinction through the self-conscious asceticism of minimalist technique. After near-silent monochrome credits, the film opens with a sex scene in an unestablished nocturnal exterior. Teenage Gerardo (played by non-professional Juan Carlos Ortuño) is performing fellatio, just out of shot, on an anonymous client in the latter's car. The camera focuses, as in Warhol's *Blow Job* (1964) (but much more briefly), on the client's face. Wiping cum or vomit from his lips with the banknotes that are his paltry reward, Gerardo next submits to a lengthy two-shot in which he (and we) is driven through the shadowy city. The couple remain resolutely blank-faced and depressingly silent, an impression ironically reinforced by the soulful romantic ballad on the car radio ('¡Oh gente!' ['Oh, people!'] by José José, the 'Prince' of 1970s Mexican pop). Here, minimalist technique (albeit leavened by luscious, grainy night shooting) is combined with existential thematics: Gerardo's alienation, apparently effected by a homosexuality that is presented here as a purely financial transaction, could hardly be more self-evident.

Blurring the boundaries between past and present, however, Hernández goes on to reveal that Gerardo's marginalization is due to more than a generalized and precocious *Weltschmerz*. As we see in flashbacks, intermittently inserted into the apparently aimless flâneurism of the present, Gerardo has been dumped by an older boyfriend who has left him a poetically enigmatic break-up note. A second scene is crucial here. As Gerardo lies frustrated on the bed in his grungy rented room, Hernández pans left over his still-clothed body. Gerardo rises to examine his morose reflection in the cracked mirror, pulls down his underpants and caresses his crotch, before retiring once more to the bed. Masturbation is, however, interrupted by remembered or fantasized scenes of love-making with the lost boyfriend. And, crucially, in spite of the typical lack of dialogue, the whole sequence is played to music sourced to the youth's old-fashioned gramophone.

The song here is 'Nena' ('Girl') by Sara Montiel, the grande dame of Spanish musicals, who also enjoyed a successful film career in Mexico. The chorus runs as follows: 'Nena . . . / Me decía loco de pasión./ Nena . . . / Que mi vida llenas de ilusión./ Deja que ponga/ con embeleso/ junto a tus labios/ la llama divina/ de un beso' ('Girl, he would call me, mad with passion; girl, who fills my life with hope. Let me in my enchantment place on your lips the divine flame of a kiss'). The novelistic lyrics go on to tell of a man who swore eternal love to the singer, only to be separated from her by death: if his dark eyes shine even brighter now than the first time they pierced the singer's soul, it is because they now burn with mortal fever. The relatively graphic frontal nudity of this sequence is thus juxtaposed with the stylized and tortured romance of an earlier era (the song is taken from the soundtrack of *The Last Torch Song* [*El último cuplé*, 1957], a Spanish variant on *A Star is Born*, directed by Francoist stalwart Juan de Orduña).

What is striking in this sequence is not so much the willed incongruity between image and soundtracks as the appeal to perhaps the most transnationally accessible figure of Spanish-language camp icons. Gerardo may be confined to his little room in Mexico, D.F., but his obsession with Sarita (who would also feature as a gay youth's ego ideal in Almodóvar's *Bad Education* [*La mala educación*] released the following year) places him in the familiar mainstream of gay fandom. Homosexuality, squalidly commercial in the opening sequence, is now presented as solitary and narcissistic, but mediated by fantastic identifications that are experienced as collective by the target audience, if not by the character himself. Gerardo, who talks with characteristic vagueness of 'some old Spanish movie', is shown to be unaware of the song's source, even as he submits in time-worn style to the seduction of its extravagant masochism.

A third and final sequence offers yet another contradictory image of homosexuality. When Gerardo cruises a stereotypically masculine man on the city outskirts, Hernández exploits the squalid urban locations that are so successfully aestheticized by his cinematographer: soulless highways, deserted train tracks and walls intricately scarred by graffiti. Here, lengthy, silent takes are combined with frequent camera movement (tracks and pans) and directive editing strategies (point-of-view shots and cross-cutting) to create a compelling, if slow-moving, chase sequence. The erotic pursuit leads, however, not to the expected embrace but rather to a punch in the face that will leave our impassive hero attractively bruised for the remainder of the film.

The sexual exploitation of the first sequence and the narcissistic camp of the second are here joined by a violence that is clearly eroticized, but not, however, presented as pleasurable to its victim. And once more, and for a third time, the source music tends to distance us from the social implications of the scene. For this queer bashing is set – with transparently ironic intent – to a choral liturgical soundtrack. Now, there are hints elsewhere in the film that Gerardo's doomed erotic and romantic odyssey is in some way spiritual. An older, deserted queen tells him he should look to the sky or heaven: 'We are nothing, but He is the King of Kings!' ('No somos nada, pero ¡Él es el Rey de los Reyes!'). It is not clear whether the older man is invoking the deity or the great dark-eyed man whose role is, as ever, to seduce and abandon the gay beloved.

I have already argued that Hernández attempts to walk a tightrope, striking a balance between the national and transnational, the homosexual and the universal. Here also he tries to distance himself from the sociopolitical arena to which much Latin American cinema has found itself confined, especially by foreign critics, even as he invokes those cinematic memories of underdevelopment in his favoured locations. One further technique exemplifies this disavowal, which (barely) preserves what it seeks to deny. Cinematographer Diego Arizmendi often favours an extreme shallowness of field which tends to isolate the protagonist, shot in loving, sculptural close-up, from his fleeting, blurry background, a visual effect that perhaps echoes the 'thousand clouds' of the title or, indeed, Ayala Blanco's 'fugacidad' ('fleetingness') of Mexican cinema.

It is thus true that Hernández bears some witness in his narrative and locations to social deprivation and exploitation (from poverty to homophobia), an emphasis likely to be expected in a Mexican movie by European or US audiences, who have tended to value such films in socioeconomic rather than aesthetic terms. But Hernández clearly signals through his technique that this localist reading of his film may be to some extent necessary but is by no means sufficient for its interpretation. Familiar elements of social realism (authentic locations, amateur actors, vernacular dialogue) are thus preserved under erasure, fleetingly glimpsed only to be masked by the equally familiar, but often incompatible, aesthetics of the transnational art movie (monochrome photography, off-centre framing, extended takes with little camera movement).

Hernández has recently said in interview that in Mexico he is regarded as 'Julián, the one who makes films about homosexuals, fags, or queers' ('Julián el que hace películas de homosexuales, jotos, o maricones'), while abroad he is thought to be simply 'a film-maker with . . . a recognizable and demanding style' ('un realizador que . . . tiene un discurso reconocible y nada complaciente') (Zonadiversa, 2012). Clearly his has not always been an easy position in his home country. I would suggest finally, however, that it is precisely through those elements of his *oeuvre* that appear to be of restricted or minority interest (homophilia, cinephilia) that Hernández has managed to construct a transnational gay auteurism that has achieved wider distribution than has more commercial Mexican cinema.

It remains to be seen whether Hernández, who has at the time of writing completed three features, will be able to build a more substantial body of work and turn himself into that rare creature, a Mexican 'career director', who would fully justify the precocious arthouse status to which his films clearly aspire. There is little doubt, though, that he is already a unique and distinctive artist, and one who has been able to take up a significant position within a globalizing Mexican film industry, even as he holds fast to the marginal status of the cinematic outlaw.

4

A Case Study in Genre and Nationality: Guillermo del Toro's *Pan's Labyrinth* (*El laberinto del fauno*, 2006)

Exploring Horror

Pan's Labyrinth takes place in 1944, the fifth year of peace, and recounts the exciting journey of Ofelia (Ivana Baquero), a young girl of thirteen, who along with her mother, Carmen (Ariadna Gil), whose condition is frail because of her advanced state of pregnancy, moves to a little village where Vidal (Sergi López) is based. He is a cruel captain in the Francoist army and Carmen's new husband, for whom Ofelia feels no affection. Vidal's mission is to finish off the last traces of Republican resistance, hidden in the forests of the region. Also in the village stands the mill that serves as Vidal's headquarters and where Mercedes (Maribel Verdú), the young housekeeper, and Dr Ferreiro (Alex Ángulo), who will take charge of Carmen's delicate state of health, are awaiting the family. One night Ofelia discovers the ruins of a labyrinth in which she meets a faun (Doug Jones), a strange creature who reveals something incredible to her: Ofelia is really a princess, the last of her line, whose family have been waiting for her for a long time (Figure 4). In order to return to her magical kingdom, the girl must undergo three trials before the full moon. During this mission, fantasy and reality join hands to give free rein to a marvellous story where the magic that surrounds Ofelia transports us to a unique universe, one that is full of adventures and charged with emotion (*Clubcultura*, 2006; translation mine).

Figure 4 *Pan's Labyrinth* (Guillermo del Toro, 2006)

There seems little doubt that *Pan's Labyrinth* is one of the greatest critical and popular successes of its decade. It was the winner of seven Goya awards in Spain (including Best Original Screenplay, Best Cinematography and Best New Actress), nine Ariels in Mexico (including Best Picture, Best Director and Best Actress), and three Oscars (Best Cinematography, once more, and Best Art Design and Make-up). It was seen by 1,682,172 viewers in Spain, thus making it the third and ninth most popular local feature in 2006 and 2007 respectively (Ministerio de Cultura, 2010), while its cumulative gross of over $37 million made it one of the most popular foreign language films ever at the US box office. The UK gross earnings of £2,723,276 were also unprecedented (Gant, 2009). Uniquely, for a Spanish-language fiction feature, it has also inspired a large bibliography in specialist journals of psychology and psychiatry (see Cook, 2010; Rohde-Brown, 2007; Segal, 2009).

Yet beyond these bare facts, *Pan's Labyrinth* exhibits continuing contradictions. Although the Spanish Ministry of Culture website defines it simply as a 'drama', the film was generally received as a horror title; and IMDb (2010) lists its multiple genres as 'drama, fantasy, mystery, thriller, war . . .'. Conversely, director Guillermo del Toro was clearly identified as *Pan's Labyrinth*'s auteur, a film-maker with a personal style and vision uniquely capable of crossing national frontiers and generic borderlines (in an interview included with the UK DVD extras, he claims that it is his 'most personal' film). Accepted as a Spanish film in Spain and a Mexican movie in Mexico (hence its eligibility for both Goyas and Ariels), it is in fact a co-production between del Toro's own Tequila Gang and Picasso Studios, the successful feature-making arm of Spanish television broadcaster Tele 5.

While the Spanish Ministry of Culture website is enviably precise about the proportion of the film that can be allotted to each country (based on the budget, 78 per cent of the credit goes to Spain and 22 per cent to Mexico), the cultural allegiance of *Pan's Labyrinth* is more difficult to apportion. Indeed, IMCINE's website (which hosts the Mexican equivalent to the Spanish database, but does not give budget or box office statistics) attributes the nationality of the film to 'Mexico, Spain, United States', in that order (IMCINE, 2011b). The fact that del Toro had already made an earlier feature charting the Civil War through the eyes of a child, *The Devil's Backbone* (*El espinazo del diablo*, 2001), and presented this second film as in some way a sequel to the first, could be seen as making *Pan's Labyrinth* yet more markedly his own cinematic property. And in an interview del Toro admitted to risking 'cliché' by connecting the violence in his film to a supposed 'Mexican sensibility' (Kermode, 2006). Yet by locating a genre film for the second time at a precise and traumatic moment in Spanish history, del Toro encouraged spectators to read the fantasy format that generally transcends time and space within a very particular context. And by making his young protagonist female in this second film, del Toro also raised the question of gender (claiming *Pan's Labyrinth* as a 'sister' to the 'brother' movie of *The Devil's Backbone* [Kermode 2006]), a question that, as we shall see, has transformed academic understanding of horror film in recent years.

Genre, then, as a set of formal characteristics that function as triggers of recognition for competent audiences, intersects in complex and unstable ways with a number of different factors: nationality, history, industry and sexuality. In this fourth chapter I argue that *Pan's Labyrinth* deserves to be read within a particularly Spanish context that is ambiguously connected to Mexico. Beginning by raising the question of whether there is a specific kind of horror in the Spanish audiovisual sector (both cinema and television), the chapter then makes reference to varied and influential precursors in the field (including Narciso Ibáñez Serrador's *Stories to Keep You Awake* [*Historias para no dormir*, 1964–82], Víctor Erice's *The Spirit of the Beehive* [*El espíritu de la colmena*, 1973], and del Toro's own *The Devil's Backbone* [2001]) and places *Pan's Labyrinth* within that context. Particular attention should be paid here to *Pan's Labyrinth*'s principal production companies, mentioned earlier, the transnational specialist film enterprise with the mockingly Mexican name Tequila Gang and Spanish national TV channel Tele 5, whose Estudios Picasso was at the time the most successful audiovisual producer in Spain. The chapter finally offers a close textual analysis of *Pan's Labyrinth* itself, calling attention to the points at which it coincides with, and those at which it diverges from, the transnational tradition of horror and its unique Spanish variant.

To begin, nomenclature is not simply a question of classification but also of production and reception. In Spanish (where the English 'horror' is in any case normally translated as 'terror'), the requisite term, irreducible to foreign taxonomies, is 'cine fantástico' ('fantasy film'). Vital for an understanding of the genre is the international festival of that name held in Sitges since 1968. An unpaginated leaflet published for that founding event, grandly titled *Índice analítico del cine fantástico* (*Analytical Index of Fantasy Film*) and written by the festival's first director Antonio Cervera (1968), attempts to set out the parameters for a body of previously neglected films. Yet, as in IMDb's description of the many genres of *Pan's Labyrinth*, categories proliferate. The leaflet lists no fewer than forty-two variants or sub-genres of 'fantasy': from vampires, werewolves and witches, through myths, dreams and fantasies, to 'personification of the abstract', the 'incarnation of death' and 'the invented past'. Signalling the open-ended nature of the account and the impossibility of fully encompassing the genre, the final category reads simply 'Y . . .' ('And . . .').

Modern scholars of this wide and indefinable field are indebted to one Spanish researcher who, uniquely, has championed what he has baptized '*Cine fantástico y de terror español*' ('*Spanish Fantasy and Horror Film*'). Carlos Aguilar's invaluable collection of that name is divided into two volumes (1900–1983 and 1984–2004), each prefaced by an excellent introduction (1999, 2005). What is most significant here is that, going well beyond the taxonomic remit of Sitges, he links formal characteristics to the historical, political and industrial factors that inform and constrain them. Aguilar begins his account of the 'hot, black blood' ('sangre caliente, negra') of Spanish 'fantasía' with an unequivocal assertion that a specifically Spanish 'cine fantástico' definitely exists. The latter encompasses its own multiple conceptions of the genre, its more or less specialized auteurs, its high and low points, and its masterpieces and minor works (1999: 11). Aguilar estimates the corpus of such films as 200, with fully half of them released in the period 1968–74 (after Sitges was set up as a genre showcase) (1999: 13).

Two factors mark Spain's 'anomaly' in the field. The first is a characteristic belatedness. In literature, Romanticism, the origin of terror narratives, took (weak) root in Spain only in 1830, when it was already on the way out in Britain and France (1999: 14). Stymied by the strength of the Catholic Church, film horror with its typical archetypes and obsessions did not infiltrate Spanish cinema until the 1960s, decades after such pioneers as German Expressionism and the 'splendour' of Lon Chaney and Todd Browning (1999: 15). And the Francoist regime allowed the shooting of supernatural stories only if they took place outside Spain.

The second feature of Spain's 'anomaly' for Aguilar is its 'crudity'. From genre specialists Jésus (Jess) Franco and Narciso Ibáñez Serrador to (the unexpectedly cited) Alex de la Iglesia and Alejandro Amenábar, Spanish auteurs embrace the putrid, sickly and sordid, having little taste for science fiction and pure fantasy (for speculation and wonder) (1999: 16). The interaction between eroticism and violence or sex and death is thus held to be the most recognizable characteristic of Spanish horror (here rendered as 'terror') in all periods of film production.

In the introduction to his second volume, Aguilar historicizes this broad model, asking what happens when the Spanish fantastic genre becomes 'modern'. Ironizing at the expense of the PSOE government, which came to power in 1982, Aguilar lauds the Socialists for downgrading the influence of the Church and armed forces and liberalizing access to pornography, but attacks the new cultural policy imposed by the 'finos' ('refined') politicians (2005: 12). The effect of the subsidy regime of the Miró Law of 1983 was, he writes, to abolish the middle ground in which fantasy film had thrived: now there were only the two 'irreconcilable' currents of expensive 'important' films (financially backed by officials and benefiting from the best technical facilities and most prestigious casts) and despised 'sub-products' (made by tiny crews and professionals out of sync with modern trends and destined for straight-to-video distribution). The continuity and renovation of the horror genre thus proved impossible during the lengthy PSOE era.

For Aguilar, the sad fate of fantasy is no accident. The Socialists hated anything that fell outside 'pure rationalism' and, encouraged by the awards won by 'important' films at foreign festivals, cultivated the 'rural drama' and 'social realism' (preferably in plots adapted from classic novels) as new stereotypes for a dignified national cinema (2005: 13). Ironically coinciding with their Francoist predecessors, then, the PSOE proved that the Spanish 'contempt' for the fantastic genre is 'impermeable', irrespective of varied political positions.

Fortunately, the genre revived in the 1990s (with the help of Mexico). For Aguilar, one recent film project that transcends persistent Spanish binaries and preconceptions precisely is del Toro's *The Devil's Backbone*, a co-production between Spain and Mexico that fuses 'historical realism' with 'traditional fantasy' (2005: 41). Another is a cross-media hybrid: *Films to Keep You Awake (Películas para no dormir*, 2005) is a series of six feature-length episodes made for TV (like *Pan's Labyrinth*) by Estudios Picasso, based on classic television drama by Ibáñez Serrador but helmed by cinematic auteurs such as de la Iglesia (2005: 42). This hybridity or difficulty in firmly locating horror within a single genre, territory or medium is confirmed by an idiosyncratic feature of Aguilar's style: his frequent appeal to foreign loan words or phrases such as 'fantastique', 'wonder sense' (*sic*), 'soft core' and 'ghost story'. This suggests that the films he focuses on are not quite at home in the Spanish language, even as he insists on the unique characteristics of Spain's form of 'terror'. (For the same reason, a later, less magisterial study written in Castilian is actually given the English-language title of *Spanish Horror* [Matellano, 2009].)

Aguilar, sympathetic to his chosen subject, offers the opportunity to re-read a much-despised genre in a way he himself defines as 'artistic-historical-industrial' (2005: 13). He establishes a broad canon of Spanish directors that range from those firmly pigeonholed in a neglected genre to the most respected in general film-making: thus in the second volume Julio Medem is included on the basis of his propensity towards 'real dreams' (2005: 199–218). But there is little doubt that the Mexican del Toro is a significant figure in this context and one who benefits from this new form of analysis. As mentioned earlier, *The Devil's Backbone* receives close study by Aguilar who, always sensitive to hybridity, praises its status as a co-production (a phenomenon to which other Spanish scholars are often hostile) and its fusion of painful 'Spanish reality' (the Civil War) with the 'ghost story' format that is held to be of 'Anglo-Saxon origin' (2005: 503). The film's creative process is equally impure, based as it is on the fusion of two separate narratives: a Spanish-set story of an unexploded bomb and an originally Mexican project located in a boarding school (2005: 504).

Clearly, although Aguilar does not state it explicitly, it is del Toro's foreign status and financial independence that make him immune to the 'impermeable' Spanish contempt for the genre in which he specializes and render him undeterred by the 'artistic-historical-industrial' complex that has hitherto hobbled Spanish film-makers drawn to the genre. As an outsider, del Toro can also bridge the divide established in a previous decade between the 'important' films that monopolized big budgets and technical and artistic talent and the straight-to-video 'sub-genres' that (barely) preserved the anarchic vitality of sub-genres such as horror movies.

It is a bridging function of which del Toro makes good use in marketing, as well as in production, in a range of countries: as *Sight & Sound* wrote, *Pan's Labyrinth* 'charmed both the hardcore horror . . . fans at [specialist festival] FrightFest in London . . . and the upmarket critical cognoscenti who snapped to attention following his Palme d'Or nomination at Cannes' (Kermode, 2006). In *Pan's Labyrinth*, horror motifs typical of the sub-genres are thus combined with technical mastery (the Oscar-winning prosthetic make-up of Catalans David Martí and Montse Ribé) and prestigious casting (respected thespians Maribel Verdú, Ariadna Gil and Sergi López). The participation of such technicians and artists serves to underwrite the 'importance' of a film that was claimed by its auteur as the first over which he had complete artistic control.

Del Toro also embraces multiple 'variants' of the fantastic, beyond the stricter definitions of Anglo-American 'horror', diverse elements that were already proposed in Sitges in 1968. *Pan's Labyrinth* thus encompasses revamped versions of traditional monsters (a hideous toad, the 'Pale Man' with eyes in the palms of his hands), with mythical creatures (the Faun and fairies) and more abstract 'personifications' (Captain Vidal as the embodiment of sadistic machismo and the incarnation of death), all set in an 'invented past', del Toro's brilliantly stylized re-creation of a corner of Spain in 1944.

In spite of the breadth of his definitions (and his inclusion of auteurist directors such as Medem in the canon of the 'fantastique'), Aguilar does not mention the clearest Spanish antecedents of del Toro's twin Civil War-set dramas – art movies with genre influences that view 'Spanish reality' through the eyes of a child. Erice's *The Spirit of the Beehive* (*El espíritu de la colmena*, 1973) not only incorporates a fragment of James Whale's *Frankenstein* (1930) as a basis for its own haunting narrative, it also offers clear precedents for scenes in *Pan's Labyrinth*. As I have written elsewhere, del Toro's child heroine Ana replaces a missing piece (the eyes) in the face of a figure just as Erice's did some thirty years earlier (in *Pan's Labyrinth* it is a stone image of the faun Ofelia will soon encounter; in *Spirit of the Beehive* it is the wooden figure of 'Don José', used to teach anatomy lessons) (Smith, 2007: 5).

Likewise in del Toro, as in Erice, it is the status of the monster that is at stake. For Peter Evans (1982), Frankenstein's monster is associated with Ana's somewhat distant father (Fernando Fernán Gómez), a reading later contested by Jo Labanyi (2010), who associates the monster rather with the 'living dead', forgotten victims of history. Likewise the Faun is the object of the child's fascination, but also of her fear, as Ofelia finds herself, like Ana (and following Evans' title), 'growing up in the Dictatorship'. It is a reference not lost on the film critics of the Spanish press: the reviewer in national daily *20 minutos* (2006) claimed that *Pan's Labyrinth* had more in common with the 'childhood regressions' of Erice than with recent 'magical-mythological spectacles' like the *Harry Potter* and *Chronicles of Narnia* franchises.

Significantly, several, less haunting films on this theme that followed *The Spirit of the Beehive* and preceded *Pan's Labyrinth* employ not girls but boys as uncomprehending witnesses to historical horror, boys whose sense of loss is often focused on father-figures. In Montxo Armendáriz's *Secrets of the Heart* (*Secretos del corazón*, 1997) nine-year-old Javi explores a haunted house in the Basque country in which the voices of the dead (including his father) can still be heard, while in José Luis Cuerda's *Butterfly's Tongue* (*La lengua de las mariposas*, 1999) it is Galician schoolboy Moncho who sees his Republican teacher (Fernán Gómez once more) taken away to his death. In Cuerda's subsequent *The Blind Sunflowers* (*Los girasoles ciegos*, 2008), also Galicia-set, child Lorenzo witnesses his father's suicide when the latter's hiding place is revealed to the Francoist authorities. Only in this last film is there a link between the small corpus of 'important' (self-important) films on childhood and dictatorship and the still underrated genre movie: Roger Príncep, the fearful son of *The Blind Sunflowers*, had recently featured as the vulnerable child in the hugely successful horror hit *The Orphanage* (*El orfanato*, J. A. Bayona, 2007), a feature for which del Toro himself took a high-profile producer credit as 'presenter' of the film. It seems likely, then, that, given his professional history, del Toro is steeped in the tradition of the specifically Spanish 'fantastic film', as well as the Mexican equivalent for which he has also expressed antiquarian interest (as we saw in chapter 2, he curated a sidebar of horror movies, both Mexican and foreign, at the Guadalajara Festival in 2011).

For Spanish audiences, however, the most pervasive horror strand is one derived from television: Narciso Ibáñez Serrador's *Stories to Keep You Awake* are low-budget studio-set dramas (now re-released on DVD) whose grainy black and white photography and claustrophobic sets (so different to the expert production design of del Toro) no doubt heightened the horror they instilled in faithful Francoist audiences. The fact that, as mentioned earlier, the *Historias* were later remade by cinematic auteurs, proves that they remain essential as a context within which Spanish audiences view the genre. Ibáñez Serrador's one-off dramas show their allegiance to the 'Anglo-Saxon' roots of the ghost story in the same manner that Aguilar suggests that del Toro employs foreign settings (the creator himself, who regularly introduced the episodes, is like del Toro of Latin American origin, in his case Uruguayan).

Just as important as this pervasive sense of foreignness attached to the fantastic genre is the fact that the *Stories* often featured child protagonists, early precursors of del Toro's tortured infants. Thus in one tale (*The Doll* [*El muñeco*, 1966]), loosely alluding to *The Turn of the Screw*, a disturbed girl in Edwardian England ecstatically communes with her dead governess before murdering her father by sticking pins into a doll. Ibáñez Serrador's few feature films (generally held to be less compelling than his work in television) also focus on minors: in *The House that Screamed* (*La residencia*, 1969) girls mysteriously disappear from their boarding school, while in *Who Could Kill a Child?* (*¿Quién puede matar a un niño?*, 1976), a murderous band of children terrorizes an adult couple. Such works thus create a context for del Toro's more prestigious but still genre-based works. The fact that both films were originally shot in English but set in France and the Balearics respectively contributes to the sense of cultural and geographical dislocation which del Toro will also exploit.

But it is in his focus not only on a child but on a female heroine (relatively rare in Spain), that del Toro coincides with academic trends that have vindicated the role of young women in the horror genre. As is well known, Carol Clover's influential *Men, Women, and Chainsaws: Gender in the Modern Horror Film* (1993) seeks to refocus attention from sadism to victimhood as sources of pleasure for young (and mainly male) audiences. Beginning with an account of Brian de Palma's *Carrie* (1973), which was based on a novel by Stephen King, Clover suggests that, first, the central figure (a schoolgirl who wreaks havoc after she is bullied on first getting her period) is at once victim, hero and monster; and second, that the intended viewers of this female-focused narrative (who King claims 'had their gym shorts pulled down' as kids) are clearly male (1993: 5). For Clover, slasher and rape-revenge movies provide strong yet ambiguous heroines for boys to sympathize with in a form of identification different from (and hostile to) the sadistic-voyeuristic and fetishistic-scopophilic looks that were previously attributed by feminist film theorists to male spectators (1993: 8). In this newly slippery film world, 'we are both Red Riding Hood and the Wolf; the force of the experience in horror comes from knowing both sides of the story' (1993: 12).

Clover suggests that the horror that harks back to an archaic 'one-sex' model of physiology, in which male and female cannot clearly be separated (1993: 13), is sensitive nonetheless to changes in historical circumstance. Indeed, she cites Stephen King himself on *Carrie* as a fearful response to the challenge posed to men by feminism in the 1970s (1993: 5). This challenge is embodied in the figure famously dubbed by Clover the 'Final Girl' (1993: 35), the distressed female who fights back against the monster. What Clover offers us here, then, is a chance to re-read both gender and history in a filmic genre often considered to have its roots in misogyny and myth. It will prove especially apt for addressing del Toro's reworking of Spanish (and Mexican) horror.

Masked Cuts and Sound Bridges

We have seen thus far how genre intersects in complex and changing ways with such factors as nationality, history, industry and sexuality. And we have addressed the question of the specific kind of horror in the Spanish audiovisual sector (both cinema and television). We can now go on in the second half of this chapter to carry out a textual analysis of *Pan's Labyrinth*, informed by the historical and theoretical debates outlined above.

Pan's Labyrinth begins with titles over a black screen, clearly specifying the film's time, place and historical situation (the struggle of the maquis or resistance against victorious Francoist forces). The opening sequence, however, works to unsettle that specific setting. Anticipating the final shot of the film (and reversing chronological time), blood flows back into the nostril of heroine Ofelia (newcomer Ivana Baquero). Guillermo Navarro's camera, in the first of many physically impossible shots, penetrates her eye to reveal a fantasy location, reinforced by voice-over: in a vast palace set (actually an expert miniature made by Spanish special effects veteran Emilio Ruiz del Río), Ofelia is a princess in exile who must return to her father, the king. The cinematography remains unusually mobile and fluid as we cut to the first sequence proper in the real world: Ofelia's arrival with her sickly pregnant mother Carmen (Ariadna Gil) at the mill where she will meet her brutal stepfather Vidal (Sergi López). The camera soars over the spectacular ruins of a devastated village, cuts in close to see Ofelia replace the missing piece in the Faun's monolith, and flies behind the insect following the family's car, which will metamorphose into one of Ofelia's 'fairies'.

From the very beginning of the film, then, fantasy and reality are inextricable and we are provided with no clues, either narrative or visual, as to which of the elements we see are to be read as part of the child's imagination. What I would suggest, however, is that this unique film, which has already established itself in a generic hinterland between drama, fantasy, mystery, thriller and war movie, recreates in its fluid diegetic and filmic texture that national and generic border crossing held to be so typical of its auteur.

Yet nationality is inseparable from history. *Pan's Labyrinth*'s vision of Fascist violence, embodied in López's terrifying Captain Vidal, was read in Spain as an intervention in the debate on historical memory that had dominated contemporary Spanish politics in recent years. Thus while foreign viewers will find the film's hostility to the dictatorship uncontroversial, some local spectators read it as supporting the PSOE's policy of promoting awareness of the continuing legacy of the Civil War. One hostile conservative viewer (Rodríguez Pardo, 2007) branded the film 'inverosímil' ('implausible') not because of its appeal to fantasy, but for its hostility to a regime for which he clearly remained nostalgic. While it is easy to dismiss such views as marginal in democratic Spain, the important point is that the discursive context in which *Pan's Labyrinth* was received was more urgent and precise than outside the country in which it was shot, namely what this writer brands 'el pensamiento Zapatero' ('the philosophy of [Socialist President] Zapatero').

If *Pan's Labyrinth* is a historically specific intervention in Spain (with little political repercussion in Mexico), it is also industrially anomalous within the Spanish tradition of the fantastic. I have already suggested that its melding of quality production values and generic narrative formulae would have been inconceivable under an earlier Socialist cultural policy. *Pan's Labyrinth* puts to rest the two charges laid against Spanish 'terror' by its champion Aguilar. Hardly behind the times, it employs the most up-to-date technical effects (albeit as often animatronic as digital) to give an impression of modern professionalism as perfectly realized as any Hollywood blockbuster. By rejecting the 'crudity' also held to be typical of Spain, *Pan's Labyrinth*'s vision of the erotic is subtly displaced into disturbing elements of *mise en scène*: Vidal's fetishistic love of his black leather boots and gloves or the pure Ofelia's repeated immersion in the abject fluids of mud and blood.

If sex does indeed lead, in traditional style, to death (Ofelia's mother will die giving birth to the baby fathered by the monstrous Vidal), then that sex remains off-screen. Ironically, then, *Pan's Labyrinth*, which rejects the rationalism or realism of an earlier mode of

Spanish quality cinema, is in part a re-creation of the refined rural drama that was the favoured format of the 1980s. The Goya-winning film was thus acceptable to the Spanish cinematic establishment as it appeared to reconcile social or historical realism with fantasy in a way anticipated to some extent by the 'real dreams' of such iconic auteurs of the 1990s as Julio Medem.

This supposed 'Spanish reality', familiar since at least the time of Erice, is of course seen through the eyes of a child, in this case a girl, whose perspective is consistently privileged throughout the film. As I have written elsewhere (Smith, 2007: 8), the main technical devices of *Pan's Labyrinth* are the masked cut (where the fluid shift between real and fantastic locations is achieved by such techniques as the camera passing behind a tree) or the sound bridge (where the same movement is effected by the audio of one space, such as the clicking of the fairy-insect, merging with that of another, such as the ticking of the Captain's stopwatch).

But this expert blurring of boundaries is based on our identification with Ofelia's point of view as internal narrator. For example, it is only when we hear her tell her unborn brother the tale of a magical flower that the camera penetrates the mother's womb to show us that brother and flower. Or again, the most generic sequences (such as the child's encounter with the monstrous toad and Pale Man) are filmed using the most classical point-of-view shooting style which sutures our look in with that of the terror-struck, yet plucky, protagonist.

As is revealed by Ofelia's response to her three trials, she is as much hero as she is victim. And the male viewers who still make up the majority of horror fans are encouraged to identify with her in her distress, rather than taking voyeuristic pleasure in her sadistic treatment at the hands of the Captain. But although Ofelia dies protecting her baby brother, the avenging force of the Final Girl is projected onto another major female character who does indeed survive: Maribel Verdú's steely housekeeper Mercedes slashes Vidal's face, saying he is not the first pig she has gutted. If, as Clover suggested, horror comes from knowing both sides of the story, then those two sides (victim and heroine) are distributed by del Toro to his twin active female protagonists. Archetypal characters and situations (fauns and fairies, dreams and trials) thus come up against a modern conception of feminism that has, since the 1970s, threatened some men with their worst fears. And in spite of its physically immature heroine, *Pan's Labyrinth*, like *Carrie*, is haunted by the prospect of menstruation: shot in the belly in the final sequence, Ofelia drips blood onto the full moon that is reflected in the puddles deep in the labyrinth.

The film thus clearly follows classic horror in its enduring attachment to the archaic 'one-sex' model: a bifurcated curving design, based on the Fallopian tubes, recurs throughout the *mise en scène*. The faun and his attendant fairies are sexless, as is the pre-pubescent Ofelia, who scorns the feminine fripperies of pretty dresses and shiny shoes. The narcissistic Captain, who prefers not to sleep with his wife, holds a lavish dinner for local worthies such as the priest, who have sublimated erotic pleasure into gluttony. Although one critic (Edwards, 2008) has claimed that Ofelia's assumption of the maternal function is 'conventional' (unlike Lewis Carroll's Alice whom he claims as her sister), del Toro's plot strips horror of its classic misogyny and mythical trappings, reinscribing gender roles into a challenging and troubling historical context.

Moreover, *Pan's Labyrinth* avoids the focus on father-figures that so preoccupies the strand of Spanish cinema in which children bear traumatized witness to the legacy of the Civil War. Ofelia repeatedly insists, at the start of the film, that the Captain is not her father. Only at the end will she return to the fantasy realm where her real parent (Federico Luppi, a ghostly Argentine revenant from *The Devil's Backbone*) is barely glimpsed. Distancing himself from the father fixation of earlier films on the violent legacy of the dictatorship, del Toro also takes care to cut quickly away from scenes of surgery or torture in *Pan's Labyrinth*, images on which recent body horror, in Spain as elsewhere, dwells at considerable length.

Beyond the changing taxonomies of film genre and their academic re-readings, however, *Pan's Labyrinth* is also a cross-media hybrid. One telling detail for older Spanish audiences is that Francisco Vidal, the actor playing the small role of the gluttonous priest was, a lifetime ago, the kindly padre in one of the most celebrated series in the history of Spanish television, *Chronicles of a Village* (*Crónicas de un pueblo*, Antonio Mercero, 1971). Likewise Alex Ángulo, who plays the larger part of the doctor, has been a popular regular in high-profile TV fiction for some twenty years and remains best known for over 100 episodes of Tele 5's ground-breaking workplace drama *Journalists* (*Periodistas*, 1998–2002). Given these triggers of televisual memory, it would thus seem appropriate that *Pan's Labyrinth* was mainly funded by Tele 5, under the Law of Cinema that requires TV stations to subsidize the loss-making feature film sector, and of which (as we saw in chapter 2) Mexican movie professionals are so envious. And media cross-fertilization works both ways: it is no coincidence that the most innovative television format to premiere in 2007, the year after *Pan's Labyrinth*'s high-profile success, was a mystery-horror title which is rare in that medium. *The Boarding*

School (*El internado*, Antena 3, 2007–10) boasted a cast of teens and infants terrified by the monsters that lurked in the forest that surrounded their school and in the 'labyrinth' of tunnels beneath it (the series was later broadcast in Mexico by Azteca). *Pan's Labyrinth* is thus not simply a prestigious feature film; it is also a prime example of a newly converged Spanish-language audiovisual sector.

In 2009 Kim Newman, the best-known horror critic in the UK (perhaps the British equivalent of Carlos Aguilar), wrote that amidst the 'localized, nationally distinctive' scenes in Europe 'only in Spain is the horror film simultaneously thriving in its classic and modern forms, delivering gruelling ordeals of survival and pointed ghost/ fantasy stories' (2009: 38). Industry commentator Charles Gant also noted in the same year that Spanish and Latin American horror films have a unique 'track record' in the UK in bringing together arthouse audiences and genre fans. In the light of J. A. Bayona's *The Orphanage* and Jaume Balagueró's *REC* (both 2007), more recent and no less successful than *Pan's Labyrinth*, it might perhaps be better to talk of a Catalan connection: there now exist a cluster of specialist technicians based in Barcelona on whom Spanish and Mexican directors can rely. Whatever the case, it is clear that, as a horror film, *Pan's Labyrinth* engages with a special matrix of nationality, history, industry and sexuality that is found only in what Spaniards considered to be its home country. But the masterpiece of del Toro, the Mexican nomad, not only refers, as we have seen, to the rich and complex cinematic legacy of the past. It has also established a unique and invaluable model for the future of Spanish-language genre film.

Jump Cut 3

21 Grams (Alejandro González Iñárritu, 2003)

An unnamed town in the US, the present. College professor Paul (Sean Penn) is awaiting a heart transplant. His English wife Mary (Charlotte Gainsbourg) is hoping to get pregnant through artificial insemination. Middle-class housewife Cristina (Naomi Watts) comes home to find her husband Michael (Danny Huston) and two young daughters have not yet arrived. Reformed jailbird Jack (Benicio Del Toro) lives in poverty with his wife Marianne (Melissa Leo) and two children and is obsessed with religion. Jumping backwards and forwards in time, the film recounts the consequences of a traffic accident in which Jack runs over and kills Cristina's husband and daughters. Paul is given Michael's heart, Cristina spirals into despair and drug abuse and Jack, overcome with remorse, gives himself up to the police. Paul finds out who his donor was and, breaking up with Mary, begins an affair with Cristina. He also discovers that his new heart is being rejected. Cristina tells Paul that they owe it to Michael to kill Jack. When Jack is released from prison he remains tortured by guilt and leaves his family to stay in a motel. Paul and Cristina follow Jack, but Paul is unable to kill him. When Jack breaks into their motel room, Cristina attacks him, but Paul's heart gives out and he shoots himself in the chest. They rush together to the hospital, where Cristina learns she is pregnant.

A. O. Scott of the *New York Times* recently wrote that when he sees a film at a press screening he tries to look at it twice: once as a film-goer who simply experiences the film and once as a critic, reflecting self-consciously on that immediate experience. There can be few films that demand this double vision so much as *21 Grams*, Alejandro González Iñárritu's hugely ambitious drama in which the lives of a professor dying of heart disease (Sean Penn's Paul), a young suburban mother (Naomi Watts' Cristina), and an ex-con who has found Jesus (Benicio del Toro's Jack) intersect after a tragic accident. In one of the opening fragments, Jack shows an apprentice hoodlum how a life can fall apart by having him remove a piece from a precarious pile of wooden blocks. The pieces cascade down. Testing formal fragmentation to the limit, González Iñárritu and screenwriter Guillermo Arriaga risk just this kind of collapse in the first half-hour when there seems no way of holding the pieces of the film (or of the three lives) together. But they offer another teasing analogy: Paul plays electronic chess in his hospital bed. As spectators we are required to participate in *21 Grams*' very serious game, facing the challenge that the filmmakers have posed for the audience as well as for the characters.

For lovers of González Iñárritu's magnificent first feature, *21 Grams* might seem at first sight to be *Amores perros* times two, and not just in its premise of three lives linked and separated by a car crash. Breaking for the border, González Iñárritu brings his creative team from Mexico, but each of their contributions is intensified. While in Arriaga's earlier script the three strands were developed separately and rarely intersected, here they are cross-cut kaleidoscopically from the start. Rodrigo Prieto's hand-held cinematography was nervous and edgy in *Amores perros*. Here it is positively vertiginous, swinging between the distraught actors for much of the picture. And the grainy, degraded texture of the image, varying with the use of different film stocks, is more emphatic than before. Even Brigitte Broch's production design seems intensified. She has said that parts of the set which will never be seen (such as drawers which will not be opened) are dressed as diligently as those that are in sight. And there is a dense authenticity to these natural locations: sterile suburbs, raucous singles bars, grungy motels and hell-hole prisons. Shot in anonymous Memphis, a city whose stubby downtown towers few viewers are likely to recognize, and in the scrubby, featureless New Mexican desert, *21 Grams* is convincing both as a middle American document and as the universal moral drama that it aims to be.

This curious combination of veracity and abstraction holds for the characters too. It comes as something of a shock to learn that Penn's gravely stoic Paul is a mathematics professor: we know nothing and care less for his professional background. The press notes tell us that Watts' Cristina, who switches from one scene to the next between squeaky clean suburban mum and dirty blonde drug-addled wreck, had substance abuse problems before her marriage. I had assumed she began to take drugs only after the accident. Only del Toro's alarmingly thick-set Jack is provided with a fully fledged back-story: after a life devoted to booze and crime, he has embraced religion with alarming ferocity. As his wife (the excellent Melissa Leo) confesses, she no longer knows who he is.

In spite of these virtuoso performances, the focus of the film is more on abstract issues. *21 Grams* tackles huge, unfashionable questions rarely posed in current cinema: if there is a God, why does He allow evil things to happen? What is the nature of human identity? How do we cope with guilt? One leitmotif is the line: 'We have to go on living.' Potentially clichéd, here it reveals the true cost of survival, its brutal and visceral effects. As in Almodóvar's *All About My Mother* (whose soundtrack Gustavo Santaolalla seems to cite in a wistful accordion theme), organ transplants are used as a metaphor for the all-too physical way in which people touch one another's lives, bringing love and death unerringly in their wake. Paul literally confronts his own heart, pickled in a jar after the operation. 'Is that my heart?' he says, adding wryly, 'The culprit.' In González Iñárritu's relentlessly austere universe even vital organs have their guilt.

For all the brilliance of his plot construction and the seriousness of his moral enquiry, however, González Iñárritu remains primarily a poet of the visible world. Among the glittering, inexplicable shards of the opening sequence is a brief shot of birds rising, black against a blood-red sky. At the end we are treated to its mirror image, with a flock falling like leaves over a sky that is now streaked with blue. After a shattering climax which has brought the three main characters together for the first and last time, this is the clearest sign from this bleak triumph that there is still hope even after that cruellest and most banal of tragedies: a traffic accident.

Sight & Sound (March 2004)

Battle in Heaven (*Batalla en el cielo*, Carlos Reygadas, 2005)

Mexico City, the present. Marcos is the middle-aged chauffeur of a general. As the film begins, we learn that he and his wife have kidnapped the baby of Viky, a friend of the family. The kidnap has gone wrong and the child has died. Marcos picks up Ana, the general's young daughter, from the airport. He drives her to the 'boutique', an up-market brothel where she works part-time. Marcos tells Ana about the botched kidnapping. When he informs his wife of this, she says Ana should be taken care of. Marcos and Ana have sex. Marcos tells his wife that he is going to turn himself in to the police. Marcos, his wife Viky and their children drive out to the country. Marcos climbs a hill and looks down on the valley below. They return to the city. Later Marcos turns up at the flat of Ana and her boyfriend. He knifes her to death and then takes part in the pilgrims' procession to the Basilica of the Virgin of Guadalupe. His wife, brought there by the police who are searching for Marcos, enters the church. When she touches Marcos's shoulder he falls to the ground, apparently dead.

With his second feature Carlos Reygadas confirms his status as the one-man third wave of Mexican cinema. Rejecting both the old-style auteurism of Ripstein and the new more audience-friendly manner of Cuarón and González Iñárritu, Reygadas ploughs a lonely and very distinctive furrow. Like *Japón* (2002), his inexplicably named debut, *Battle in Heaven* (whose title is equally enigmatic) employs a very particular technique. Long takes and 360-degree pans are matched by idiosyncratic framing and sound design. For example, an early scene shows only the podgy, care-worn faces of middle-aged chauffeur Marcos and his wife against a neutral background. An annoying alarm plays throughout their laconic dialogue. It is only after some time has elapsed that we realize, as the camera pulls back, that the couple are selling cakes and clocks (hence the alarm) in the Mexico City metro.

The tight framing is especially troubling in the frequent explicit sex scenes. Obese and sweaty body parts have rarely been shown as closely as here and, although an already notorious blow-job sequence has been trimmed since *Battle* was shown in Cannes, some genital close-ups are positively gynaecological. As in *Japón*, which featured a lengthy sex scene with an aged rural dowager, the use of amateur actors here raises tricky ethical questions. Did the beautiful young Ana Mushkadiz, who plays a part-time teenage prostitute, and the dumpy Marcos Hernández, a morose and murderous chauffeur, really know what they were letting themselves in for? While the former claims in interview to be even more 'excessive' than her character, the latter worries that he may have problems with his family when they see the film. Hernandez's real wife might not be too pleased at her husband's visible excitement while in bed with the 'excessive' nymphette. The fact that the amateur actors keep their original names in the film only increases this confusion of life and art.

While *Japón* was rural, shot in a desolate ravine as remote as Mars from modern Mexico, *Battle* is defiantly urban and even makes gestures towards current social problems, such as kidnapping. Frequent driving shots are oddly reminiscent of *Amores perros*, as is the distinctive milky-white light of the polluted megalopolis. Reygadas tops and tails his film not just with repeated shots of the blow job, but with the military police raising a huge flag in the Zócalo, Mexico's equivalent of Trafalgar Square. The very prominent use of this daily ceremony, as familiar to Mexicans as the Changing of the Guard is to Londoners, seems another obscure provocation by Reygadas. Is he setting out to desecrate the potent symbols of nationalism by juxtaposing flag and fellatio? Or is he simply suggesting that such icons no longer have any power? The last sequence is also shot in a familiar and symbolically charged site: the Basilica dedicated to the Virgin of Guadalupe, Mexico's national patron. As the hooded and bare-chested murderer Marcos shuffles on his knees to the altar, is he truly penitent? Or is Catholicism, like nationalism, just another empty ideology?

Throughout his film Reygadas insists on such enigmas. While the plot synopsis of *Battle* reads like melodrama, the shooting and cutting style wilfully sabotage narrative tension and dynamism. The kidnapping and death of the child are not shown, but only impassively recounted by Marcos and wife in the sterile Metro setting mentioned above. The Viky from whom the maudlin couple attempts to extort a ransom appears to be a friend of the family, of modest means, an unlikely target for kidnapping. We never find out why bourgeois Ana decides to prostitute herself (is this just a nod to Buñuel's *Belle de jour*?) and we barely see Marcos's boss, Ana's father. Moreover, Marcos and his family seem comfortably off, so their reason for kidnapping the child is obscure.

As Reygadas knows full well, this lack of back-story prevents the audience from identifying with his characters and understanding their motivation. Often Reygadas's camera will linger on inexplicable details, as if testing or tempting us to work out their meaning. We are shown extended scenes of a football match on television (to which Marcos inexplicably jerks off) and prints of paintings by Stubbs and Vermeer in the wealthy Ana's apartment. Like the portentous title of the film, it seems that any element in *Battle* can mean everything or nothing.

Reygadas has denied that the sex scenes are pornographic. But his practice of film-making, with its radical rejection of narrative, relies on a distinguishing feature of pornography: the sheer physical presence of actors and acts before the camera. Indeed, Reygadas has said that the people in his films do not act, but simply *are*. Beyond porn, this ontology of the photographic image also has a long philosophical pedigree and illustrious cinematic precedents. Reygadas's preference for the long take seems to aspire to the tradition of Bazin, Welles and Warhol (the press notes cite Rossellini and Titian). Although *Battle* bears a marked family resemblance to *Japón*, it is much more proficient than its amateurish predecessor (the soundtrack is particularly well crafted). But while there can be no doubt that Reygadas has invented a unique blend of austerity and sensationalism, the jury is still out on whether his films are metaphysical investigations or all too fleshy provocations.

Sight & Sound (November 2005)

KM 31 (Rigoberto Castañeda, 2006)

The outskirts of Mexico City, the present. After an argument with her boyfriend Omar, Agata drives along a deserted road at night. Believing she has hit a child, she stops her car and is herself run over and taken to hospital. Her twin sister Catalina arrives with her Spanish friend Nuño and Omar. Although Agata is in a coma, Catalina seems to hear her sister calling for help. Omar returns alone to the site of the accident, where he senses a child's presence and encounters Ugalde, a brusque policeman. When she stays the night at Omar's house, Catalina believes she can hear her sister calling to her from inside the sewer below the street. Catalina tells Nuño that her mother had schizophrenia and that she blames herself for her mother drowning when the twins were children. The three friends drive once more to the scene of the accident. As the men argue, Nuño runs a woman over (later it is revealed the victim was already dead). Nuño is taken away by the police. When he is released the next day, he returns with Catalina to the forest. They spend the night at the house of an old woman who tells them the origin of the ghostly disturbances: in the colonial period a child was drowned by an Indian mother abandoned by her Spanish lover. Meanwhile Omar visits Ugalde, who shows him a file documenting years of mysterious accidents at the site. Returning to the road, Omar confronts the ghostly child at a river. Catalina discovers from a press clipping that the old woman at whose house she has just spent the night had in fact committed suicide years earlier. She drives back and finds the now ghostly Omar who leads her to his own dead body. Nuño and the policeman return to the old lady's house: it has suddenly become deserted and decrepit. Catalina drives to the sewer, the modern site of the river where the colonial mother and child drowned. She is followed by Nuño and the policeman. The old woman and Catalina's dead mother appear to her. Spurred on by these ghosts, Nuño bludgeons Catalina to death with a rifle and apparently shoots himself. But he wakes up in hospital, handcuffed to the bed as a murderer. As he does so, Agata also awakes from her coma, calling out to the lost child she never had.

First-time director Rigoberto Castañeda has said that his ambition is to make a Mexican horror movie as technically proficient as any from Hollywood. And it seems that he has succeeded. His slick ghost story *KM 31* (the title refers to a milestone marking the distance on the haunted highway from the city centre) gained some three million admissions in its home country, a result no doubt helped by a rather creepy promotional gimmick: a realistic dummy of a child was curled up on cinema floors in front of posters advertising the film. And if the production values are excellent, then the shooting and cutting are also dynamically paced. The opening sequence establishes the premise and three main characters even before the credits have rolled: accompanied by swirling smoke and urgent strings, Iliana Fox's Agata suffers a traumatic accident and is visited in hospital by her twin sister (also played by Fox) and two male friends. She will remain unconscious throughout the film and at first it seems that the true horror may come simply from the hospital setting. Agata's mutilated body (her legs have been amputated) is uncannily accompanied by the ticking and buzzing of life-support machines in a ward empty except for a lugubrious doctor and nurse in a nun's habit.

As we move into the second act, Castañeda skilfully stokes the tension. Even as Catalina rehearses the twins' back-story to her comatose sister (they had lost both parents in mysterious circumstances), the ghostly child makes his appearance, unseen, behind her and reaches out his bony finger to touch her back. Throughout the film Castañeda expertly exploits such hallowed horror techniques. Shallow focus (much of the film is shot in tight close-up) leaves room for blurry apparitions behind his likeable young principals, while nameless horrors tend to scurry across the screen to linger just out of shot. The cold blue and grey palette could not be further from the retina-searing colours often associated with Mexico, while aerial shots of the winding road and thick pine forest could almost be of Norway. Although the film was shot close to the sedate suburbs south of Mexico City (the forest ominously named 'the Desert of the Lions' is in fact a national park housing historic ruins), the locations look consistently scary. When Catalina finally descends into a sewer to confront the ghosts who torment her, she goes down a huge spiral staircase into a vast concrete silo.

These impressive effects and settings are reminiscent of a more experienced Mexican horror maestro: Guillermo del Toro. The digitally degraded ghostly child could be the cinematic brother of the one in del Toro's *The Devil's Backbone*, another film that explores the overlap of the historical and the supernatural. And as *KM 31* develops, its unusual fusion of American form and Mexican content comes into focus. Castañeda's premise reworks perhaps the best-known legend in Hispanic folklore, the Weeping Woman or La Llorona. (Venerable local rock band La Lupita even gives her a name check in the song that plays over the closing credits.) La Llorona is a ghostly suicide victim who mourns the children she has herself drowned. Castañeda, screenwriter as well as director, artfully reshapes the traditional story, making his version of the murderous mother an Indian betrayed by a Spanish colonist in the seventeenth century who calls out to Catalina and her Spanish boyfriend in the twenty-first. Typically, the sylvan stream of the colonial period has now become the foul sewer in which the climactic struggle is staged.

But this premise also justifies the casting of cute Spanish sitcom star Adrià Collado as Catalina's initially dour but ultimately deranged friend. Composer Carles Cases is also, like the Barcelona-born Collado, a distinguished veteran of Catalan cinema. While such casting is normally just a condition of foreign funding (one of the film's two production companies is indeed Spanish), the nationality of Collado's character, highlighted in the dialogue, is for once essential to the plot. Many Latin Americans are currently resentful about what they see as renewed colonialism from the Spain that has been buying up companies throughout the continent. So the real cultural connection of *KM 31* may be not so much with the America whose genre conventions Castañeda borrows as with the Spain that once colonized the New World and now funds so many Latin American films. Whatever the case, although its final scenes succumb to Grand Guignol, *KM 31* remains for the most part admirably economical with its gore, offering horror aficionados some authentic chills and arthouse fans enough genuine mystery to fuel a Mexican retread of Lynch's *Lost Highway*.

(*Sight & Sound*, December 2007)

Part III

Marginal Subjects

5

Youth Culture in Mexico: *Rebel* (*Rebelde*, Televisa, 2004–6), *I'm Gonna Explode* (*Voy a explotar*, Gerardo Naranjo, 2009)

Founding Contradictions

> Mientras mi mente viaja donde tú estás
> Mi padre grita otra vez
> Que me malgasto mi futuro y su paz
> Con mi manera de ser
> Aunque lo escucho ya estoy lejos de aquí
> Cierro los ojos y ya estoy pensando en ti.

(While my mind wanders to where you are/ My father shouts at me again/ That I'm ruining my future and his well-being/ With my attitude./ Though I hear him I'm far away/I close my eyes and I'm thinking of you.)

From the theme tune to *Rebelde*

This fifth chapter looks at two audiovisual texts, one a popular TV series and the other an auteur feature film, which would appear to come under the heading of 'Mexican youth culture'. In their very different ways both raise questions of nationality (the telenovela's format was imported from an Argentine original; the film draws stylistically on French New Wave) and of cultural distinction (the TV fiction, with its massive audience, was widely criticized at home; the art movie was praised at prestigious international festivals). I will argue, however, that there is much in common thematically between the two texts, especially with regard to the linked themes of family and friendship, and sex and violence; that this crossover illuminates their respective media; and that both, transnational and hybrid as they are, serve to transform the already protean youth genre.

While, as we shall see, relatively little research has been carried out on recent audiovisual fictions on or for young people in Mexico, there is clearly an awareness of the importance of the theme. As the distinguished sociologist Rosanna Reguillo wrote in 2000:

> El fortalecimiento de los ámbitos de las industrias culturales está en la construcción y reconfiguración constantes del sector juvenil. El vestuario, la música, el acceso a ciertos objetos emblemáticos, constituyen hoy una de las más importantes mediaciones para la construcción de identidades. (cited in Torres San Martín, 2011: 192)

> (The strengthening of the scope of cultural industries lies in the constant building and remodelling of the youth sector. Fashion, music and the access to certain symbolic objects form one of the most important mediations today for the construction of identities.)

Yet IMCINE's statistical yearbook for 2010, otherwise admirably exhaustive, makes no reference to youth as a criterion of production or reception, other than noting that, ironically enough, young audiences are less likely to pay attention to the official rating system, which is designed to exclude them from viewing certain titles, than are older spectators (2010: 131). Economist Mariana Cerrilla Noriega, writing in 2011, documents that 78 per cent of the Mexican public never attend movie theatres because of restrictive factors such as income, social exclusion and geographical location (2011: 40). Although the new cinema audience is (as we already noted in chapter 1) wealthier, more educated and more urban, the question of age (as a positive or negative factor) is not addressed here.

Social exclusion, whether on the basis of class, gender or age, is hardly relevant in relation to free-to-air television, now almost universally accessible. Indeed, according to IMCINE, the great majority of Mexican film, both past and present, is consumed via TV broadcasts or pirated DVDs (2010: 63, 76). But youth television has received even less attention than youth cinema, and in recent scholarly research in the US the question of youth media seems to raise significant contradictions. Thus in *The Changing Portrayal of Adolescents in the Media since 1950*, edited in 2008 by Patrick E. Jamieson and Daniel Romer, contributors warn that (contrary to expectations perhaps) there has been little interest in the topic of teens and screen violence in the last decade, and a neglect of the role of verbal, as opposed to physical, violence in the media (Potter, 2008: 244). More expectedly, they argue that teen sexuality, that other perennial topic, was in 1990s American TV presented as a 'game', as habitually extra-marital (albeit with a 'norm of exclusivity'), and shown to have no harmful risks or consequences (Stern and Brown 2008: 328). While, according to this statistical analysis, the portrayal of teen sexuality varies according to medium, decade and genre, current representations are based on a fundamental 'ambiguity':

> We want teens to 'wait' but often expect that they will nevertheless engage in sexual activity. Parents and educators promote abstinence, and yet teens' peer culture often suggests that only nerds and prudes abstain. On the other hand, teens, especially girls, learn quickly that having sex might hurt their reputations. (Stern and Brown, 2008: 335)

Even contributors to this volume, intended to produce policy proposals for educators, acknowledge that such messages, invariably inconsistent, cannot fully be accounted for by quantitative measures: they need 'context and a sense of the whole' (Stern and Brown, 2008: 336). For example, movie depiction of youthful sexual behaviour may well discourage experimentation rather than promote it (2008: 336). In the conclusion the editors argue that there is a fundamental contradiction here that transcends age: 'the cultural blurring between adulthood and adolescence' (Jamieson and Romer, 2008: 447). Thus 'the need to invest time and resources to achieve success' is combined with reminders that 'immediate gratification is the source of happiness'; 'the culture of youthful hedonism poses conflicts for adolescents who are held in limbo by . . . the delay of adult responsibility, a condition that effectively extends adolescence into the third decade of life'; or, again, 'our culture wants youth to mature into adults, but wants adults to remain youthful' (2008: 447).

This 'cultural confusion' is most evident in the case of women, with 'tweens' sexualized and, conversely, adults 'increasingly portrayed as youthful and even childlike' (2008: 448). The central contradiction here is that women 'must work hard and produce and achieve success and . . . live impulsively . . . be constantly and immediately gratified' (2008: 450). Sex and food are of course vital in this context: 'Girls are promised fulfilment both through being thin and through rich foods . . . through being innocent and virginal and through wild and impulsive sex' (2008: 450; citing Jeane Kilbourne).

It is interesting to compare this US material with rarer Mexican studies of local youth culture. A survey by Francisco Javier Millán (published in 2006 by a festival in Guanajuato), which the blurb hopes will both 'end our innocence' with regard to the theme of cinematic childhood and youth and 'promote rebellion', recites common features of the genre: teachers who act as guides to children lacking in affection; the growth of gangs and street kids; the burden of machismo and routine; and, finally, the return to the past and (in a specifically Mexican context) the commemoration of Tlatelolco, the massacre in 1968 that put an end to youthful revolt (2006: 'Índice', unnumbered). More broadly, the book's themes are said to be apprenticeship in life, the negation of childhood (by social exclusion), the search for self and the retrieval of youth through memory (2006: 13).

Beyond such broad brushstrokes, a content analysis of youth in Mexican cinema can be pieced together through dissertations on the topic submitted over some twenty years and held in the Cineteca archive, Mexico City. Thus one thesis in sociology examines the image of youth gangs in the capital in local film (Hernán de Jesús Becerra Pino, 1986). It includes a 'glossary' of youth speak (1986: 85), 'direct observation' of subjects (1986: 89) and a content analysis through a five-fold 'typology' (1986: 89). There is also an interview with a self-described gang member from Santa Fe, now a glitzy business district, then a distant slum. 'Andrés' claims that youth gangs were born of unemployment and constitute a 'political organization', independent of any state agency or party (1986: 272). Since the state has responded repressively to such gangs, the latters' response will necessarily be violent as befits class struggle (1986: 272). In spite of his vernacular language, carefully reproduced in the transcript, and his boast that the state apparatus will never coopt a movement, which, he claims, has links with agricultural workers outside the city, 'Andrés' may not be a typical gang member. Admitting to the relatively advanced age of twenty-six, he also claims to have completed nine semesters of psychology courses (1986: 273), while boasting that real learning or apprenticeship ('aprendizaje') comes from practice not school (1986: 273).

If the quest for lived youth rebellion proves muddy here, then the contours of the cinematic genre are also obscure. The researcher also includes his somewhat embarrassing interview with Carlos Monsiváis, perhaps the best known of cultural commentators. Monsiváis, damningly, tells the student that his focus on Mexican film noir and musicals is absurd and will lead to disaster for his thesis (1986: 227). Rather, he should investigate US teen novels, the creation of a youth market in the 1950s and the concept of 'rebellion in education' ('rebeldía educativa') (1986: 227). The nature of the field thus proves problematic.

A second thesis in Communication Studies examines the image of youth from 1960 to 1969 in Mexican commercial cinema (Miranda Duarte, 1999). Here, beyond the anecdotal, the young scholar seeks to analyse the ideas and values transmitted by the national film industry in a decade synonymous with both student activism and the proliferation of youth movies (1999: 4). Once more there is a question about the limits of the research corpus, which is large (eighty-three features) and of difficult access, even though the conclusion acknowledges that such films remain alive in the popular imagination as at least one of them is revived each week on local broadcast television (1999: 120). However, the final verdict is negative. Of two patterns of teen behaviour, one has dominated: the 'authentic' and 'non-conformist' political youth has been eclipsed by individualism, consumerism and ignorance (1999: 120).

The cinema of the 1960s, then, with its frequent song and dance numbers, was closer to traditional moralism than to real-life youth subculture (1999: 123). With the exception of just three films, fashionable singing stars of the 1960s were thus 'incorporated' (1999: 123), with commercial cinema failing to produce new figures for a new time: Angélica María, former child star, was already well known (1999: 124). The key image that emerges from these features, made in a decade that culminated in violent state repression, is thus that of the 'loyal' youth: dynamic and joyful, but apolitical and uneducated (1999: 125).

A third thesis treats youth in four features from then current Mexican cinema, all but one shot in the capital, ranging from box office comedy *Sex, Shame, and Tears* (*Sexo, pudor, y lágrimas*, Antonio Serrano, 1999) to drama *Amores perros* (María Teresa López Martínez, 2001). This conscientious content-analysis works through the characteristics of the chosen films' young protagonists (professional, personal and private), before offering a commentary on selected scenes and drawing a 'sociological evaluation'. Yet even here the conclusion stresses that 'youth' cannot be spoken of in the singular, heterogeneous as it is (2001: 134) and drawing on multiple realities as it does (2001: 135). And if the films re-confirm that characters and conduct are conditioned by (urban) environment (2001: 136), they still stress the variety of youth subcultures and those who participate in them, given here in an untranslatable macaronic enumeration: 'rockeros, jipis, chavos bandas, darks, punks, yuppies, campesinos, obreros, estudiantes' (2001: 139).

A final thesis examines the questions of consumption and exhibition, offering recommendations for the promotion of art cinema amongst youths (Sara Eny Curiel Ochoa, 2003). Based on informant interviews, this study offers valuable insight into the opinions of young viewers. The scholar discovers with 'surprise' that interview subjects are well aware of the existence of art movies and can define the genre in opposition to Hollywood, but fail to go to see such films because, so they claim, they lack information on where they are screened (2003: 96). Beyond this question of diffusion, the thesis recommends education in reception or the provision of tools for the understanding of such films to young people (2003: 100). Interestingly, informants claim that art movies address the same themes as commercial films, but with a different treatment: less visually overwhelming and more austere or homely ('casero') (2003: 110). Aware of the differential aesthetics of cultural distinction, they are also cautious in their recommendations as to how art film could be made more attractive to viewers like themselves. The most widely shared opinion is that art movies are too slow, 'high' ('elevado'), and 'deep' ('profundo'); but informants also qualify such populist opinions by suggesting that movies of this kind should not become 'too fast' in rhythm or too easy to understand. Young informants recognize that such qualities are the main characteristics of art cinema (2003: 112).

We have seen, then, that the thematics and aesthetics of youth media are complex and contradictory, even at the level of content. Later I will give an account of exceptional work by two scholars of youth audiences in Mexican film and television that go beyond content analysis to raise questions of media pedagogy and apprenticeship in both the restricted and the general sense of the words. But first I offer a preliminary account of production and reception in my chosen fictions.

Two Audiovisual Case Studies: Production and Consumption

> Y soy rebelde
> Cuando no sigo a los demás
> Sí soy rebelde
> Cuando te quiero hasta rabiar
> (And I'm a rebel/ When I don't follow the rest/ Yes I'm a rebel/ When
> I love you like crazy)

My two case studies are teen telenovela *Rebel* (*Rebelde*, Televisa, 2004–6) and Gerardo Naranjo's feature film *I'm Gonna Explode* (*Voy a explotar*, 2009). The former was arguably the most successful youth telenovela in history, stretching to some 440 episodes in its three seasons. Adapted from the Argentine original, *Rebelde Way*, it was produced for Televisa by Pedro Damián, a former actor known for his Midas touch in the genre. 'Damián' (the name is a pseudonym) frequently appeared on talk shows, introducing the young cast and presenting himself as the auteur of the series.

It seems fair to say that for professional commentators, if not for its massive and still faithful audience, *Rebel* remains notorious as an example of the culture of youthful hedonism in which any possibility of 'authentic' and 'non-conformist' political youth has been eclipsed by individualism, consumerism and ignorance. I will argue, however, that as a text it is (like the category of 'youth' itself) more heterogeneous than might be expected, giving its audience access to multiple realities. For example, in its frequent musical numbers, this telenovela offers an ecstatic or utopian release that is clearly at odds with the everyday nature of its setting and the domestic mode of consumption. Moreover, the unusual delay imposed on the audience in waiting for the requisite romantic resolution (*Rebel* played over three years, rather than the normal six months) suggests that immediate gratification was a source of happiness neither for the public outside the fiction nor for the characters within it.

The four protagonists are, however, set up with the Manichaean dichotomies of the most traditional telenovela (Figure 5). Thus Mía

Figure 5 *Rebel* (Televisa, 2004–6)

(singing star Anahí) is the most popular girl at the Elite Way (the name is given in English) boarding school outside Mexico City, as pretty as she is superficial. The daughter of a neglectful businessman (her mother is dead), she favours pastels, voluminous hair extensions and a shiny adhesive star on the forehead. (All of the girls spice up the formal blazers of their uniform with micro-mini skirts and exposed midriffs.) Conversely Roberta (Dulce María), Mía's deadly rival, is something of a punk or Goth, with her spiky tartan-dyed hair and fondness for piercings and black mesh. Her mother is a famous performer who dresses with conspicuous sexiness, while her father is once more missing.

The two boys are also contrasted. Earnest working-class Miguel (Alfonso 'Poncho' Herrera), from distant provincial Monterrey, is the handsome dark-haired boy-next-door who is dependent on a scholarship to attend the school. His secret mission is revenge: he blames Mía's father for his own father's suicide and his family's subsequent ruin. Blond playboy apprentice Diego (Christopher Uckermann) has an equally troubled but different back-story. He is the son of a corrupt politician who maltreats his family with macho bullying. Diego's style is notably swisher than Miguel's. While both keep their shirts and ties provocatively undone, Diego sports shiny silver trousers in one of the series' many party scenes. Rivalling the girls in the sexual objectification stakes, in the first season both boys are surprised in just a towel by their on-off girlfriends or strip down to their bathing suits to cool off in the picturesque lakes or inviting swimming pools that always seem to be close at hand. Once the inevitable sexual tension is set up between the two unlikely couples (trivial Mía and serious Miguel, rebellious Roberta and daddy's boy Diego), the stage is set for near interminable emotional drama.

It is striking, though, that however sexualized the girls are in their revealing costumes (blurring the boundary between adulthood and adolescence), they refuse immediate gratification. In the first season the flirty Mía, after lengthy hesitation, will not submit to pressure to have sex with an attractive bad boy, who subsequently turns out to be a drug dealer. The show thus promotes abstinence even at the risk of prudishness. And violence is mainly verbal (the girls trade insults, vicious poison-pen letters circulate), with the exception of that meted out by the school's masked and hooded secret society. 'La Logia' ('The Lodge') submits initiates to rigorous hazing and threatens scholarship students like Miguel with physical punishment. *Rebel* even dips its well-shod toes into the violence of social exclusion. In one unlikely plotline, punky Roberta unwillingly adopts a grubby street kid, whom she keeps hidden in an abandoned truck in the school grounds. Such cute infant performers are of course the stock-in-trade of adult serials in Mexico and here signal a target audience that is extending beyond the series' primary teen demographic.

More innovative than these stereotypical characters and plotlines (not to mention the often exaggerated performance style) is the brand extension associated with the show. The producers, like the characters in their agonizingly slow love lives, clearly recognized the need to invest time and resources to achieve success. And they are well aware of the value of fashion, music and symbolic objects for their target audience.

Thus when the first episode was screened in a restaurant in the capital, the producer claimed that the show's 'message' was that teens should look for their own identities, for their own way in the world; and he added that his modest intention was not to provoke controversy but rather to provide a story well told (Rodríguez González, 2004). However, on *Rebel*'s final night (when the students 'graduate'), *El Universal* interviewed Damián once more and faithfully reported on his marketing successes. *Rebel* had inspired comics, calendars, clothing, jewellery and even a charitable foundation. Most important was the bestselling pop group RBD, made up of the four main stars with the addition of two sidekicks. Sell-out tours had taken place throughout Latin America, Spain and the US, all territories to which the series was exported. And testimony to the brand's transnational selling power had been the frequent cameos by established music stars: from rocker Lenny Kravitz (who signs a guitar onscreen for the semi-fictional RBD) to British animated group Gorillaz and US teen actress-singer Hilary Duff. Damián called attention to the fact that a series initially aimed at teenagers had in fact attracted all age groups: an enviable multi-target audience from 'aspirational' infants to senior citizens. He claimed, immodestly, to have thus broken the mould of youth television (Cano, 2006).

A further article gave a commercial context for this varied success. The head of licensing in Televisa explained that the secret of *Rebel*'s broad appeal was not only the music, with which teenagers 'identified', but the show's allegedly 'everyday' nature: it was, she claims, less over-acted than most telenovelas. Here the list of branded products, stocked in the show's candy-coloured sets and aimed at distinct segments of the public, include food and drink items (fruit juice, cookies and chocolates), school supplies (backpacks and pens), beauty products (shampoo and gel), and even household goods (bed covers and slippers). *Rebel*-related promotions included joint campaigns with the American Coca-Cola, Pepsi and Kellogg and Mexican brands such as Calzado Andrea shoes and Jumex drinks (Ulloa, 2006).

This 'everyday' angle seems somewhat implausible in the case of *Rebel*, given the show's secluded setting: the Elite Way location is actually an upmarket housing and leisure development, complete with golf course called Bosque Real Country Club, well connected for the new office towers of Santa Fe. Luxurious class outings in season 1 gave opportunities for exotic location shooting in a beach resort on the Caribbean island of Cozumel and a winter sports facility in the Canadian Rockies. But the perceived 'realness' of the young cast, however improbable, was reaffirmed by a pseudo-reality sitcom that followed the series proper. *RBD: La familia* (*RBD: The Family*, 2007) claimed to give the still-faithful audience access to the six stars' lives as they cohabited in a Mexico City apartment. The young friends' mediated apprenticeship in life thus continued after the telenovela itself was concluded and in a show in which they performed versions of themselves.

As is the way with volatile and vulnerable teen phenomena, not everything went smoothly. When three fans were killed and many injured at an autograph-signing session in Brazil, future promotional events of this kind were cancelled (*El Universal* [staff], 2006). Sociologists lined up to critique *Rebel* in the press. Guisela Frid of the UNAM was quoted as attacking 'stereotyping' in *Rebel*, which she defined, ironically enough, in words reminiscent of the show's theme tune and the statements of its producer. Stereotypes, she said, are patterns of behaviour that generalize 'forms of being' for an age group which prioritizes the 'search for identity' (Cano, 2006). Florence Toussaint, also of the UNAM, apparently ignorant of the show's Argentine origins and indifferent to the aspirations of its young viewers, claimed that these rich kids 'didn't seem Mexican' and would be more at home in *Beverly Hills, 90210*. The show's set-up was 'classist' and its vision of 'rebellion' was hardly revolutionary. Its characters wanted not to change the world but merely to follow a different lifestyle (Cruz, 2005). This would-be damning verdict was confirmed by the show's official website, where Televisa guided discussion towards such undemanding topics as 'What do you most like about RBD's concerts?' ('¿Qué es lo que más te gusta de los conciertos de RBD?'), what is 'the RBD song that touches your heart' ('la canción de RBD que te toca el corazón'), and 'What would you do if you came face to face with [the six stars]?' ('¿Qué harías si estuvieras frente a Anny, May, Dul, Chris, Poncho, Ucker?') (RBD Sitio Oficial, 2011).

While the show was attacked by journalists and academics, its actors also faced problems in the press. Flat-stomached Anahí confessed to having suffered an eating disorder and campaigned on television against the tyranny of a body image that she herself had helped promote (in the series her best friend is an overweight girl mercilessly teased by others) (Fundación Televisa, 2012). When Christian Chávez, who played initially bleach-blond (and latterly pink-haired) class clown Giovanni, was forced out of the closet by the threat of blackmail, however, he was supported by fellow cast members and fans alike. The press, now with good reason, called his statement 'rebellious' (Cano, 2007). Soon he and Anahí were rebranded as disco divas for an anthemic plea for sexual freedom entitled 'Libertad' ('Freedom') (christianchaveztv, 2011). Chávez promoted the song live at Mexico City's LGBT Pride with a drag queen imitating his absent colleague. A series notable for its stress on traditional sexual morality was thus extended by accident in quite a different educational direction. But, in spite of the evidence provided by his homoerotically charged video clip, Chávez's media narrative hardly promoted wild and impulsive sex: the photos the blackmailer threatened to release were of his wedding some time earlier during *Rebel*'s location shoot in Canada (same-sex marriage was not at that time permitted anywhere in Mexico).

Meanwhile the suspicion that *Rebel* was a unique phenomenon was confirmed after the third season came to an end. Damián's next series was not a hit: his lucky streak was over. In 2011, at the 9th World Summit of Telenovelas and Fiction Series, held in Miami, delegates argued that the main challenge for the industry now was how to reach the youth audience, which had now turned its back on the genre (EFE, 2011).

It would seem, then, that *Rebel*'s stars coincide with the sanitized musical teens of Mexican cinema of the 1960s: dynamic and joyful (in spite of frequent bouts of weeping by both boys and girls), but apolitical and uneducated (in spite of intermittent guidance from often clueless adults). One of the series' bitterest critics was a contemporary film-maker with a growing reputation, Gerardo Naranjo. In press coverage for *I'm Gonna Explode*, his third feature (often described in the press as his second), the writer-director repeatedly calls attention to the irony that a band (*sic*) called 'Rebelde' should be a group of 'empty-headed' kids ('*descerebrados*') without any ideas. This was in spite of the fact that several plotlines of his art movie coincide with the telenovela he so scorns.

Thus, like *Rebel*'s orphaned teens, Naranjo's young rebel Román has lost a parent, in this case his mother, and he blames his neglectful father for the loss, which resulted from a car crash. (*Rebel* had also begun with a drunken car crash.) Confirming *Rebel*'s main theme of cross-class romance, rich Román (the son, like *Rebel*'s Diego, of a corrupt politician) will hook up with poor Maru, whose father is also absent. Making an attempt, pathetic or comic, to run away from home, the couple will pitch a tent on the family roof before fleeing in a stolen car (*Rebel*'s Diego will make it further, when he escapes with a girlfriend from school in the capital to the neighbouring city of Puebla). Both fictions also feature that stereotype of the teen genre, the sympathetic pedagogue who understands adolescent rebellion. Naranjo's twin leads will drop in on Román's adult confidant as their escape falters; Televisa's troubled ensemble will be advised by their Argentine teacher of ethics, the only adult who escapes ridicule or worse when giving advice on vital matters such as sex, drugs and violence. Proving the paradox that our culture wants youth to mature into adults, but wants adults to remain youthful, such rare moments of education in *Rebel* are undercut by this teacher's youth and hotness: unlike *I'm Gonna Explode*'s grizzled ex-revolutionary (who admits to taking part in 1960s student activism and still boasts a poster of Che Guevara on the wall), *Rebel*'s telenovela-attractive teacher is romantically bearded and long-haired.

Of course the main difference between the TV series and the auteur movie (apart from its textual composition, which I examine later) is the latter's successful bid for cultural distinction. *I'm Gonna Explode*, described by its director as 'candy with poison' ('un dulce con veneno') was shown at the most prestigious international festivals, including Venice and Berlin, where it was included in the specialist Generation 14 Plus section, whose jury is made up of teenagers. Naranjo hoped in this case that a film about youth would share the young audience's 'sensibilities' (Olivares, 2009). Such festivals are, of course, the main source of legitimation for Latin American art cinema. On its acceptance at New York and Toronto, the director said that *I'm Gonna Explode* was about what rebellion ('rebeldía') means at the current time, when counter-culture symbols have been 'assimilated' and the pop group Rebelde represents anything but what is properly designated by that name (Molina Ramírez, 2008).

Paradoxically, however, Naranjo's own rebels, searching vainly for a reason to live, also have no cause: they revolt not against injustice but against the fact that they have nothing to fight for. Reflecting perhaps the cultural blurring between adulthood and adolescence noted earlier, young people, the director says, now have no enemies (Molina Ramírez, 2008). In Naranjo's art movie, as in the telenovela, neglectful parents (including the central recurring figure of the corrupt politician-father) are more concerned with their own public image than with their children's welfare. And in both fictions the conflict between children and parents is presented not in political but rather in personal terms. Similarly the inter-class love story in *I'm Gonna Explode* (as in *Rebel* before it) carries little or no charge of class conflict.

As in many recent Mexican auteur films, Naranjo's leads are amateurs, plucked from secondary school for their first (and to date only) feature roles. Unlike telenovela actors, trained from an early age at Televisa's own academy in a recognizably declamatory style of performance, Naranjo's unpractised stars offer naturalistic line readings that match their coarsely vernacular dialogue, even as their story spirals into tragic melodrama. (Is it, however, a wink at telenovela that Román's stepmother is played by an actress who had hitherto specialized in that genre?)

Yet *I'm Gonna Explode* rejects the dominant current of Mexican art movie production, which can be described as 'realist' or 'minimalist', and which (as we saw in chapter 1) combines non-professional actors with festival-friendly technique: long takes, lack of non-diegetic music and references to such austere European predecessors as Dreyer, Bresson and Tarkovsky. In interview, Naranjo says his 'ideal' is rather to combine 'festival films' with appeal to a general audience (Olivares y Agencias, 2008). Indeed, he claims that 'revolutionary cinemas', such as Italian neo-realism or French New Wave, relied not only on directors but also on their publics in a joint quest for national identity. This is something which Mexico, according to the director, now lacks (Franco Reyes, 2009).

The impossible rebellion of youth today would thus seem to be echoed by the quixotic revolt of the would-be innovative film-maker, feted in foreign festivals but deprived of a sympathetic audience at home. Once more, television is said to be responsible here: Mexico is described as the 'kingdom of telenovela' ('el reino de la telenovela') where local cinema is difficult to promote (Olivares y Agencias, 2008). Naranjo's cinematic nostalgia for the decade of the 1960s thus coincides with his political longing for a time when engagement had not been coopted by consumerism (an argument we have also seen in Mexican theses on youth culture). *I'm Gonna Explode*'s promotion strategies, clearly limited by budget, also invoked rebellions of the past. The director posed moodily for the press with dark glasses, extravagantly wind-blown hair and ironic moustachios. With equally studied eccentricity, the film was advertised virally with stencilled graffiti throughout Mexico City. In 2011 (when I carried out the research for this chapter), one was still visible on the wall outside the Cineteca, the National Film Institute in Coyoacán.

I'm Gonna Explode thus focused on the same themes as commercial fictions like *Rebel*, but with a different treatment. And responding perhaps to the youth audience's boredom with art movies, it was faster, flashier and less homely than its rivals, while maintaining that aspiration towards elevation and profundity by which auteurism is recognized. But just as the film's form combines art-movie aesthetics and commercialism (Naranjo inveighs against 'boring' and 'inaccessible' films as well as television), so its ideological address is flexible and accommodating. Although Román's and Maru's revolt is presented as existentially absurd (backed up by those references to France in the 1960s), it is also more precisely political and local. As shooting began, Naranjo reminded readers of the leftist *La Jornada*, a sympathetic audience, that his location of Guanajuato (the home state of both the director and ex-President Vicente Fox) had seen no fewer than three sex scandals by members of the rightist Partido de Acción Nacional in the past year (Rodríquez, 2007). He stated that his film was an accusation ('denuncia') of the hypocrisy of men in power.

Typically, foreign viewers identified *I'm Gonna Explode*'s stylistic hybridity but not its submerged political implications: *Variety*, accurately predicting success at 'Euro art screens', compared the 'punchy explanation of unattributable teenage angst' to 'Nicholas Ray meets Jean-Luc Godard' (Weissberg, 2008). The *New York Times* also compared this 'small sometimes confusing movie' to early Godard (Holden, 2009). In such cases, the retrieval of youth, or at least its media lineage, is derived from the transnational cinephile memory shared by director and critics alike.

Crucial in a Mexican context, however, was that *I'm Gonna Explode*'s production company was Canana, the shingle set up by iconic young actors Gael García Bernal and Diego Luna, who get first credit amongst the many executive producers of the film. Their partner Pablo Cruz set out their aims to *La Jornada*. On the one hand, he said, local audiences are avid for 'quality cinema' made in Mexico; but, on the other, film-makers and producers should attempt to make films that people want to see (Rodríguez, 2007). The balancing act between sensibilities (high and low) is thus also a tension between two conflicting cultural economies (art and commerce).

A working hypothesis for this chapter, then, would be that the teen genre, exploiting as it does the commercial patterns of telenovela that are so familiar to the Mexican masses, offers a unique possibility for an artistic restructuring of national cinema that does not turn its back on the popular audience. But before turning finally to a close textual analysis of *Rebel* and *I'm Gonna Explode*, we must look more closely at two rare studies of the elusive youth audience. Both raise the question of audiovisual education, broadly defined, in Mexican film and television.

Media, Youth, Apprenticeship

> Y soy rebelde
> Cuando no pienso igual que ayer
> Y soy rebelde
> Cuando me juego hasta la piel
> Si soy rebelde
> Es que quizás nadie me conoce bien.
> (And I'm a rebel/ When I don't think the same as yesterday/ And I'm
> a rebel/ When I take a gamble on my life/ If I'm a rebel/ Maybe it's
> because nobody knows what I'm really like.)

Patricia Torres San Martín is the author of a recent monograph on cinema, gender and youth in contemporary Mexican cinema (2011). While her book is focused specifically on the reception of two well-known movies with teen protagonists (*Amores perros* and *Y tu mamá también*) and uses data derived from Mexico's second city (Guadalajara), it also raises general questions about youth representation and audience in the country as a whole. Thus Torres gives an invaluable account of scholarship on spectatorship in Mexico, writing that such research (very recent) shows three trends: cinema as a constructor of identities, the characterization of the audience, and the development of the national film industry (2011: 53).

Empirical work, undertaken at Torres' own University of Guadalajara, gives valuable evidence of the tastes of audiences, broken down by age, educational level and social class. Thus viewers aged thirty to forty-five, with only secondary education and of a lower class, watch films on video (thinking movie theatres too expensive) and enjoy current Hollywood fare, especially action movies, and Mexican films of the Golden Age (1940s and 50s) (2011: 79). Lower middle-class youth (aged eighteen to twenty-two), with a somewhat higher education level, prefer movie theatres to home viewing, claim to be hostile to Hollywood, and find local production too commercial and generic. Finally, upper middle-class spectators in their twenties with college degrees, also hostile to Hollywood, believe with practised discrimination that Mexican movies are successful in their artistic ambitions (narrative and style) but cling to outdated topics. In the light of this 'typology', Torres concludes that recent Mexican cinema has indeed attracted young, educated audiences, but remains out of touch with a society that has changed radically in recent years (2011: 80). This is in spite of the fact that the two films she examines in detail have reinvented national film trends for the millennium, positioning themselves within a 'new wave' of Mexican youth culture

(2011: 99, 129). Films that actively target the youth audience may be subject, however, to a 'social use' by that audience quite different to the one intended by the directors (2011: 144).

Here Torres' own qualitative data, based on informant interview and focus group discussion, is also invaluable. Thus teen boys saw *Y tu mamá* simply as a raucous comedy, identifying especially with the film's distinctive youth argot. Conversely, viewers aged eighteen to twenty-seven employed negotiation, resistance and reflection in their responses, attacking the 'values' of the protagonists, for which uncultured Mexicans are said to be unprepared, but also reading the film as an 'exaggeration' or 'allegory' of national fantasies (2011: 163–4). Likewise, young working-class female viewers of *Amores perros* were 'disgusted' by the image it presented of their country, while older wealthier women, comfortably able to take their distance, commented that the film accurately depicted the 'reality' of lower-class life and the 'culture of poverty' (of which they, of course, had no direct knowledge) (2011: 165).

Class, gender and age thus intersect in complex ways, especially at a time when what Torres calls the 'crisis in patriarchy' is ambivalently presented in films which remain, she says, 'patriarchal' in ideology (2011: 167). Torres concludes that the recent 'regeneration' of Mexican cinema (which she does not call into question) in both production and exhibition is structurally related to its new targeting of a youth audience that it has seduced back into the theatres (2011: 190). Yet while that audience has correctly identified and enjoyed the innovations of such films (especially their frank and unmoralizing treatment of sex), the 'discursive form' of cinema, having identified its audience, still imposes limits on interpretation, determining modes of 'cinevidencia' (2011: 190).

This last term is coined by analogy with the 'televidencia' (i.e. mode of TV watching) coined by a prolific and distinguished scholar on television, youth and education, Guillermo Orozco Gómez. Recent research by Orozco would appear to be negative about the potential of mass media. Thus he writes, repeatedly against the falsely optimistic vision of digital technology, that it has led rather to 'dis-ordering' of communication, to social 'un-power', and to disruptions in the experience of time ('des-ordenamiento', 'despoder', 'destiempos'). Social actors are thus in need of 'processes of apprenticeship' or, simply, 'learning' ('aprendizaje') to catch up with media exuberance (2001a). In *Televisión, audiencias, y educación* (*Television, Audiences, and Education*) he argues that 'mediatization' and 'audiencization' of social subjects have led to the appropriation of time and space by media, inhibiting other forms of civil participation (2001b: 126). TV has also split the audience into 'fragments'.

Yet even here there is some possibility of positive change. One of Orozco's examples of 'un-time' is the Zapatistas, who drew attention to age-old injustice via the internet. The new 'fragments' of the television audience are also realigned in unexpected ways: citing the title of a famous series, Orozco claims that 'the rich also weep' ('los ricos también lloran'); that children ask questions about programming that is in theory reserved for adults; and (a favourite example, repeated elsewhere) that mothers who sit stony-faced through tragic news bulletins cry to their heart's content ('a gusto') over the next chapter of their favourite telenovela (2001b: 26). And in *Televisión y audiencias: un enfoque cualitativo* (*Television and Audiences: A Qualitative Approach*), Orozco asserts the relative autonomy of the audience (1996: 67) and its construction of strategies of viewing (1996: 79). Such strategies involve multiple levels of interaction (from the normative to the pragmatic), reliant on various types of decision (aesthetic, informative, emotional and functional), which are based in turn on needs that are both cognitive and affective (1996: 73). Orozco writes here and elsewhere that communication is not determined by media; and it is striking how often he appeals in his theory to language drawn from drama: plot, dialogue and 'escenario' ('stage', 'setting' or 'scene').

'Televidencias' (i.e. practices of watching television) can thus be rearticulated pedagogically, even though groups such as the indigenous, the homeless, dissidents, women, youths and children (minorities that constitute a numerical majority) are regularly excluded from TV programming. Reworking, relearning or talking television – Orozco's varied definitions of this pedagogy – would not a priori exclude any television type or genre. Indeed, this pedagogy (the interconnection of television, audience and education) is always, potentially, taking place. As Orozco writes, albeit with some ambivalence:

> La televisión educa y seguirá haciéndolo, aunque no se lo proponga; las audiencias aprenden de la televisión . . . aunque no se percaten de ello; su educación se realiza y se seguirá realizando muchas veces de manera inadvertida. (2001b: 111)

> (Television educates and will continue to do so, although that is not its intention; audiences learn from television . . . although they are not aware of it; their education will take place and will continue taking place in a way that often goes unnoticed.)

Thus, while Orozco writes that children are especially vulnerable, demanding as they do immediate gratification, he also notes that age as a mediation is a factor that is subject to debate (1996: 86). Following Jesús Martín Barbero, Orozco argues that such mediations or, more simply, identities, are neither monolithic nor determinist. Here once more, telenovela is the preferred example. It is not perverse when Latin American mothers recommend to their children that they should learn about life from series melodramas. Rather, this is the manifestation of a perceptual mediation (2001b: 49). Put more simply, a mother's tears at a fictional drama do not prevent her from being concerned for the present and future of her children but rather provide her with a means for expressing and negotiating that concern (2001b: 46).

As in the case of cinema reception, however, such opinions and tastes are influenced by social class. According to Orozco's empirical research, female informants who believe that telenovela serves a positive function (a significant apprenticeship ['aprendizaje'] for social performance ['actuación']) tend to be working class and locate any harmful effect in the children themselves. Middle-class mothers, on the other hand, fret that too much fiction and fantasy will harm the child's own potential for imagination: it is TV itself that is to blame (2001a). Press hostility to youth media also appeals to such class-based generalized hostility. But by using these twin paradigms from Torres and Orozco we can now go on to re-read *Rebel* and *I'm Gonna Explode* more closely in the light of a reception theory that transcends the negative content analysis to which fictions on and for young people are so often subjected.

Rebel: Pleasures and Pedagogies

Episodio 1 (4 de octubre de 2004): En la Ciudad de México, escuela Elite Way School [*sic*], el director da un discurso por el fin de cursos. Mía se molesta porque su padre no llegó a la ceremonia de clausura, por lo que en lugar del espectáculo que tenía planeado baila un streaptease [*sic*] muy sensual para vengarse. Alma Rey, una cantante grupera, le dice a su hija Roberta que su padre quiere que le busque una escuela para que tenga una buena educación. Franco Colucci [padre de Mía] le dice a Mía que lo que hizo fue vergonzoso y en castigo no saldrá de vacaciones, ella le dice que lo hizo porque lo estuvo esperando para la ceremonia y nunca llegó.

(Episode 1 (4 de octubre de 2004): In Mexico City's Elite Way School, the principal is giving the end-of-year address. Mía is annoyed because her father didn't come to the closing ceremony, so instead of the dance performance she had planned she does a very sexy striptease in order to take revenge on him. Alma Rey, a *grupera* singer, tells her daughter Roberta that her father wants to find her a school where she'll get a good education. Franco Colucci [Mía's father] tells Mía that what she did was shameful and she'll be punished by not going on vacation with him. She tells him she only did it because she was waiting for him at the ceremony and he didn't come.)

Episodio 2 (5 de octubre de 2004): León [padre de Diego] le dice al director que hace falta más seguridad en el colegio, que si la gente se entera que no es capaz de controlar a su hijo, cómo van a votar por él para gobernar un país. Mía le dice a Roberta que no crea que se va a quedar en ese colegio, que es muy exclusivo. En la central camionera de Monterrey, Miguel se despide de su madre y hermana, pues viajará al distrito federal para ingresar al colegio. León le entrega un citatorio a Diego y le dice que tendrá que resolver sólo su problema, que lo denunció porque la prensa lo acosa, además destruyó un carro y pudo haber matado a alguna persona; Diego le responde que lo único que le importa es su imagen pública.

(Episode 2 (5 de octubre de 2004): León [Diego's father] tells the principal that they need more security at the school and if people find out he can't control his own son, they won't vote for him to run the country. Mía tells Roberta that she doesn't think she'll stay in the school, as it's very exclusive. In the bus station in Monterrey, Miguel says goodbye to his mother and sister as he's leaving for Mexico City to go to school. León gives Diego a citation and tells him he'll have to solve his problem on his own and that he reported him as the press is hounding him about it. Moreover he smashed up a car and could have killed someone. Diego replies that the only thing his father is concerned about is his public image.) (Wikipedia 2012)

Guillermo Orozco has an essay (2006) on the decline of telenovela in Mexico, which he claims has changed from being a cultural expression to a mere marketing product. Unsurprisingly, perhaps, his case study here is *Rebel*. Beginning with a vindication of the history of the genre as both an important phenomenon in Latin American everyday life and a media product of national and international reach (2006: 12), he argues that telenovela can redeem communication within the family and promote the exchange of affects in a mass audience. Evidence here of this national conversation is the ratings table for the top ten prime-time shows for the week 14–20 November 2005, when *Rebel* (which was coming to the end of its first season) scored an audience of almost three and a half million and an enviable share of 31 per cent (2006: 13). While all of these shows are Mexican productions, three of them (including, of course, *Rebel*) are derived from foreign formats, whether Argentine or Spanish. Orozco writes that although telenovela can foster the recognition of multiple identities, it also perpetuates undesirable traits such as machismo and 'anachronistic' virtues such as virginity (2006: 14). Condensing the popular and the melodramatic, practices of knowledge and of behaviour, the genre allows us nonetheless to understand the link between the commercial logic of its industrial production and the logic of consumption embedded in its viewers' communicative competence.

Now, writes Orozco, a narration based on social reality (or at least the collective memory of *mexicanidad*) has been replaced by one based on empathetic sociality: moods, feelings and emotions (2006: 16). In *Rebel*, moreover, narrative is shattered into 'fragments' (small 'spots', whether formal, sensorial or linguistic) whose aim is solely to facilitate ease of consumption. Attractive images (half-naked male and female bodies, fashions in clothing or language) promote mercantilization over aesthetic value, technical quality or innovative storytelling (2006: 17). Popularity is now unrelated to the skill of the stars' performances, which are increasingly improvised (2006: 18). And, as proof of this impoverishment, as Televisa's profits have gone up, so its budgets have gone down – to just $70,000 per hour of drama, as opposed to $100,000 per hour in rival Brazil. If telenovela is no longer watched but simply consumed, then it has 'come out of the screen' to be everywhere – in marketing trinkets and on displays in shop windows and public places (2006: 19).

Orozco gives a valuable periodization of production since 1951, identifying successive stages he names as 'initial', 'home made', 'industrial', 'transnational' and (the most recent) 'mercantile' (2006: 24–30). He notes specifically Mexican characteristics such as the obsessive focus on the trials of impossible love to the detriment of both sex and politics (2006: 25, 26). Now, however, plot strands and protagonists have multiplied. Where once nothing happened (with characters rehearsing to one another on interior sets the way they feel), now, as in video clips, action is all, with exterior scenes increasingly common, and tone irregular, with the irruption of fantastic or farcical elements (2006: 31). Seduction is thus replaced by excitation; and a dominant leitmotif (such as rebellion) need not be 'authentic' or require something worth rebelling against (2006: 31). It is simply a question of 'reacting' and 'confronting the other', a refusal to obey and to adjust to the minimal social rules of cohabitation ('convivencia') (2006: 32).

What is striking here is that Orozco does not allow viewers of *Rebel* the active competence that he ascribes to spectators in earlier 'stages' of telenovela; that he denies the possibility that affect could be a form of cognition, guiding young viewers to a new understanding of their social status; and that he is unwilling to ask what pleasures and profits the new aesthetic might offer. He also seems to posit an 'outside' of mercantilism which is difficult to imagine, given the marginal status of public broadcasting in Mexico since TV service began and the inseparability of the history of the genre from the commercial monopoly and later duopoly of broadcasters (Televisa and Azteca) which has hosted that genre. In the close reading of the first season of *Rebel* that follows, then, I seek to use Orozco's own more friendly account of 'televidencia' (in which viewers learn about life from their favourite shows) against his unsympathetic version of recent teen drama.

The first episodes of *Rebel* waste no time in setting up the linked themes of family and friendship, and sex and violence. After a brief voice-over set to pseudo-home movie footage, we first see popular Mía on the gaudily coloured school set, rejecting a clumsy suitor, to the acclaim of her less attractive female friends. Meanwhile serious Miguel (first shown in a high-angle shot sprawled melancholically on a mattress on the floor) is shown explaining to his little sister that a 'bad man' (Mía's father) 'took their father away from them'. Soon, in one of those fragmented 'spots' which Orozco so dislikes, Mía is stripping down to her black underwear on stage to the pleasure and horror of the assembled school community. When her father arrives late at the improvised performance, he tells her to 'respect the rules', but she replies, tearfully, that he is more concerned with the fact that she made him look ridiculous than with how she feels about his failure to turn up on time. Ironically, then, for a show which was so criticized for its promotion of superficial looks, the moral of the opening episodes is that inner values trump external appearances.

Next, sullen Roberta arrives with her underdressed but over-attentive mother, whom she treats with some scorn. When Mía kindly (or cattily) offers to change the new girl's look, Roberta replies that Mía should change her brain instead. Competing characters are here shown by their duelling wardrobes: the denim-clad punk pours a can of soda over the fluffy pink sweater of the archetypal *fresa* (entitled rich kid). Meanwhile, earnest Miguel is saying goodbye to friends and family at Monterrey's unaesthetic bus station. His traditionalist mother gives him a medallion of the Virgin of Guadalupe to keep him safe in the capital. And rich blond Diego, having been (like Mía) neglected by his father, drunkenly ploughs a sports car through a street market, injuring himself and older female friends. Finally, when new kid Miguel arrives at school, he first catches sight of Mía, who will be his target in the revenge plot against her father. There is much slow-motion head-turning and hair-tossing here, with a song playing full length on the soundtrack to signal this as a momentous moment.

What can we learn from this set-up? The stress on costume, not just exhibited but thematized here (the make-over dialogue), suggests that the show will indeed be a formidable marketing vehicle (the cast's selection of bracelets, customized with such slogans as 'México' in Spanish and 'Love' in English, will prove especially desirable and accessible to cash-poor teens). Moods, feelings and emotions are also clearly privileged over reflection (Mía shifts from one moment to the next between sexy bravado and sarcastic taunting to child-like petulance and tearful misery). The texture is fragmentary, broken up, as Orozco says, into pop video-like 'spots' apparently independent of the 'deep' continuing plotlines. (Much later, testing verisimilitude to the limit, the show will break into Japanese-style animation or stage a musical performance on the frigid ski slopes of Canada.) The tone is also irregular from the start, with high melodrama mixed with low farce. Finally, rebellion is presented as excitation (the pupils' and parents' fevered reaction to Mía's striptease) and instinctive reaction (the young people's refusal of all social and parental rules).

Yet clearly there is something else happening here. The show may praise virginity (we later learn that sex should come only when accompanied by true love) but it clearly contests machismo (Diego's politician father, who will encourage his son to beat up a rival, is presented as a monster). The sets at Televisa's San Ángel studios may be as excessive as the wardrobe (the lavish dormitory rooms boast internal spiral staircases), but there are also frequent everyday exteriors and expensive action sequences (the bus station, the car crash). And if the narrative seems to express Orozco's 'disordering' (dislocations in time and space), then it also offers young viewers processes of apprenticeship to negotiate those discontinuities. It seems plausible that teen fans (like the TV viewers Orozco interviewed elsewhere) are relatively autonomous of the text, engaging different levels of interaction according to the series' changing tone and making aesthetic or informative decisions in relation to clues in the *mise-en-scène* (costume and setting) or the varied plotlines (romantic, familial and educational).

To take an obvious example: the editing is contrastive. We cross-cut between broodingly handsome scholarship boy Miguel – serious in both style and performance – and his more privileged classmates: mischievous Mía and drunken Diego. Miguel's loyalty to his family is implicitly contrasted with the latter's dysfunctional relationships.

Combating machismo once more, Mía will definitively fall for the boy she first dismisses as an impoverished provincial 'cowboy' ('charrito montaperros': literally, 'dog-rider') only when she sees how kindly he is to her overweight friend. And if Miguel attacks amoral Mía (who actually proclaims herself in the first episode 'beyond good and evil') it is because such privileged people 'crush the weak'.

'Televidencia' can thus be rearticulated pedagogically to help viewers negotiate gender and class conflict in ethical terms (we remember that the one teacher who features prominently and sympathetically in the series gives a class on ethics). And if *Rebel* stays loyal to Mexican telenovela's historical stress on impossible loves (the frequency of tight close-ups of weeping youths is remarkable), it ventures from the start, and surprisingly, into politics. Diego's corrupt political candidate of a father, fearful of bad publicity from his son's drunk-driving, personally presents him with a summons, albeit with a punishment limited to community service. But the politician will also use his influence to get the police to arrest the poor father whose infant son humiliates Diego during that service, a transparently unjust outcome. Conversely, selfish Roberta, whose reactive rebellion is expressed through rejection of her doting mother, will end up reluctantly adopting a street kid and thus learning a lesson about both social exclusion and maternal devotion.

But can we re-read (re-view) the most fanciful element of *Rebel*, the kids' transformation in the course of a single season from a bunch of argumentative students into a bestselling pop group who give a (real-life) climactic concert at Mexico City's Palacio de los Deportes (Sports Stadium) to an audience of some 20,000? It is significant that, throughout the series, vital moments take place on stage: Mía flaunts her (brief and fragile) independence with the initial striptease; her rivalry with edgy Roberta is played out through respective dance teams (Mía's features micro-miniskirts, Roberta's hospital gowns and wheelchairs); and the girls' (provisional) reconciliation with their respective boyfriends is shown through a slow dance at an elaborately staged joint birthday party, witnessed and applauded by the whole school. But given the conventions of teen musical fiction (stretching back at least to films of the 1930s), such scenes can perhaps be read as an apprenticeship ('aprendizaje'), however utopian, in social performance ('actuación'). And it is important here to remember that while *Rebel*'s form is fragmented, its audience is not: the series successfully attracted a 'multi-target' national public, from infants to seniors.

Music and dance thus provide a framework for the transcendence of social exclusion, even as the narrative calls attention to the existence of stubborn problems rarely shown even in Mexican cinema. One long-running plotline of tragic love between Jewish boy and Gentile girl is (barely) resolved when the pair are rewarded by their faithful classmates with an unofficial wedding ceremony, as extravagantly staged as it is legally invalid. By promoting the easy visual consumption of such scenes (white costumes, roses and doves shown with virtuoso camera movements) *Rebel* guides its young audience towards a perhaps unexpected final moral: that of *convivencia* or peaceful cohabitation. Form here may be mercantile, but it is also inseparable from content. Like Orozco's weeping housewives, *Rebel*'s teen fans are thus not perverse: rather, they can combine intense pleasure in visual and aural stimuli (stylish wardrobe and aspirational décor, professionally produced soft rock and ballads) with perceptual mediation (an acknowledgement of the social and political determinants without which the narrative that stages that pleasure could not take place). While such storytelling may not be innovative, nor can it be dismissed as empty-headed.

I'm Gonna Explode: A Finely Balanced Rebellion

Guanajuato, Mexico, the present. Teenage Román is the son of a Congressman, who caused the car crash that killed his mother. Román is expelled from boarding school when his diary, which contains plans for a murder-suicide bid, is discovered. At his new school he hooks up with classmate Maru, who lives with her mother and sister. The couple plan to run away together and make a pact to meet if they are separated. They end up living in a tent on the roof of Román's family home. Román's father and Maru's mother search for their runaway children. Román makes crank calls to the radio and to his father, giving false leads as to their whereabouts. Román's stepmother discovers where they are hiding but says nothing. The teenagers steal a car and sneak out to a party in a nearby town. They are briefly separated but then spend the night at the home of Román's favourite teacher. Returning to the roof, they are surprised by a police raid. Román, who has stolen a gun, shoots Maru in the confusion. True to their pact, Maru, who is seriously wounded, escapes from hospital to meet Román. When he also escapes from the mental institution that is holding him to join her, she is already dying. (Smith, 2009a)

Bare-chested in his bedroom and shot in luscious black and white, adolescent Román broods over his diary, a single tear trickling down his still smooth cheek. The voice-over repeats the words he traces in a rounded childish hand: 'Bastards. Go ahead and laugh. We'll see who laughs last.' Tight (too tight) close-ups and a slowly circling camera give way to a fast-paced montage of the youth's plan in action: stealing money, phoning his father (a corrupt Congressman), shooting a loathed teacher and turning the gun on himself.

Naranjo next cuts to a colour sequence of Maru, also writing in her bedroom. This time darkly shadowed eyes are enhanced by a red filter. A slow pan over a bleak landscape shows the same girl leaving a truck where she's just spent the night against her will with an ex-boyfriend. The voice-over, gently spoken, says: 'Everything I do turns out bad. I think I'm gonna explode. Then I saw him.' Those last laconic Spanish words fill the screen in scarlet ink: 'Y lo vi.' A mystery youth has arrived at school in a luxury sedan, eyeholes cut in the red scarf he wears as a mask. A reverse shot shows the tearful girl, framed by ominous black, from the boy's POV.

But Maru doesn't stop there: 'He exists. But I also made him up.' And we soon discover that Naranjo, screenwriter as well as director, is quite capable of playing with narrative too. Although we are apparently deep in *Bowling in Columbine* territory, the footage of the shootings is actually a dream sequence: Román did not execute his plan and has simply been expelled from his elite private school when his ultra-violent diary was discovered. Lightning-fast cuts give us glimpses of its self-consciously gory contents. A little later, when the two kids run away together (Figure 6), the account we are given is equally unreliable. We know that Román steals a car and Maru gets

Figure 6 *I'm Gonna Explode* (Gerardo Naranjo, 2009)

herself expelled. But as she notes in impassive voice-over: 'There are conflicting versions.' Her own words are imprecise but dreamily evocative: 'A boy with a scarf on his head, two bullets, a Volkswagen, a little rain . . .'

The opening sequences of *I'm Gonna Explode* thus have elements in common thematically and even formally with *Rebel*, elements that make this art movie easily consumable by its youthful target audience, whom we know to be sceptical of such films. The feature film and the TV series share shots of handsome bare-chested boys, idiosyncratic fashion choices (Román's scarf-mask, Maru's jaggedly cut androgynous hair), and a somewhat archaic emphasis on the written word rather than mobile telephony (Román's 'album of gore', the diaries and poison-pen letters that are a leitmotif at Elite Way). The *coup de foudre* between Naranjo's teens is signalled by lingering looks as traditional as those exchanged between Mía and Miguel; indeed, playing on his name, Maru repeatedly calls her young suitor 'Romántico'.

Like Mía too, the virginal Maru will save herself for some time before giving in to sex with the youth she loves. She thus resists immediate gratification even as she sleeps with her tousled-haired boyfriend in an orange tent whose colour is as garish as any set in *Rebel*. If *Rebel*'s teens are granted an exotic vacation to Cozumel (where they even get to swim with dolphins), *I'm Gonna Explode*'s more modest provincial rebels, who pine for Mexico City, take a trip only to the roof of Román's family home. The latter, however, is as luxurious as any in telenovela (although rainwater drips ominously from a hole in the ceiling down the shiny chandeliers). Sunbathing, barbequing and drinking tequila, Maru claims 'It's like we're on the beach.' And Naranjo does not deny us spectacular landscape shots of the historic city of Guanajuato behind them, with its lush green hills stretching into the distance.

More importantly (and of course Naranjo is well aware of this), would-be authentic adolescent rebellion is once more channelled through public performance. Mía's well-practised choreography is echoed at the start of the film by Maru's desultory dance moves as an incongruous sailor in a school play. And Mía's rebellious striptease is reworked in Román's expert staging of a mock suicide by hanging at the same event, to the alarm of the parental audience. Ironically, the pace of the telenovela is much more leisurely than the art movie, requiring as it does constant repetition and deferral so as not to reach too soon the definitive romantic resolution. Moreover, the average shot length of the feature is, in its first act at least, as abbreviated as in any video clip. Indeed, the use of black and white and of coloured filters, of jump cuts and odd camera angles, is unusually showy, especially in the contemporary context of a Mexican art cinema that is reliably minimalist.

In a related crowd-pleasing move, Naranjo uses music to heighten and fragment his text still further, creating autonomous 'spots' within the fiction, similar to those criticized by Orozco in the case of *Rebel*. Thus, when the kids first escape in a car, we are shown diverse, discontinuous images, in a manner reminiscent of the French New Wave: travelling shots from the windows, portraits of the protagonists staring straight into the camera, and ecstatic shots of fluffy white clouds in a blue sky and vivid flowers in a green field. What plays over the sequence, however, knitting it together but also separating it off from the rest of the film, is a lushly incongruous Baroque adagio by Albinoni. Earlier Naranjo had essayed the same technique. A Mahler Lied plays throughout as the kids frolic in bed on the roof, an electric storm flashes across Guanajuato's night sky, and the camera cranes down to the lush, hushed living room where, under the dripping chandelier, the parents drink and fret. Elsewhere, and with typical eclecticism, the music on the soundtrack is as cosmopolitan as anything in *Rebel*: the narcissistic 'Hope in the Mirror' by UK electro band Zoot Woman and the fey surrealism of Andalusian indie Pin' La La's 'Naves que dan vueltas a un balón'. Citing (reworking and undoing) Mexican romance, Naranjo's lovers will even dance drunkenly at a *quinceañera* party to the most classic and slyly erotic of boleros, 'Sabor a mí'.

After the pace slackens in the second act, Naranjo gives us in the third the tragic, even melodramatic, ending we have been waiting for: Román, reunited with Maru after escaping from the institution to which he has been confined, is just too late to save her life (the Albinoni recurs here as she lies bloodily in the back of the car where her lover has carried her). The effects in this final sequence (distorted sound and vision, evoking Maru's loss of consciousness) are also found in scenes in *Rebel* where characters are near death.

Given all these parallels, it is not surprising, then, that there is a discourse on television explicit in the film's diegesis, as well as implicit in its narrative and stylistic choices. We are shown how Román's neglectful politician father would rather watch sports on his TV set than the video on how to cope with a missing family member helpfully provided by the clueless police. When Maru momentarily turns on Román, she attacks his taste in the movies that he watches on TV; and says he must love the Paty Chapoy show (a gossip programme by Azteca's showbiz reporter). But revelling in an amoralism and nihilism that has so many precedents in high culture, *I'm Gonna Explode* does not care to offer the audience the education in ethics which we saw in *Rebel* and which Orozco identifies in some forms of televidencia. While the critique of the politician-patriarch is as transparent in the feature film as in the telenovela, the former glories in the self-destruction of its anti-heroes, in an ecstatic mix of sound and image and of bared bodies and colourful *mise en scène*, a mix that tends to promote ease of consumption over considered reflection. It seems improbable that, in the unlikely event that Orozco's working-class mothers were to see *I'm Gonna Explode*, they would find much material to educate their children for their future lives, as they do in the case of their favourite telenovelas.

But here we should return to Patricia Torres' research on youth cinema audiences in Mexico. What mode of 'cinevidencia' is implied by Naranjo's film, what kind of identities does it construct? *I'm Gonna Explode* would seem to be ideal for the young, educated audiences that Torres claims have been behind the regeneration of Mexican film: at once hostile to Hollywood and wary of local movies that are too commercial and generic. The richest and most literate of these youthful spectators, we remember, considered recent Mexican films to be successful in their artistic ambitions (narrative and style) but outdated in their subject matter. The transparent bid for aesthetic distinction in Naranjo's film would thus coincide with the tastes of those eighteen- to twenty-seven-year-olds who, like the bourgeois family depicted in *I'm Gonna Explode*, can afford to buy regular tickets at the newly upmarket theatres now located in the shiny shopping malls where the poor would not be made welcome.

Perhaps, however, such consumers employed their typical strategies of negotiation, resistance and reflection here. Released some years after Torres' case studies, *Amores perros* and *Y tu mamá también* (films which had come to symbolize the 'new wave' of local production), the teen-set *I'm Gonna Explode* might no longer seem like a reinvention of national film trends. Nonetheless, with its prominent political critique, Naranjo's film could still present itself as an 'exaggeration' or 'allegory' of national fantasies in the same mould as the films by González Iñárritu and Cuarón. And if it lacked those features' concern for the culture of poverty (a milieu which the middle-class public could watch with such professional dispassion), it did share the frank and unmoralizing treatment of sex that young audiences praised and prized in the earlier movies.

Experimental but easily consumable in its technique, challenging but familiar in its subject matter, *I'm Gonna Explode*, a film that combined unknown protagonists with one of the most consecrated of Mexican actors (Daniel Giménez Cacho as the father), thus embodied a mode of 'cinevidencia' situated in the middle of the current cultural field. It was a position that, ironically enough, owed much to television, the dominant medium for youth fiction, even as it targeted TV as a key part of that conservative culture against which the film's photogenic stars aimed their gratuitous and doomed revolt.

The Impossible Dream

> Alguno de estos días voy a escapar
> Para jugarme todo un sueño
> Todo en la vida es a perder o ganar
> Hay que apostar sin miedo
> No importa mucho lo que digan de mí,
> Cierro los ojos y ya estoy pensando en ti.

(One of these days I'm gonna escape/ To stake it all on a dream/ Everything in life is up for grabs/ You gotta be brave and take a chance/ I don't care what they say about me/ I close my eyes and I'm thinking of you.)

The lyrics to *Rebel*'s theme tune are ambiguous. On the one hand they stress the quest for identity (the young person's 'way of being') and his/her reflexive rebellion against the parents (the father whose complaints are unheard). On the other hand, the fearless wager on freedom or flight from the everyday (risking the social ostracism of 'what they say about me') is wholly dependent on the love object, on whom the subject's mind is obsessively focused. As in *I'm Gonna Explode*, then, the revolt into romance can lead only to a new, albeit more pleasurable, kind of submission.

This dialectic between determinism and free will is suggested in the first words we hear in the first episode of *Rebel*. Miguel's voice-over (playing over black and white home movie-style footage of the cast) asks both 'What is the precise moment when we begin to choose our life?' and 'When parents choose a school, are they aware that this place will mark us forever?' It is a dialectic explored in some immoralist high culture precedents of *I'm Gonna Explode*: in Albert Camus's 'absurd' and, more evidently, in André Gide's '*acte gratuit*', introduced in *The Vatican Cellars* (*Les Caves du Vatican*, 1914) when a charismatic teen rebel pushes an old man out of a moving train just for the hell of it. Cultural distinction, shared by Naranjo's art movie, inoculates and aestheticizes such nihilism, rendering it readily consumable by elite audiences. Popular narrative is less likely to opt for the death wish: unlike the fatal destiny of *I'm Gonna Explode*'s tragic twins, the revolt of *Rebel*'s rich kids is clearly motivated by a parental neglect or temporary dysfunction, both of which will be resolved by the end of the series.

Clearly I have been provocative in juxtaposing the two texts. Yet, the judgement of taste that creates cultural hierarchies is, of course, socially produced. Indeed, the struggle over aesthetics is built into both of these fictions. In *Rebel*, fashion icon Mía often dismisses rival styles as '*naco*' ('tacky' or 'gross'); and in *I'm Gonna Explode* Maru attacks Román's taste in TV and, showing her own eclectic style, teams a formal gown stolen from his mother with a cocky trilby. Perhaps one advantage for foreign scholars is that, although they may fail to spot specific references that are easily accessible to locals, familiarity has not yet bred in them contempt for ubiquitous popular successes. I have thus argued that even teenage telenovelas can (as Orozco suggested of the genre as a whole) serve as a vehicle for a media pedagogy that is at once social and ethical; and that a youth art movie (something of a contradiction in terms) may be more digestible if it assimilates themes and techniques associated with the mass medium that it must so ostentatiously reject.

Ironically, television, once thought to be ephemeral, now seems more lasting than feature film. As *I'm Gonna Explode*'s graffiti stencils continue to fade on Mexico City's walls, *Rebel* remains accessible (albeit in a choppily edited version) on DVD and in thousands of YouTube sites, lovingly curated by fans. Stars like Anahí, amongst the most popular in Mexico, have (at the time of writing, some five years after the series finished) millions of followers on Twitter. The para-sociality of telenovela (the close cohabitation of viewers with actors over three years of daily contact) has thus smoothly mutated into the yet faster and denser rhythm of social media. It is a transition that feature film, relatively removed from everyday life and in Mexico secluded in middle-class shopping malls of restricted access, finds much more difficult. Conversely Alfonso ('Poncho') Herrera, who played serious Miguel, has made the leap to the aptly named 'legitimate theatre', and was in January 2012 co-starring in a play with Oscar-nominated Demián Bichir. Cultural distinction is thus more fluid and mutable than the persistent prejudices against television as a medium and telenovela as a genre would suggest.

Therefore, if we are concerned with the specificity of Mexican audiovisual fiction we should perhaps look to television rather than cinema. *Rebel* may have been based on a resilient Argentine format (and a Brazilian version began playing as late as 2011). But there is no doubt that it connected with a mass local audience, proud to sport bracelets inscribed with the word 'México' even as they enjoyed spoilt Mía's notorious anglicisms ('Hello, daddy!'). And Naranjo's invocation of *À bout de souffle*, where Godard's somewhat older stars were also headed on an amoral journey to nowhere, was clearly more transnational than a telenovela that is reworked for each national market. After all, *I'm Gonna Explode*'s main audience was at festivals in Europe and the US. Foreign scholars should not allow our vision of Mexican audiovisual culture to be distorted by such accidents of distribution.

Finally, there is, of course, no 'outside' of mercantilism for the products of audiovisual media, no TV show or film untouched by capital. Yet not all content is the same; and only close textual analysis can reveal its specific value. *Rebel* was a rare triumph of brand extension. Given the failure of later shows by the same producer, it is difficult to argue that teens can be brainwashed into buying into any product foisted on them by media goliath Televisa. And, as I have attempted to show, *Rebel* can be re-read in the light of reception theory (Orozco's TV pedagogy), however inadvertent and unnoticed that apprenticeship was at the time. Likewise, *I'm Gonna Explode* marked an aesthetic innovation within the genre of art movies in Mexico, but one which attempted to adapt itself to the changed industrial conditions of exhibition, ably documented by Torres, and stage a dialogue with the rival and ubiquitous medium of television. It would seem – finally – that in the field of Mexican media, as in the world of its teen fiction, rebellion remains as impossible as it is necessary.

6

Lady Killers in TV Fiction: *Women Murderers* (*Mujeres asesinas*, Televisa, 2008–10), *The Aparicio Women* (*Las Aparicio*, Argos, 2010–11)

Ladies of Silence?

In 2006 Juana Barraza, a forty-eight-year-old single mother, was arrested under suspicion of being the 'Mataviejitas', or 'Little old lady killer', who had committed thirty-two murders in Mexico City. Barraza also performed as a masked wrestler under the professional name 'la Dama del Silencio' ('the Lady of Silence'). The press, assuming her guilt, commented on a continual history of abuse (beginning with her being raped as a child) and speculated on the origin of her pathology (the murders supposedly resulting from the anger she felt towards her neglectful alcoholic mother, who had allegedly exchanged her young daughter for 'three beers') (Arvizu, 2007).

Elena Azaola, a distinguished criminologist and psychoanalyst, whose works include the significantly titled *El delito de ser mujer* (*The Crime of Being a Woman*, 1996), is cited in the UK daily *Guardian* as commenting on this 'unheard of' case: 'How much our society must have changed if it can produce a [female] *mataviejitas*' (Tuckman, 2006). Conversely Susana Vargas Cervantes, a graduate student at McGill University, argues in an article in the academic journal *Crime, Media, Culture* that the case of Barraza is an example of policing and performing *mexicanidad* ('Mexicanness'): 'reinforcing but also revealing the limits of Mexican masculinity and femininity' (2010: 185). Here Barraza's actions are said to redress the social factors of race, class, gender and sex that have historically prevented marginal subjects such as her from attaining full citizenship.

Whether invoked as 'Mataviejitas' or 'Dama del Silencio', Mexico's first female serial killer is thus at once singular and universal: an index of both revolution and reaction, of radical social change and stubborn political stasis. Moreover she is positioned at the crossroads between the psychic and the social: is this troubling phenomenon the result of a pathological aetiology or a purely political complex?

The year 2006 also marked the beginning of the six-year term of President Felipe Calderón, which would be marked by unprecedented drug-related violence and the continuing *feminicidio* (or mass murder of women) in Ciudad Juárez, which had resulted in scores of female victims. It was perhaps curious, then, that, following on from the Barraza case, Mexican television should end the decade with two unique fictions that also focused on women as aggressors rather than as victims and that achieved mass audiences, critical acclaim and retransmission in the US. These series, which remain to my knowledge unstudied, treat their common theme of female fatality with notable differences both in their approach to the issues of gender and nationality cited above and in their engagement with production processes and formats.

Women Murderers (*Mujeres asesinas*), shown on dominant network Televisa and produced by independent Mediamates, is an evening series screened just twice a week in which each of the episodes dramatizes a single case, allegedly based on a true story. The only recurring characters are the officers of the fictional DIEM (or 'Department of Investigation Specializing in Women'), headed by director Sofía Capellán, played by the steely Rosa María Bianchi (who had a small part in *Amores perros*). Femmes fatales of the week have included such distinguished film actresses as María Rojo and Diana Bracho (Figure 7). The show, which at around forty-three minutes filled an

Figure 7   *Women Murderers* (Televisa, 2008–10)

hour-long time slot, ran for three seasons with a total of forty episodes between 2008 and 2010. When the second season premiered in the USA, Televisa claimed that a show that was 'made in Mexico' had, with 4,600,000 viewers, the highest rating in its 10 p.m. timeslot, bigger even than the offerings of the English-language networks (Guzmán, 2010).

My second text, *The Aparicio Women* (*Las Aparicio*), is a daily serial based around an all-female household made up of women whose many husbands have died in suspicious circumstances. Thrice-widowed matriarch Rafaela is joined by her three daughters: Alma, a psychologist who runs a cultural centre and male escort service for women; Mercedes, a feminist lawyer; and the youngest, Julia, an aspiring actress who embarks in early episodes on a lesbian affair with her best friend (Figure 8). The 120 episodes of *The Aparicio Women*, a series that promoted itself as self-consciously daring, were made by independent producer Argos and shown outside the dominant duopoly of Mexican broadcast TV (Televisa and Azteca) on upstart rival Cadena 3. It found support from an unusual quarter: the DVD box cited master screenwriter Guillermo Arriaga (*Amores*

Figure 8   *The Aparicio Women* (Cadena 3, 2010–11)

perros) as praising the series' cinematic timing, moderation and realism.

With their common stress on women's agency and even sadism, both series would seem to transcend the passivity and masochism thought to be embodied by the heroines of traditional telenovela or (the industry's preferred term) series melodrama. Yet telenovela has itself demonstrated for at least a decade a split between romantic and realist sub-genres, with the latter frequently engaging with urgent sociopolitical issues, from abortion to ecology. And one-off series have challenged the hegemony of serial narratives. In 2011 Televisa's afternoon scheduling boasted such titles as *The Rose of Guadalupe* (*La rosa de Guadalupe*): narratives of popular piety, as when a mother's prayer to the Virgin retrieves a lost child used as bait by kidnappers; and *As the Saying Goes* (*Como dice el dicho*): narratives of folk wisdom, as when a daughter sexually harassed by her prospective stepfather is not heard 'even by God' because she fails to speak out.

In spite of these provisos, the still exceptional theme and production context of *Women Murderers* and *The Aparicio Women* would suggest an initial hypothesis for this sixth chapter: that the 'unheard of' phenomenon of the female murderer coincides with the status of the two series as different forms of 'quality' or 'event' programming, unique in the first case for its high production values (promoted as 'cinematic') and in the second for its unprecedented thematics (unapologetically pro-feminist and pro-gay).

Yet *Women Murderers*, unlike *The Aparicio Women*, is clearly ambivalent where gender is concerned. Mealy-mouthed taglines on the DVD boxes state that although the heroines are predators, they are also 'victims'; or again, although they are guilty, they are also 'disturbingly innocent'. And while *The Aparicio Women*'s unusual premise is locally sourced, *Women Murderers* is loosely adapted from an original Argentine format, albeit indigenized for Mexico (the third season was, however, based directly on domestic stories, including that of Juana Barraza).

As mentioned earlier, *Women Murderers* benefited from the strength of its hegemonic broadcaster, while *The Aparicio Women*'s outsider status was bolstered by its upstart network (the press reported that Televisa had even blacklisted Cadena 3's stars for their temerity in working for the new rival [*Premiere*, 2010]). Finally, while *Women Murderers* enjoyed the luxury of rare production values proper to a one-off, twice-weekly series, *The Aparicio Women*, for all its ambitions to novelty in aesthetics as well as thematics, was restricted to some extent by the rigour of the daily production schedule typical of telenovelas. As we shall see, however, the tension between cinema and television (or, more broadly, between innovation and convention in a TV context) is played out in both fictions and, indeed, constitutes a great part of their interest.

Beyond content analysis and production history, however, the question arises of what theoretical paradigms are adequate to these two exceptional cases. Three scholars can guide us here. Jesús Martín Barbero has long been a strong defender of a genre that is no longer mere entertainment for 'housewives' (the term 'amas de casa' remains widely used in this context) and has extended his pioneering book on Colombian television and melodrama (1992) into a continuing international research project. In the original study he examined in huge detail the structure and dynamic of production (including professional mentalities [1992: 30]), reception or social uses and ways of seeing (including cultural competency [1992: 33]) and textual composition (including forms of narration and TV syntax [1992: 36]). More recently Martín Barbero has proposed that the supposedly 'anachronistic' genre of melodrama is, in a televisual context at least, not distanced from or a substitute for everyday life but rather touches it, or is even, in its rhythmic recurrence, structured like it (2012).

Hugh O'Donnell has also analysed this incursion of popular fiction into social reality in an admirably large selection of countries. Thus he shows how in Sweden two separate models of soap opera can coexist simultaneously; and how an apparently controversial scene (a gay kiss) can promote a society's self-image of tolerance that was achieved in the real world some time before the scene was shown ('anachronistically', once again) (1996a). Meanwhile, in the Iberian Peninsula, he writes, soaps have moved 'From a Manichean World View to the Kitchen Sink' (1996b), a division O'Donnell studies elsewhere (2007: 125–6) in the competing textual compositions of Latin American telenovela and Basque and Catalan soaps. The melodramatic mode of the former (he claims) requires stylized *mise en scène*, fatalistic characters and a spectator content to sit back and observe the highly coloured spectacle, while the social realist text of the latter (derived from British working-class soaps) promotes a naturalistic register and characters and audiences who actively participate in their everyday plotlines.

It is, however, Milly Buonanno, a scholar of the much-despised Italian television, who provides perhaps the most useful approach for my Mexican texts. Buonanno has called attention to the linked paradigms of space, time and narrative typical of what she calls *The Age of Television* (2008). Thus, arguing against the cultural imperialism model, she writes that imported formats (like that of *Women*

Murderers) are travelling narratives that are radically indigenized by distinctly national TV ecologies (2008: 85, 101). She further claims that the much-proclaimed liveness of TV is eclipsed in fiction at least by a desire to transcend time boundaries and give viewers access to temporalities that are (like televisual geographies) distant from the spectator (2008: 119).

Buonanno also locates those time-frames in two distinct strategies that correspond to the different formats exhibited by my case studies here: the series and the serial. The series seeks, by beginning its narrative again each week, to ward off death by making no 'bridge-crossing' definitive. Conversely, the serial manages mortality by putting off the final, inevitable conclusion for as long as possible. *Scheherazade*-like, then, TV fiction consoles us for fatality even as it reminds us of its inevitability (2008: 128). This is clearly a key insight for *Women Murderers* and *The Aparicio Women*, which are, respectively, a series and a serial founded with unusual explicitness on the twin premises of male death and female transcendence of time.

Women Murderers: Overview

The most striking feature of Televisa's female murderers is the variety of ages, social classes and geographical locations they exhibit. The thirteen women of the first season alone are young, middle-aged and elderly; of wealthy professional, middle or working class; and based in the city centre, suburb or dusty hacienda. The main conflict, however, is one unacknowledged in the series itself: that between the psychic and social etiologies. Thus some protagonists are defined in episode titles by their temperament ('pitiless' ['desalmada'], 'trapped' ['acorralada'], 'vengeful' ['vengadora'], 'hopeful' ['esperanzadora'], 'rebellious' ['rebelde']); some by their modus operandi ('poisonous' ['ponzoñosa'], 'toxic' ['tóxica'], 'asphyxiating' ['asfixiante'], 'knife-wielding' ['cuchillera'], 'corrosive' ['corrosiva']); and others by their profession or life-style ('cook' ['cocinera'], 'gold-digger'['trepadora'], 'seamstress' ['costurera']).

Characteristic motifs of both kinds recur. Thus at least two women ('pitiless' and 'vengeful') are traumatized victims of the sexual abuse of a father; while, coinciding with recent social trends in demography, many of the heroines, of varied age and social status, are married to abusive husbands but lacking in children, a state which goes unremarked within their respective episodes. While both the psychic and social paradigms could prove deterministic, depriving even femmes fatales of agency, one final feature of the textual composition works against this negative tendency: in the last shot of each episode, the murderess, having just committed her crime in flashback, stares straight into the camera, challenging the viewer's gaze. The ladies may be silent here, but clearly they remain defiant.

Frequently the actors who embody these roles are long-time telenovela heroines, playing very much against type. Thus in the second season, Angélica María, child movie star of the sixties, is a mother who pimps for her daughter, played by her namesake Angélica Vale, once also a youthful TV actor and subsequently the appealing heroine of the Mexican version of *Ugly Betty* (*Yo soy Betty, la fea*). In such stories the sexual graphicness of the series, so different to the romantic school of telenovelas, is notable (*Women Murderers* premiered on premium cable, where censorship is laxer than free to air). In successive episodes an ageing prostitute offers hand-jobs to an elderly client and refuses to be 'burst' ('reventada') by four johns at one time. A child obliges with oral sex on her abusive father (who is excited by watching her pee); or, again, a middle-aged female police officer, who insists on sex with a teenage suspect and is disappointed by his lacklustre performance, resorts to rubbing cocaine on her breasts and genitals to excite him. Patricia, the avenger, is provided with a gay brother, as maltreated as herself, who is spied on by their father as he has sex with his boyfriend in a nightclub bathroom. In the episodes which I study in detail a little later, the jealous wife of a surgeon tortures her young rival with a scalpel at some length (more urination here), while the hard-pressed wife of a dead-beat singer submits with transparent disgust to repeated and unromantic penetration by their landlord in lieu of rent.

Clearly the series could be accused, in line with its ambivalent taglines, of a faux feminism here. While its protagonists frequently rebel against the cruelty and perversity of patriarchs, their predicaments also provide ample opportunity for male voyeurism and for morbid fascination with the desecration of once revered cultural icons such as the aptly named Angélica María. And sometimes the series would seem to blame its victims: tough Sofía tells the avenger's timorous mother that women who fail to denounce a husband's or father's abuse must acknowledge their own share of the responsibility for male violence.

Moreover, at the time the show was playing, Televisa was being attacked not only for its pernicious stranglehold on Mexican broadcasting in general but also for its misogyny in particular. The controversial Laura Bozzo had been imported from Peru for a Jerry Springer-style talk show, a format new to Mexico, in which she had spouted such slurs as 'putita' ('little whore') at her guests. Televisa's television for women (with a prime-time schedule still dominated by series melodrama) might seem to be edging closer to television against women. Invoking the name of the series, the director of Mexico City's Women's Institute said that Bozzo was 'encouraging [male] violence' against women who did not wish to become 'Women Murderers' themselves (Baños, 2011). When a real-life mother and daughter were accused of murdering the latter's boyfriend in order to profit from the insurance policies they had taken out on his life, the series was, once more, cited by one commentator as a precedent (*El Imparcial*, 2010), to prove that real life was stranger than fiction.

Beyond this ideological ambivalence (feminism or misogyny?), the hybrid format of *Women Murderers* can also be read as an attempt to reconcile the US procedural, with its emphasis on mainly male technicians, with the Latin American telenovela, which is overwhelmingly female in its cast and target audience. As mentioned earlier, unlike in, say, *CSI*, the criminal investigative agency in the series is dedicated exclusively to cases involving women and is headed by a female director. This factor attempts to neutralize another nationally specific element: the lack of successful cop shows on Mexican TV, an absence evidently deriving from the public's perception of pervasive corruption in the force. The series' reassuring Sofía, an incorruptible female officer, is, however, undercut by an ex-colleague in episode 11 of the first season ('Cristina the rebel'). Here an impressive Daniela Romo plays the spectacularly immoral drug-dealing policewoman, who, as mentioned earlier, preys sexually on her teenage suspects.

Given the inquisitorial system of justice in Mexico, where cases are investigated at length by judges in sessions that are often closed, the show also lacks – of necessity – the dramatic adversarial courtroom scenes on which US equivalents such as *Law & Order* rely so heavily. This national difference might also perhaps explain the curious lack of suspense in the series' plots. Viewers know from the start that the victim (generally glimpsed in a teasing pre-credit sequence) has been murdered by the star-protagonist of the week. Thus the lengthy forensic scenes at DIEM, reminiscent of US procedurals in its high-tech *mise-en-scène* and stylized palette (gun-metal blue and grey), are deprived of surprise and seem somewhat perfunctory.

Of course there is little reason for the series to display evidence of cultural imperialism from north of the border. *Women Murderers* remains a Latin American franchise (with excursions to Italy and Romania). Rumours of a remake in the US, spread by the producer, proved unfounded (Silva, 2009). While the US connection is tenuous, Mexican producer Mediamates took care to rebrand the Argentine show for its own market by adapting even the promotional materials. Thus the original black butterfly logo for the series was replaced by a red insect, reminiscent perhaps of the Monarchs of Michoacán, dripping blood as it flutters through the expert credits. In such details, the twin factors of gender and nationality interact with each other to ambivalent effect.

How does this kind of content analysis intersect with industrial and theoretical questions? Some initial observations stand out. Although *Women Murderers* was broadcast by Televisa (the juggernaut of the telenovela genre), the structure and dynamic of production (including 'professional mentality') seems in this special case to be derived more from independent Mediamates. Producer Pedro Torres is presented in press materials as the undisputed auteur or star of the Mexican *Women Murderers*, immodestly described as a 'recognized visionary' in trade materials (*Directorio Producción* [2010–11: 112]). Secondly, the chief screenwriter claims that he had considerable autonomy in adapting the Argentine scripts, credited as he is with his own 'versions' of them, even as he notes that, unlike in his own work as a playwright, he was subject to constant scrutiny by the series producer and the episode director (*Vanguardia*, 2009). Thirdly, Torres contrasts the relatively low budget of this his first drama (Mediamates was previously known for reality shows), which, even with its high production values, is considerably less than those available to his Hollywood rivals; while US series with their added resources can extend to eight or nine seasons, the 'natural length' of his Mexican equivalent is just three (*AM*, 2011).

Finally, there is evidence of an argument for auteurism on the part of the female stars. Already beloved by audiences, they are the key selling point of the show. According to the screenwriter, Torres commented ironically on one actress who claimed that the method of murder she was allotted went against her 'spirituality' (he asked rhetorically what forms of killing might indeed be compatible with such moralizing) (*Vanguardia*, 2009). But the producer willingly acknowledges that without his female protagonists there would be no audience. And a star like María Rojo (who appeared in two episodes) brings not only a prestigious curriculum vitae in national cinema (features with directors from Cazals to Hermosillo, not to mention the much-loved popular success *Danzón* [María Novaro, 1991]), but also a high profile as a politician in both federal and local assemblies (*Informador*, 2010).

The fullest account of the production process is an extended interview with Pedro Torres ('Death Becomes Him' ['La muerte le sienta bien']), published in business magazine *CNNExpansión* (Tavira, 2009). This profile is accompanied by publicity shots of the protagonists, reminiscent of those for *Desperate Housewives* (ABC,

2004–12), where the stars appear not in character but rather soigné in blood-red gowns. Here the success of the show is attributed to its status as a 'Monster of Marketing' with the 'renowned' actresses announcing their crimes on billboards, hoardings, buses and radio and TV spots (where their red gowns gave way to virginal white, splattered provocatively with blood).

The novelty here is that it is not the broadcaster, Televisa, but the production company (previously known for commercials, games shows and 'advertainment') that took responsibility for promotion, thus turning the show into a 'product' like any other. Proudly defining himself as 100 per cent advertising man ('publicista'), even when it comes to promoting himself, Torres recounts that he first bought reality franchise *Big Brother* for Mexico. The format cost for *Women Murderers*, which was his next travelling narrative, was cheap (just $15,000 per episode), but the price of production was high. At $300,000 per hour it was three times the budget of Televisa's novelas. The sceptical broadcaster was thus willing to bring just 35 per cent of the budget to the table, with the rest being made up by cablers TVC, Sony and AXN and, crucially, US Spanish-language network Univisión.

The series' high concept and luxury cast also brought precious free publicity, valued here at 40 million pesos in press coverage for the first season alone. Pioneering too was Torres' use of Facebook and Twitter (acknowledged he says by the *New York Times*): each murderess had her own page and feed. Product placement was paid for by the Nextel telephony company, with the article claiming that the brand was integrated into the content and its appearances were not forced. After the initial screenings, the episodes were sold on to nineteen different territories at a price said to be comparable to that of US dramas; uploaded to an official YouTube channel, for which sponsorship was sold; and made available for downloading from iTunes for $1.99. Such international sales and the 'long tail' of syndication meant that income reached an exceptional twenty to thirty times the cost of production.

But success had been by no means assured. As mentioned earlier, a wary Televisa had initially turned down funding *Women Murderers*; and all of the sources interviewed in the article claim they were 'terrified' before the unprecedented ratings and sales were achieved. Clearly this was a case, then, in which, in Martín Barbero's terms, a new 'professional mentality', based on the primacy of promotion, made itself felt even within the rigid TV ecology dominated for so long by Televisa. But, beyond this content analysis and production history, what remains to be addressed, before we examine specimen episodes, is the series' reception or social uses and ways of seeing (its 'cultural competency'), and its textual composition (its 'forms of narration' and 'TV syntax').

Unsurprisingly, *Women Murderers* gave rise to richly detailed internet discussion. On the main forum, celebrating the show's first anniversary, two taglines acknowledge the links between the show's brutalized protagonists and its attentive and sharp-eyed spectators: the first is 'The wound will never heal' ('La herida jamás sanará') and the second 'To judge, you [first] have to be a witness' ('Para juzgar hay que ser testigo') (Mujeresaseinas, 2012). Taking great pleasure in the relatively novel series format, forumers compare and contrast different episodes and actresses, displaying close and active knowledge of the show's varied run. One viewer even devised a multiple-choice test, inviting fellow fans to compete in their specialist subject. While participants (who claim to include a number of boyishly young males) fail to debate directly questions of gender and sexuality, they often discuss the stars' different acting styles (perhaps as a proxy for female behaviour), arguing that some actresses are too (or conversely too little) emotional in their performance.

The national, even nationalist, agenda is more prominent. Many Mexican viewers prove to be familiar with the Argentine original and much prefer the local style. It is left to one forumer to write that it is a 'mistake' to compare the two: if the Argentine is more downbeat in its textual composition, less showy than the Mexican, it is because it is attempting a greater realism. But both forms of narration or TV syntax are equally valid. While such social uses of the series are occasionally parochial or even chauvinistic (viewers react venomously to the casting of a Spanish supermodel in a late episode), the ways of seeing documented here reveal more often a surprisingly sophisticated cultural competency.

Part of that competence is, as Martín Barbero suggested, an awareness of the connection between reception and production. Forumers are conscious of the fact that, although the producer and screenwriter remain the same, the directors change from one episode to another. They wonder aloud if this intermittence accounts for a perceived variation in quality. And unlike O'Donnell's passive spectators of telenovelas, they see themselves as participants in these one-off dramas, vigorously arguing their case in the internet courtroom. Following Buonanno, also, they experience the indigenization of the narrative (its adaption from Argentina) as by no means negative but rather part of the distinctive pleasure the series offers a local audience.

Unsurprisingly, forumers are more troubled by mortality, however. One unpopular thread asks squeamishly, which is the bloodiest episode. But the compulsion to repeat the murders on the bulletin boards (to rehearse and contrast them) confirms Buonanno's suggestion of the palliative function of the TV series format. By miming death over and over, the show (and its faithful audience) transcend time boundaries and learn to ward off the sense of a definitive ending. Mortality is thus domesticated, reintegrated, with the series itself, into the regular rhythms of everyday life. Indeed, it is telling how often the murders in the series take place in that most nurturing and protective of locations: the kitchen.

What of the text of the show? The relatively high budget allows for varied and effective locations, both interior and exterior, even though recognizable streets or buildings of Mexico City are never shown. In episode 2 Mónica ('trapped' ['acorralada']) is the downtrodden daughter of a bed-ridden ex-movie star. The two women live in a luxury duplex crammed with photos and mementos of past glories, boasting a spiral staircase that is evidently unsuitable for the handicapped mother (the daughter must carry her down). Another precisely chosen detail of *mise-en-scène* here is the gilt chain of a designer handbag, which serves as a flashy murder weapon.

In contrast, the very next episode takes place in a gloomy and primitive hacienda, to which distant location the whole team of DIEM has somewhat implausibly transferred in search of the missing niece of a politician. Here Margarita ('poisonous' ['ponzoñosa']), the turbaned elderly priestess of a cult, lords it over submissive male minions before lengthily dispatching her victim in a bleak field in a spectacular rural manner: the repeated bites of a venomous snake hidden in a box.

Further episodes feature lavish suburban interiors (the comfortable home with extensive garden where the patriarch beats his gay son and abuses his daughter Patricia); or ominous urban exteriors (the sticky, trash-strewn streets where prostitute Cándida, 'hopeful' ['esperanzada'], turns her tricks at night). Wardrobe is also vital here. Patricia boasts the carefully tousled hair and defiant piercing of the young yuppie rebel. Cándida (played by proud telenovela heroine Lucía Méndez) sports the red vinyl mini-skirt and perilous heels of the ageing whore.

Expert *mise-en-scène* is matched by top-notch cinematography, which generally favours (in O'Donnell's terms) kitchen-sink naturalism over highly coloured Manichaeism. But the single camera set-up allows for some flexible pseudo-cinematic techniques. Wide shots of those evocative locations contrast with extreme close-ups of spectacular wounds or weapons. And sometimes technique is used to expressive rather than social realist effect. In several episodes explanatory flashbacks are shot in bleached-out colour, especially effective when, as so often, they document the childhood abuse of future murderers. Sordid sex between the policewoman and a teen criminal is shown reflected in bedroom mirrors, a notably art movie-style device. The last venom-fuelled minutes of the cult victim are shown with blurry focus and jump cuts, heightening her fatal predicament and promoting our emotional identification. In pre-credit sequences, a steadycam drifts in dreamy slow motion through the crime scene (for example, the bloody remains of a showbiz party at the apartment of Mónica's mother). And throughout the series, in contrast to the UK or Catalan soaps analysed by O'Donnell, the incidental music (swelling strings, heavily reverbed guitar or even a heavenly chorus) is almost as prominent as in the most melodramatic novela.

Textual composition is thus inconsistent. At some points *Women Murderers* encourages viewers to participate in the fiction through an everyday naturalism (even the prostitute will commit her crime in the cosy kitchen of her protector), while at others it invites us to witness in horror a highly coloured spectacle over which we (and the characters) have no control. Significant here is the thematization within the fictional world of the conflict between the contrasting aesthetics of single-camera film location shooting style and multi-camera TV studio set-ups. Replaying Gothic movie classics like *What Ever Happened to Baby Jane?* (Robert Aldrich, 1962) the 'Mónica' episode stages a deadly rivalry between a modest daughter, concerned only to pass her exams and gain her independence, and an extravagant mother still blinded by cinematic stardust and obsessed with half-forgotten triumphs with Buñuel (or was it Ripstein?).

The barely disguised moral here is that the old-time prestige of cinema is now challenged by a new claim to distinction by television's quality or event programming, of which *Women Murderers* is such an evident example. But the clearest contradiction in the series, at once artistic and ideological, is the one revealed by the two specimen episodes I examine below.

Women Murderers: Specimen Episodes

'Sonia, desalmada'

Temporada 1, capítulo 1; estreno 16 de junio de 2008
Sonia es una mujer casada en primeras nupcias con un médico. En apariencia, el matrimonio parece funcionar como un perfecto engranaje; hasta que ella comienza a sospechar que su marido lleva una doble vida. Desgraciadamente, lo que era una suposición se

convierte finalmente en una realidad: una enfermera del hospital parece ser la amante de su esposo. Desilusionada y desencajada por el triste descubrimiento, Sonia empieza a elucubrar la manera de deshacerse de su competencia. Los celos, la rabia y la sed de venganza se apoderan de esta mujer, que termina llevando a cabo un plan siniestro: secuestra a la joven y la mantiene durante varios días en cautiverio, sometiéndola a terribles torturas. Para Sonia, ésta es la manera de que la enfermera expíe sus culpas por apoderarse de su marido. La situación llegará a un horrible punto de inflexión que desencadenará en un trágico final.

'Emilia, cocinera'

Temporada 1, capítulo 9; estreno 15 de julio de 2008
Emilia es víctima de los hombres, hasta que se convence de que una cruel receta cambiará su existencia. Su casero don José la acosaba sexualmente, ya que le debía tres meses de renta y se cobraba así, su esposo se hacía de la vista gorda para no tener que conseguir dinero para la renta, entonces termina ahorcando a su casero con una cuerda y en su fonda lo terminó haciendo tamales. La condenaron a 20 años de cárcel.

'Sonia, pitiless'

Season 1, episode 1, first broadcast 16 June 2008
Sonia is a woman married for the first time to a doctor. Apparently, her marriage seems to work like clockwork, until she begins to suspect that her husband is leading a double life. Unfortunately, it was an assumption that eventually becomes a reality: a nurse at the hospital seems to be the lover of her husband. Disillusioned and distraught by the sad discovery, Sonia begins to plot how to get rid of her competitor. Jealousy, anger and revenge take over this woman, who ends up carrying out a sinister plan: kidnapping the girl and holding her for several days in captivity, subjecting her to severe torture. To Sonia, this is the way for the nurse to atone for the sin of stealing her husband. The situation will come to a terrible turning point that will trigger a tragic end.

'Emilia, cook'

Season 1, Chapter 9, Release 15 July 2008
Emilia is a victim of men, until she becomes convinced that a cruel recipe will change her life. Emilia's landlord, Don José, was sexually harassing her, as she owed three months rent and he took his payment

in kind. Her husband turned a blind eye so as to avoid having to raise money for the rent. She ends up strangling her landlord with a rope and making tamales out of him in her little restaurant. She is sentenced to twenty years in prison.

Breaking the audience in gently, the very first episode of *Women Murderers* keeps close to the conventions of telenovela. Bleach-blonde Leticia Calderón is a thirty-year veteran of series melodrama and her Sonia here, a neglected bourgeois wife in a sharply tailored Chanel-style jacket, is the spitting image of the genre's villains. While the teaser pre-credit sequence seems social realist (a homeless man discovers a body in a dumpster), the initial set-up is purely Manichaean. We see Sonia's surgeon husband Fernando, telenovela-handsome in his white scrubs, romancing a young and pretty brunette resident, Marcela.

But soon reality (or realism) intrudes. Marcela has been receiving threatening phone calls and her mother cautions her to take a taxi from a rank ('sitio') to work, considered safer than one flagged down on the street. Far from being romantic, sexual relations in the hospital are brutally pragmatic. Naïve Marcela's more knowing colleagues are well aware that Fernando has worked his way through the available young women, who are positively eager for his attention. When Sonia confronts her husband at work he claims she is frigid and should find a good plumber to give her a 'roll in the hay' ('revolcada').

Soon Sonia has kidnapped Marcela off the street in her car (one of many exterior sequences in the series) and taken her to the large house which once belonged to her parents and which she is now redecorating (hence her husband's plumber reference). The rest of the episode is thus dedicated to the wife's extended torture of her younger rival: tied to a chair, refused water and a bathroom, burned with a cigarette, and cut with a scalpel. The latter detail is emblematic. Frustrated professionally as well as sexually, trophy wife Sonia had been a resident herself, with a future assured as a surgeon when she met her husband-to-be. Curiously (perversely), however, the professional aspect is combined here with a parody of the domestic: Sonia tells Marcela she is a guest in her house and thus deserving of special treatment; she makes the girl up and cuts her hair as if playing with a doll.

Mock hospitality or domesticity here signals pathology. When the terrified Marcela pees herself, Sonia is transported back to the past in that same family home where she was abandoned by her mother and sexually abused by her father. And now textual composition echoes thematic exposition. When Sonia binds Marcela to a chair, the camera takes up a canted (Dutch) angle; when she carves a bloody cross on her chest, the scene is reflected in a distorting bevelled mirror; and when she flashes back to infantile trauma the colour palette is coldly bleached out. Enviably free of material constraints, like so many telenovela heroines (gifted even with a spare house to use as a torture chamber), Sonia is thus tormented only by a toxic psychic inheritance, resurrected by marital neglect and reinforced by a self-conscious TV technique.

Manichaean melodrama (sadistic wife versus saintly lover) is, however, cross-cut with the relative realism of the procedural genre. When Marcela's mother complains to DIEM of her daughter's disappearance, the unit engages in some high-tech investigation, analysing bloodstains and tracing phone calls. The victim's whereabouts are hardly a mystery, though, as the husband is well aware of his wife's presence in her old home. Chillingly, however, the final scene of the murder (set at night in the city with a train clattering overhead) reveals that the victim was still alive when set alight in the dumpster. As she walks away from the conflagration, Sonia proudly displays to the camera her white T-shirt, splattered with blood.

What is striking here, then, is not simply the intensity of sadism, surely unseen in any telenovela, however modern and transgressive. It is the combination of familiar factors (a well-known actress, an adulterous love triangle, a comfortably bourgeois *mise en scène*) with new and troubling elements, most of all the suggestion that Sonia, however pitiless, is herself a victim, of father and husband alike. Moreover, even in this stylized setting, troublingly everyday moments intrude: the genuine fear of a rogue taxi driver, the sexual cynicism of eager young nurses and randy doctors. Even Sofía, director of DIEM, is sceptical of Sonia's purity, asking the latter's mother if her daughter can be truly as 'innocent' as she says. The certainties of melodrama, even here at their most extreme, thus come up against the contingencies of social realism in a conflict that is at once ideological and textual.

My second specimen episode takes the opposite tack to arrive at the same mixed conclusion. María Rojo's Emilia, in episode nine, is a cook in a working-class barrio far from Sonia's lush suburbs, with a face apparently unenhanced by surgery and unkempt hair falling over her face. The pre-credit sequence here involves cross-cutting reminiscent of Soviet analytical montage: workers dress pig carcasses in a slaughterhouse (otherwise unseen in the episode), a kitchen knife vigorously chops vegetables, and a dog overturns a brimming trash can to chew on a headless human torso.

As we soon learn, dowdy Emilia does all the work at the tiny restaurant that her husband Felipe claims will boom just as soon as

CONCORDIA COLLEGE LIBRARY
BRONXVILLE, NY 10708

he perfects his singing voice with the musical trio whom he regales with free beer. Meanwhile Emilia submits with scarcely veiled scorn to the repeated sexual advances of her landlord don Pepe (the couple rarely even bother to lie down), as payment in kind for the rent her husband cannot provide. Here sex is yet more brutally pragmatic than in the previous episode's hospital setting, and certainly far less pleasurable. Authentic urban locations also offer a sometimes literally raw slice of life: on her visits to a crowded market Emilia fingers the slabs of meat at a butcher's stall with professional dispassion.

Men are thus condemned for their pretensions (the husband's hopeless aspiration to be a 'performer') and their predations (the landlord's unwelcome sexual advances). Yet in Rojo's brave performance the female killer remains wholly unsympathetic. Unlike Sonia, she is given no psychological back-story to justify her crime. And, if Sonia parodies hospitality (with a tortured 'guest' in her home), Emilia reworks domesticity: a lengthy sequence shows her dismembering, chopping and slicing the landlord's body (just out of shot) before feeding the flesh into a hand-operated grinder. Regular clients (including the victim's brother) claim that her tamales have never tasted better.

With the agents of DIEM ineffectual, Emilia is betrayed only by the most everyday of occurrences: the fact that the (notoriously inefficient) Mexico City refuse service failed to take away her trash before the dog of the pre-credit sequence discovered the remains of the corpse. And when finally apprehended she remains unrepentant, claiming she killed only one man because she didn't have time to dispatch two; and, laughing, that men who live like animals deserve to die like animals. Hers, then, is a purely social predicament: Emilia's crime, unlike Sonia's, is the result of economic desperation. In its reworking of female domestic labour (and more specifically Mexican gastronomy), the episode takes up its place, disturbingly, within an everyday life much more recognizable to most audiences than that led in the show homes of the telenovela.

The unevenness of episodes within *Women Murderers* (noted by viewers on the internet forum) is thus not only a generic question, made possible by the still rare format of the series; it is also an ideological concern, suggesting as it does two conflicting and irreconcilable etiologies for femmes fatales. And it points also to a continuing struggle between two media. Appropriating cinematic prestige, episodes of the series were premiered at film festivals by their enterprising producer. There is little doubt that María Rojo's Emilia, although made for despised broadcaster Televisa, deserves inclusion in the gallery of feisty heroines she has created for the respected auteurs of Mexican cinema.

The Aparicio Women: Overview

With three suspicious deaths to her credit (three husbands who met their ends in violent accidents), cigar-smoking Rafaela, matriarch of the Aparicio clan, would seem to be a worthy fictional rival for Juana Barraza, real-life 'Lady of Silence'. And her three daughters (*The Aparicio Women*, we are told, never have sons) are equally femmes fatales. Psychologist and male-prostitute wrangler Alma has a husband who was mysteriously murdered, a McGuffin that intermittently structures the telenovela's 120-episode arc. Former feminist lawyer and stay-at-home mother Mercedes is obliged to go back to work when her erring husband dies in the arms of his girlfriend. Only Julia, the youngest, has avoided marriage and thus the supposed 'black widow' curse of her family. Burdened with an unfaithful footballer boyfriend, she will, in what is surely a telenovela first, wed her on-off girlfriend Mariana in a climactic episode.

The serial thus sets out, at a time of radical social change, to challenge head-on the supposed crime of being a woman and to redefine the boundaries of performing *mexicanidad*. And, unlike *Women Murderers*, it will intervene directly in urgent contemporary issues: not just the legalization of same-sex marriage in Mexico City but, more ambitiously perhaps, President Calderón's bloody war against the narcos, which plays out mainly outside the capital.

Curiously, however, *The Aparicio Women* combines the sociopolitical with the fantastic. Drawing on the supernatural tradition of her native Veracruz, faithful retainer Aurelia keeps a small altar to the family's dead males, displaying photos and burning candles, and warns her housemates that the deceased must be placated. Rafaela's disapproving 'turns' or 'fits' ('vahidos'), which occur whenever a daughter leaves home to take up with an invariably unsuitable man, disrupt the water and electric supply of her large and luxurious house. And in a device reminiscent of HBO's *Six Feet Under* (2001–5), Alma's husband Máximo (in suit, tie and fedora) will reappear to his widow and mother-in-law as a mockingly persistent, and all too real, ghost. Aurelia is also allotted a voice-over at the beginning and end of each episode (like the voice from beyond the grave in *Desperate Housewives*), which offers omniscient commentary on the living and the dead.

Like *Women Murderers*, then, but in a lighter and more playful register, *The Aparicio Women* radically revises gender roles for Mexican women. And if this female family enjoys the enviable and inexplicable wealth common to clans in traditional telenovelas (social class is uniformly high), the sexual roles of its members are explicitly diverse. Here, once more, the conflict between psychic and social determination recurs, but is now distributed between two regular characters: the older sisters. Alma runs a cultural centre called, with fancy French distinction, El Atelier, in which she teaches conscious-ness-raising workshops to female students, informing them that men are still stuck in the Stone Age while women have evolved far beyond them; and offers select candidates (typically repressed or depressed housewives) private sexual therapy at the hands of the handsome male escorts she has personally trained herself. Mixing her psycho-analytic schools, Alma claims that her therapists are as reputable as any 'Lacanian analyst trained in Vienna'. Working mother Mercedes, on the other hand, fights her own battles and those of her clients in the public sphere. Her first cases include a divorced transgender parent who seeks access to her child, a stripper who complains of sexual harassment at work, and, as we shall see later, a mother whose sons died as 'collateral damage' in the drugs war.

Thus while Alma offers her clients sexual liberation by stimulating a new awareness of their own bodies and fantasies, Mercedes offers hers socioeconomic autonomy in the workplace and society by advis-ing them on their civil rights. But both women's cases of the week also have a generic function: resolved over five episodes from Monday to Friday, they insert the urgent rhythm of the series drama into the more relaxed temporality of the extended serial. In addition to this uncertain generic hybridity, the stars of *The Aparicio Women*, unlike the stellar protagonists of *Women Murderers*, were initially little known, thus adding to the risk of this innovative project.

Producers and journalists alike played up the sexual explicitness of the serial, claiming it was unprecedented in Mexico (Madrigal, 2010a). But in the frequent torrid sex scenes (often shot in a cinematic split screen), most of the nudity is male. And although Alma encour-ages her charges to see themselves as 'sexual objects', she also lectures them on women's new financial independence which gives them power over men. Enter the three male escorts, often shown eating or exercising together, who disrobe for the visual pleasure of female clients (and viewers), as does Julia's young boyfriend, to the mixed emotions of his bi-curious partner. And while all three sisters are conventionally pretty and fashionably dressed, their decorativeness is consistent with the polished aesthetics of the serial as a whole, shot as it is on handsome sets, in high-definition video and with a sophis-ticated palette of black, white and signature purple (the colour of the retro wallpaper which graces the show's publicity materials). This ambivalence (are *The Aparicio Women* feminists or fashion plates?)

extends to publicity appearances by the actresses, where they are as likely to be promoting social causes (as they did at Mexico City's LGBT Pride) as to be gracing the opening of a new boutique (as they did in the upmarket colonia of Polanco) (Gutiérrez, 2010).

The Aparicio Women's credits begin pointedly with retro materials taken from a period newspaper: eleven rules for 1950s housewives on how to keep your husband happy. Producer Epigmenio Ibarra also repeated to the press that, just as Mexican society had changed, so must the women on Mexican television: the submissive Cinderellas of telenovela are now anachronisms (Madrigal, 2010a). Episode 16, timed for Mother's Day, is a test case here in that it highlights the way that, as Martín Barbero has suggested, the supposedly anachronistic genre of melodrama 'touches' everyday life, or is, in its rhythmic recurrence, structured like it. The opening voice-over notes that motherhood begins with nausea; and the episode starts and ends with vomiting: in the story of the week, the mistress of a recently deceased man discovers that she is pregnant and, in the main narrative, Alma reacts with repulsion on learning that her chaste young daughter Ileana has fallen in love, unwittingly, with one of her mother's highly trained escorts. The only thing mother and daughter agree on is that Mother's Day is a marketing ploy. Sister Julia agrees that 'too much mother is seriously damaging to the health', while her girlfriend Mariana recounts that she called her own estranged mother in the US only to discover that Mother's Day was already over there.

As the week develops, these plotlines intersect and partially resolve. Mercedes's client, the betrayed widow, comes to an accommodation with her dead husband's mistress, allowing the latter to keep the flat he bought her and raise the child she is bearing there. Mercedes herself, however, remains distraught about her own dead husband's infidelities. *The Aparicio Women* thus provides viewers with the feminine emotions typical of telenovelas (especially in the context of motherhood), but it re-evaluates them in a new social context: it is precisely because of Mercedes's identification with her client, a characteristic that would appear to be a disadvantage within the workplace, that she wins the widow away from a male rival and achieves a satisfactory, if still painful, result for her case.

It is salutary to contrast this social plotline with the previous week's psychological case study, which focuses on another supposedly female theme, namely beauty. Episode 11 begins with Alma lecturing her students on the 'torture' that women around the world submit to in the name of a supposed physical perfection that in fact varies widely in time and place. One student, dumpy and middle-aged, is sceptical that women like her can escape the beauty myth. We cut to the roof terrace of the male brothel where the three escorts compete at exercise, reminding each other that their bodies are the only things they have to sell to female clients. Meanwhile, in a quietly affecting scene, Mariana breaks up with her girlfriend Dani, on realizing that she is in love with the (still nominally straight) Julia. Lesbianism seems to be the only relation in the serial unmediated by money or exploitation. Indeed, as Mariana, Eréndira Ibarra's slurred dialogue readings and vernacular vocabulary ('lencha' and 'buga' for 'lesbian' and 'straight') could not be further from the melodramatic performance style and stylized speech hitherto dominant on Mexican TV. (The actress, who stresses her social responsibility in the performance, is the daughter of *The Aparicio Women*'s producer and the sister of its openly lesbian screenwriter.)

By the end of the week, Alma's student, inspired by the advice that she should please not men but herself, has hot sex with one of the escorts (his body is displayed to us, while hers is not), thus regaining her self-esteem. While this 'cure' is clearly an example of wish fulfilment (indeed, the woman notes that herself), *The Aparicio Women* stresses here the powers and pleasures of fantasy, just as in the next week's episodes it will attempt to reconcile women to the realities of male neglect and infidelity. Like sisters Alma and Mercedes, the psychic and the social are inseparable.

Gender and nationality also intersect in the theme of modernity, which is subject to differing interpretations. Thus one (male) columnist of daily *El Universal* sketched an imaginary Facebook profile for a supposedly neurotic, insecure and possessive young woman, educated at the UNAM (National Autonomous University) and reader of García Márquez, who watches *House*, *The Sopranos* and *The Aparicio Women* (Castañeda, 2011). Such a girl, he suggests, will have little luck in her love life. Conversely, one female blogger, self-described as a 'modern chick' ('tía') looks forward to Ibarra's new show after *The Aparicio Women* (*The Weaker Sex* [*El sexo débil*] would treat men without women), claiming the producer is 'courageous' and writing that she is excited by the changes in Mexican TV effected by trailblazer Cadena 3 (post on *El Universal* no longer available).

Reconfirming the show's connection with contemporary trends, national newspaper *Milenio* writes of 2010 as a 'pink year' for Mexico City, with *The Aparicio Women*'s high-profile lesbian couple showing the 'other face' of homosexuality: actresses no longer fear typecasting and can concentrate on creating convincing characters. Female autonomy thus transcends fiction and embraces professional opportunities (*Milenio*, 2010). One article headlined 'Free and fearless' ('Libre y sin miedo') refers not to a character but to an actress, noting that the woman who plays lawyer Mercedes faces a suit from Cadena 3's rival Azteca alleging breach of contract: now, she says, actors should be able to work for any TV station (Madrigal, 2010b).

The Aparicio Women's bid for novelty, however (like the somewhat different innovations of *Women Murderers*), remained risky. One media commentator pits the 'David' of little Cadena 3 against the 'Goliath' of Televisa, which is scheduling a remake of an old success against the unprecedented show (Ramos, 2010). He asks if viewers are really ready for new stories or still stuck twenty years ago, when, he claims, they didn't even know about homosexuality. Meanwhile plucky producer Ibarra said that traditional telenovelas were 'digging their own grave' ('cavan su propia tumba'): remakes ('refritos'), like fairy tales, are over (Díaz Moreno, 2011). On the day of the premiere he once more talked up this contemporaneity. The aim of the show is to speak candidly ('sin tapujos') about what's happening in the country, addressing with 'absolute freedom' a series of issues previously unseen on broadcast TV (Madrigal, 2010a). Sexual and political frankness thus go hand in hand. And here, as elsewhere, the national question is also generic: the show is said to be a hybrid between Mexican telenovela and US series. Elsewhere he will say that *The Aparicio Women* combines the contemporary focus of North American shows and the irreverence of Brazil with the 'heartwarming' ('entrañable') tone of Mexico, a perilous balancing act for a new title (Amoroso, 2010).

Vital to this sense of national specificity, even in this context of hybridity, is a resource more common in feature films than TV serials: location shooting. The main setting of the women's home is an authentic house in comfortable Coyoacán, the southern suburb where Frida Kahlo's house is located (Argos's headquarters name – CasAzul (*sic*) –invokes Frida also) (*Vanguardia*, 2010a). The extensive garden, large reception rooms, sunlit kitchen, many bedrooms and ample staircase provide varied opportunities for shooting. Alma's Atelier, on the other hand, is located in a refurbished industrial brick building in the notoriously underprivileged colonia of Doctores (a sign reading 'Estación Indianilla', the real name of the cultural centre based there, is visible in some shots). Suburban luxury here gives way to edgy urban regeneration. Conversely, Alma's boyfriend Leonardo (introduced as a casual pick-up in the first episode) has an elegant and modern duplex, all glass and leather, said to be in the large central *diputación* of Cuauhtémoc, and contrasting both with the comfort of Coyoacán and the urban edge of Doctores.

Another frequent location is the rooftop terrace, with its handsome view of city towers behind, where the escorts chat, exercise or ply their trade. As we shall see, some emblematic locations (such as the Zócalo or central square) are reserved for equally special episodes. What is important, however, is that the 'realism' of the serial (loudly trumpeted by its producer) is considerably reinforced by this uncommon aspect of the production, where relatively few scenes are shot on the show's permanent sets in the Churubusco studio complex. And there is something of a productive tension here between the playful or fantastic elements of the premise (Alma's cultural centre cum male bordello is surely as fanciful as any family business in a traditional telenovela) and the sociopolitical ambitions of the serial, signalled by its attachment to recognizably real places.

Location shooting is just one aspect of self-proclaimed 'quality' television that is grafted with difficulty on to the genre of the daily serial, generally held to be of low status. The actors stress in interviews that they are fleeing the 'mediocrity' of the normal roles offered them on Mexican TV, and the show's production manager describes its impressive logistics: with two units, 150 staff, eighty people on set and lengthy work-days required by shooting night scenes in 'real time' (*Vanguardia*, 2010b). Similarly the music is especially composed for the show and does not resort to the stock scores used by telenovelas. The composers (Mexican, Argentine and adopted New Yorkers) describe their compositions as avant-garde and modern, mixing jazz, punk and tango to give an 'urban' and 'electronic' feel (Yahoo, 2010).

But this realism, hybridism and cosmopolitanism have a long history as a professional mentality at production company Argos. In an interview for trade journal *Canal 100*, where he is already described as the most important independent producer in the country (Fernández Fernández, 2000), Epigmenio Ibarra claims that the Mexican TV industry is structured like an old hacienda and charts his own pedigree. While *Women Murderers*' Pedro Torres came out of advertising, Ibarra was a foreign correspondent who first specialized in documentaries, including a famous interview with Zapatista leader Comandante Marcos. With business partner Carlos Payán (founder of leftist daily *La Jornada* and sometime politician in the PRD), Ibarra transferred his skills in non-fiction programming into fiction, introducing social concerns central to Mexican reality into old-school telenovela. A decade before *The Aparicio Women* and Cadena 3, his broadcaster was Azteca, then a recent rival for Televisa (key collaborators such as Leticia López Margalli, one of two head writers on *The Aparicio Women*, date back to this period). While the repetition in this narrative is troubling (Ibarra has the same negative verdict on current production in 2000 and 2010), his continuing stress on social justice and artistic quality is striking. Openly political, in 2010 Ibarra wrote an open letter to Mexican President Calderón, criticizing his strategy in the drug war 'for love of Mexico, for our children' ('por amor a México, por nuestros hijos') (Ibarra, 2010). Further, an awareness of his background in documentary heightens an under-standing of the thematic and aesthetic innovations that Ibarra and his crew bring to long-form fiction.

It is also impressive that such high production values (not to mention naturalistic acting and intelligent dialogue) can be achieved on such modest budgets: $6 million for the series breaks down to just $50,000 per hour, half the cost of a Televisa serial and one sixth of an episode of *Women Murderers*. But novel production processes also led to novel distribution. *Hollywood Reporter* wrote that in the US *The Aparicio Women* would be the first telenovela to premier online before its on-air debut (for just 99 cents an episode) (Guider, 2010); and broadcaster Mun2, a division of NBC Universal, claimed the show as a perfect match for its target audience: 'today's cultural con-nectors – bicultural Latinos, 18–34' (Mun2, 2011a).

Back in Mexico, *The Aparicio Women* figured in press lists of the top successes of the year 2010, reflecting the nation in its Bicentennial year 'in the language of the street' ('el lenguaje . . . de la calle') (Tolosa, 2011). Popular acclaim was also evident. The official website carefully guided the cultural competence of its target audience (*Las Aparicio*, 2012). Under the feminist taglines 'Behind every successful woman' ('Detrás de una gran mujer') and 'A whole woman doesn't need another half' ('Una mujer entera no necesita media naranja'), the site encouraged viewers to be part of the family by registering with the fan community; and, more ambivalently, to create their own ideal man from a selection of perfect body parts or to punish their man by sticking digital pins in a dummy. The Forum helpfully sug-gested such threads as 'I'm an Aparicio too' ('Yo también soy Apari-cio') (encouraging identification with the characters) but also and more explicitly 'How I came out of the closet' ('Como salí del clóset') (the most popular discussion on the site).

Unofficial forums with a lesbian bias included an international site which offered extended and playfully tendentious plot summaries: AfterEllen. This website also hosted an interview with Eréndira Ibarra (Mariana) in which the heterosexual actress said she performed with 'love, respect, and gratitude for the women in my life' (AfterEllen, 2010). The moving testimony on these forums shows that women viewers, passionate in their attachment to the characters, clearly feel themselves to be participants and not observers in this drama, however highly coloured it may be. And they long not only for a girlfriend like Julia or Mariana, but for a mother like Rafaela and sisters like Alma and Mercedes, more tolerant, wise and accepting than their own.

Such social uses and ways of seeing intersect with *The Aparicio Women*'s textual composition (its forms of narration and TV syntax). As mentioned earlier, the voice-overs that bracket each episode encourage access to a collective female subjectivity. Rather than serving as a distraction, the visual pleasures of the *mise-en-scène* actively reinforce through their distinction the transmission of the social issues so dear to its producer's heart. In O'Donnell's terms, the stylization of melodrama does not contradict the social realism of the kitchen sink (although it has to be said that the bourgeois Aparicios are provided with ample domestic help).

The lesbian couple, neither girly nor mannish, proved particularly attractive to fans; and their relationship is granted a resource not used elsewhere: Julia and Mariana's frequent scenes of tender love-making or agonizing break-ups are set to plaintive English-language ballads by female vocalists, thus signalling their special status. On the other hand, raunchy sex between independent Alma and pick-up Leonardo is scored rather with the standard incidental music, whether electric guitar or wailing 'Oriental' pipes. In such latter sequences, the image tends to break into split screen, a transparently cinematic technique.

Such intense visual pleasure may be (as Buonanno suggests) a consolation for the death that is near universal for the show's male characters. But in a serial that is at once repeatedly renewed (with new cases each week) and endlessly deferred (with deep plotlines stretching over six months), it is a valuable arm in the narrative arsenal that seeks to manage mortality for its viewers even in the apparently unpromising domain of the femme fatale or black widow.

But while *Women Murderers* thematizes the tension between cinema and television (in the episode, say, on the old movie star), *The Aparicio Women* is more concerned with electronic media. Mariana repeatedly records herself on her Flip camera (a product placement?), sending a heartfelt message to an absent Julia; and the couple miss, too often, text or voice messages from one another. Moreover, both women are aspiring actors. Julia will perform an erotic monologue for 'a new TV station', presumably modelled on the Cadena 3 whose tagline was 'more open than ever'. And, as we shall see, the most political of plotlines in the whole serial involves media mediation: an appearance on television for the dogged heroine of one case of the week.

The Aparicio Women: Specimen Episodes

Episode 1; first broadcast 19 April 2010

After the death of her husband, Mercedes Aparicio goes toe to toe with his powerful business partners. Alma makes sex her business. Julia catches her boyfriend in the act with another woman. Three generations of women share a strange family tradition: they've all become widows due to extraordinary circumstances and they only give birth to girls. *The Aparicio Women* are strong and modern women who have realized they don't need men to survive. So why do they have men? Because they can. (Mun2, 2011b)

Episode 26; first broadcast 24 May 2010

After confessing the truth, Alma defends her escort business to Leonardo. Ileana is a wreck after her break-up with Mauro and Julia finally makes her decision. Will she stay or will she go to Spain with Armando? (Mun2, 2011c)

The first episode of *The Aparicio Women* begins with a remarkable cinematic calling card: a five-minute sequence shot without a cut. The camera begins by craning down behind a tree (it is night in the Coyoacán garden), before advancing across the lawn and up the stairs in through the front door of the women's lavish house, where a convivial party is taking place. It pauses as Rafaela regales older female friends with tales of past husbands before seeking out each sister in turn in the crowded rooms: Alma gives her business card to a cute guy, Julia flinches as her boyfriend flirts with a waitress, and Mercedes is torn between rage and grief. Taking the hand of her small daughter, she says 'Let's say goodbye to daddy'. They and the camera enter a final room, where we discover her husband laid out in a coffin. The cheery party is in fact a wake; and the corpse is the latest victim of the Aparicio curse.

With three pages of dialogue and one eighth of the running time of the episode, this scene is a tour de force, a clear bid for distinction in the mediocre 'hacienda' of Mexican TV fiction. The narrative develops with equally transgressive novelty. After the opening voice-over (in which Aurelia recounts the deaths of the three women's five husbands, whether accidents or homicides), we are treated to cross-cutting between scenes that establish the sisters' characters. Thus Alma offers a strange man a drink in a fashionable bar, Mercedes struggles to communicate with her depressed daughter, and Julia is invited to a threesome when she finds her boyfriend in bed with another woman (briefly tempted, she replies with a forceful Mexican obscenity). Meanwhile Alma is now engaged in hot, split-screen sex with the pick-up, named Leonardo, who, we later learn, is actually bent on investigating the mysterious death of her husband some years earlier.

Differing attitudes to home, work, love and sex are displayed by the various protagonists. Alma strides into El Atelier, where she lectures the female students on the inferiority of men. Mercedes, in business-like suit, is at first patronized by the male board at her husband's practice (partner Claudio tells his colleagues that she is 'gorgeous' and calls her 'princess' to her face). Julia flirts with lesbian best friend Mariana as they prepare mini-quiches for the latter's catering business.

Typically, then, cooking in *The Aparicio Women* is not a domestic pursuit but a business venture. Likewise a quick cut montage of night in the city (the glamorous boulevard Reforma with its golden 'Angel' monument) introduces us to the oldest profession: a close-up of thighs in fishnet stockings precedes the revelation that it is a street-walking Alma who is negotiating with a cute guy in a car. The sex scene that follows is shot via reflections in a gilt mirror and edited with teasing fades to black. Typically, however, the writers flip our expectations here. When, after sex, Alma gives a brisk account of her partner's performance, we realize that she has been on top in more ways than one: this was an audition for her escort service. And future employee Alejandro, the trainee here, must be schooled in role-play for a bored housewife client (the series' first case of the week) whose fantasy is to be treated like a whore.

Mercedes' initial problem is more domestic, but still sex-related. Her daughter is upset that no one seems to be mourning the death of her father. But grandmother Rafaela, stating that *The Aparicio Women* are 'not hypocrites', finally tells the girl the truth: that he died in the arms of his mistress. While Mercedes struggles to reconcile the competing demands on a working mother, Julia is pulled between conflicting sexual preferences in a world where (she says), after the achievements of 1960s feminism, sex is so easy and love so difficult. A lengthy love scene between her and Mariana, drunkenly kissing on the bed, leads to the latter pulling back and saying 'La lencha soy yo' ('I'm the one who's a dyke'). The series' frankness is thus verbal as well as visual. Mercedes, on receiving a sparkly tiara as a gift from her sarcastic colleague, will reply with Mexican profanity: 'Princesa tu chingada madre' ('Princess your fucking mother'). As producer Epigmenio Ibarra had said, the fairy tale of the traditional telenovela is well and truly over (Díaz Moreno, 2011).

The first episode ends with a voice-over from nanny Aurelia, which makes the moral explicit: *The Aparicio Women* are not Cinderellas but warriors. Nonetheless Alma's case of the week seems somewhat self-indulgent. After extensive 'therapy' from escort Alejandro (as handy in the kitchen as he is in the bedroom), the wealthy housewife, now sexually awakened, is reconciled with her previously neglectful husband. Revealing the show's range, however, the run of episodes in the sixth week will see Mercedes tackle a more challenging and intractable topic: the rising tide of fatalities in Mexico's drug wars.

In episode 26 Aurelia's voice-over is devoted to a social question: reputation (Spanish 'fama pública'). The Aparicios will never get rid of the label of 'black widows' with which others have branded them. Mercedes' working-class client has a more pressing problem. In the distant border town of Reynosa, notorious for drug cartel violence, her two sons have been killed in a shoot-out between narcos and police and branded criminals by the authorities. The mourning mother seeks to clear their name. In spite of her colleagues' warnings (they tell her 'the first rule' for a Mexican lawyer is never to challenge the government), Mercedes not only takes on the case, she also invites the woman (whose unprepossessing appearance could not be further from the Aparicios' glossy look) to stay in her mother's ample home.

In this week's episodes, the other sisters' dilemmas seem superficial by comparison. Yet they also explore the question of social reputation and public image. Thus Alma, outwardly a respectable psychologist, reveals to now steady boyfriend Leonardo that El Atelier is a cover for male prostitution; and Julia, repressing her private desires for the girlfriend who has now declared her love for her, briefly emigrates to Madrid with her soccer star boyfriend. Looking out on the city towers from the escorts' flat, Leonardo ruminates on the negative implications for men of such rapid social change: from the outside everything seems to be the same, but inside it's all changed – twenty million people are living in solitude, unable to face their inability to love others. It is a point of view echoed by Alma's conservative daughter Ileana, who is saving herself for marriage, unaware that her attentive boyfriend is actually one of her mother's escorts, the sympathetic Mauro. Perhaps she should have paid more attention to the T-shirt he sports this week. Its English slogan reads: 'Fake love is not nice.'

Once more, realistic and frankly implausible plotlines seem to intersect. But as the week passes both are brought together by the reality-effect of shooting in authentic spaces. There are a number of sequences on the mean streets of the historic centre of Mexico City, where the client hands out flyers seeking support from passers-by. Mercedes confronts the politician responsible for burying her client's case (described as a 'Secretary' he bears a strong resemblance to the current President) in the most loaded of locations: the Zócalo, where a huge Mexican flag billows behind her. Twice ambushing a posse of suited males, she tells them that the authorities have admitted their mistakes in Monterrey and Juárez. Why not here too? And she angrily rejects the argument, made by both politicians and her fellow lawyers, that to criticize the authorities is to lend support to the narcos. When Mercedes' legal practice loses half its clients, scared off by her political engagement, matriarch Rafaela supports her daughter and the client: an Aparicio woman must always hold true to her convictions just as a mother must protect her children's name.

Striking here is the theme of mortality. The client's sons are already dead (the government will, finally, admit to a cover-up); and Alma's ghostly husband Máximo is an incongruous presence in these most political and concrete of episodes, playing chess with Rafaela and intruding on Leonardo's affair with his widow. The supernatural theme thus rubs up against a political critique that coincides directly, as we have seen, with producer Ibarra's attack on President Calderón's policies and the 'collateral damage' they have allegedly provoked.

After the humble but noble client has successfully appealed on television in a bid to clear her sons' names, she returns to the Aparicios' house. Rafaela tells her: 'Now is the time to cry.' The women hug and weep. Although this conclusion might seem to reinforce stereotypes of femininity, maternity and sentimentality, this plotline could also be read as promoting change in the public sphere: only when women like Mercedes take a stand will investment in the family be recognized as a political, as well as an emotional, good. And of course family structures are here redefined for a new Mexico. The client appears to have no husband; and, in the same episode, we see a drawing of 'my family', made by Julia when a child, which shows her holding hands with Mariana, her best friend. Femmes may well be fatales – the Aparicios' house is haunted by death – but women's incursion into the public sphere will change society for the good, just as their erotic emancipation will transform psychic relations between and within the sexes.

Vocal Women

Finally, *The Aparicio Women* are not killers. Rafaela may keep a loaded pistol in the cupboard, responsible, perhaps, for the bullet hole in the forehead that is barely hidden by the homburg of ghostly

Máximo, but the murder-mystery narrative recedes ever further into the background as the serial continues. As faithful fans know, the lesbian love affair, culminating in the show's final week with a glamorous wedding at Mexico City's town hall in the Zócalo, is the main plotline. As ever, tradition and innovation are reconciled in this self-consciously contemporary telenovela. And unlike the unfortunate protagonists of *Women Murderers*, the Aparicios are hardly brutalized by their travails in a society that is shown to remain sexist and homophobic. The role of women warriors, for all their fancy wardrobe and flirtations with men, is didactic: to educate their clients, whether psychological or legal, on the pleasures and profits of being a Mexican woman today.

Yet, as mentioned earlier, those pleasures and profits are shadowed by death, and the serial thus acknowledges both Milly Buonanno's insight that long-form fiction seeks, transcending time, to inoculate viewers to the threat of death (the final ending that we strive to put off for as many episodes as possible) and to shield them from a zeitgeist in modern Mexico where insecurity seems omnipresent. Even in the comfortable female household in placid Coyoacán, Mercedes' daughter has anxiety nightmares (grandmother Rafaela's instinct is to rush into her bedroom with that loaded pistol). If the Aparicios' reputation as black widows is false (retainer Aurelia had already warned us that public reputation is not to be trusted), then the positing of women as murderers also corresponds to both TV fictions' exceptional status as quality shows, respectively, in the series and serial genres.

The difference of course is that *The Aparicio Women* pushes the dramatic envelope in two ways. Unlike *Women Murderers*, which remains realist even as it engages variably with the exaggerated rhetoric of melodrama familiar on Mexican TV, *The Aparicio Women* blurs the boundaries between time-bound naturalism (vernacular dialogue, authentic settings, urgent contemporary issues) and timeless fantasy (ghosts, curses and reckonings with the dead). And while *Women Murderers* is ambiguous in its politics, suggesting that women are driven to murder by either psychic trauma or social conflict, *The Aparicio Women* is openly leftist in its ambitions, loyal to its producers' long-held convictions.

Yet there is still some tension between the show's celebration of the female libido and its promotion of liberal social attitudes. After the first series of *The Aparicio Women* ended, viewers were offered the chance to attend a conference on female sexuality chaired by the actress who played Alma (who in real life holds a degree in psychology from Mexico City's Metropolitan University) (*Excelsior*, 2011).

They were warned, however, that one aim of the event was to suggest new plotlines for a second series that at the time of writing (May 2012) was not yet in production. Consciousness-raising was thus inseparable from the more pragmatic aim of feeding the voracious narrative appetite of the daily serial.

More advanced was a projected feature film for *The Aparicio Women* (*Excelsior*, 2010). We have seen that both shows benefited from a moment of revision for standard Mexican TV fiction, whose traditional telenovelas were thought by many to be in a repetitive rut. Hybrid in narrative form (drawing on both series and serial formats), they are also mixed in technique (aspiring to cinematic production values on the small screen).

In spite of these innovations in production (made possible by the divergent professional mentalities of independents Mediamates and Argos), reception remained mixed. While, as we have seen, viewers engaged actively in the social uses of internet forums, unwilling to be confined to the position of passive observers and intent on proving their cultural competency, professional observers proved more sceptical. One researcher at the UNAM's Center for Interdisciplinary Research wrote that, in spite of the fact that *The Aparicio Women* received prizes from Mexico City's branch of the government's National Institute for Women (Inmujeres DF), it does nothing for gender equality (Vega Montiel, 2012). Rather it employs the same old sexist stereotypes disguised as modernity. Males, writes Aimée Vega Montiel, remain rational, strong and egotistic; females emotional, submissive and altruistic. Women's bodies are exploited as sexual objects in the love scenes and lesbian and gay characters are constructed from a heterosexual perspective that fails to destabilize patriarchal power. There is, she claims, no discussion of diversity, discrimination and civil rights; and any innovation in theme is a change in form not content, a sign of the voraciousness of the market in assimilating a newly diverse audience rather than an index of genuine social transformation.

I hope that my own close content analysis of the serial reveals that such reflexive criticism is unjustified. If anything, *The Aparicio Women* is too didactic in its proposal of a progressive social agenda and too Manichaean in its inversion of gender stereotypes (did the researcher not even notice the brothel staffed by submissive men that is such a prominent location in the serial?) I have argued that the show reworks private qualities gendered as feminine and perhaps considered anachronistic (familialism, emotionalism) by revealing how they can be assimilated into the public sphere and thus transform a still macho society. For example, lawyer Mercedes's altruistic care for her clients is vital to her practical success in winning cases that are transparently discussions of diversity, discrimination and civil rights.

It seems more likely that the researcher has been put off by the serial's textual composition: the transparent visual pleasure it offers, with its lush bourgeois locations and wealthy, sexy stars. Yet, as the faithful forumers attest, such highly coloured spectacle is not directed only, or mainly, to male viewers; and an attractive lesbian couple may touch everyday life, inspiring fans to be an Aparicio too. They may even be moved to write the story of how they, like Julia and Mariana, came out of the closet.

The sadists of *Women Murderers*, who do not benefit from the parasocial investments enjoyed by characters in long-running serials, remain more disturbing. María Rojo's cook Emilia in particular is a frightening reworking of the traditional nurturing function of the female. Yet, as two separate models existing simultaneously, both fictions perform *mexicanidad* in their very different ways, revealing and challenging the limits of Mexican masculinity and femininity. And, unlike Juana Barraza 'Mataviejitas', their heroines are no longer 'ladies of silence' but rather vocal vehicles of social and televisual change.

Jump Cut 4

We Are What We Are (*Somos lo que hay*, Jorge Michel Grau, 2010)

In a recent round-up of the current crop of Mexican movies, respected critic Carlos Bonfil wrote that too many young directors merely imitate maestros of the past, and that all are mesmerized by current conditions in the country. Although Mexican society may have 'collapsed' (his word), riven as it is by drug-fuelled violence, surely a national cinema could find a new topic to tackle? Although the auteurist Bonfil is no fan of *We Are What We Are* (he called it the worst film he saw at the national showcase Guadalajara Festival), Jorge Michel Grau's debut follows the critic's prescription for a Mexican new wave. Strikingly original in technique, it pays no heed to the old masters of Mexican film; alluding only indirectly to present social conditions, it rewrites the horror genre with a premise that is outrageously novel: a cannibal family hidden in the heart of the capital.

The pre-credit sequence, wholly wordless, says it all. Shot from a disorientating high angle, a middle-aged man ascends an escalator, clutching his stomach. Emerging in a sterile shopping mall, all grey steel and glass, he stumbles towards a shop window, gesturing towards the bikinied dummies within. He sees – we see – his face, bearded and decrepit, reflected in the glass. Collapsing to the floor and whimpering, he vomits what appears to be black tar. Without missing a beat, cleaners come to drag the body away, mopping up the foul liquid from the shiny floor and making the mall safe for shoppers once more. While this sequence is clearly a mordant commentary on consumerism (Mexico is now a middle-income country with a large moneyed class), it also functions perfectly in a genre context, announcing a new mode of horror that cites zombie and vampire pictures but places them in a setting that is all too everyday.

Avoiding the clichés of gore or torture porn, then, writer-director Grau convincingly establishes the banality of cannibalism. His central family may live in a memorably weird house (shabby, crowded and packed with clocks), but their lust for human flesh – only gradually revealed to the audience – is not so different from the equally pressing demands of so many households that have lost their breadwinner in the current crisis. As daughter Sabina (Paulina Gaitán) comments early on, with both urgency and mystery, 'We just have to go on like before.' Even the original Spanish title *Somos lo que hay* – which translates as something like 'We're all there is' – suggests not the defiant assertion of identity of the English version, but rather an impassive acceptance of a pre-existing predicament.

In equally original fashion, Grau implies that the basic conflict is not so much between the monstrous and the normal as among the surprisingly domesticated outcasts themselves. His females are tougher than his males: the mother (Carmen Beato) slaps and scolds elder son Alfredo for his timidity, and dispatches victims with a vigorous battering with a club. Later she prepares a corpse with her daughter, both expertly wielding hooks. (The potentially gory ritual is shot mainly through a curtain of cellophane and softened by candlelight and mirrors.) Shy Alfredo (cute Francisco Barreiro), who proves to be gay, quarrels constantly with his impulsive brother Julián, who appears to have a thing for his strong-willed sister.

The film's moral is clearly that the family that preys together stays together. But these boys are barely competent as kidnappers – victims escape their clutches with unusual ease. And when Alfredo bashfully follows a potential morsel through the city (trailing him from street to metro and into a throbbing gay nightclub), he seems more scared of his object of desire than the victim is of his predator. Who, then, is the pursuer and who the pursued?

A seminal gay novel of Mexico City was actually called *El vampiro de la colonia Roma* (*The Vampire of the Colonia Roma*, citing a now wealthy central neighbourhood). Grau's film slyly suggests that social exclusion, whether of gays or the destitute, is more of a monstrosity than cannibalism. The metaphor is made explicit when a mortician (a cameo by veteran Daniel Giménez Cacho), having found a red-nailed finger in the stomach of a corpse, comments ruefully to a policeman: 'So many people eat others in this city.' The cannibal 'ritual', much mentioned by the family but unseen, thus stands in to some extent for the cycle of violence, corruption and stasis that many Mexicans diagnose in their country. The incompetent policeman, for example, hopes that if he solves the case he will be congratulated by the President for contributing to the latter's (spectacularly unsuccessful) war on crime. And at another point a character refers to the Bicentennial Projects intended to spruce up the capital for 2010, the much heralded 200th anniversary of the start of the struggle for independence from Spain.

Needless to say, the vision of Mexico City offered by the film is more dystopian than these optimistic public works would suggest. The shopping mall at the start is contrasted with a more colourful traditional market, where the family makes a doomed attempt to sell watches. But more typical urban locations in the film are the shadowy spaces beneath highway bridges, where the homeless live and the cannibals lurk. Yet Grau's technique prevents us from reading his film as a genuflection to old masters of urban grunge such as the adoptive Mexican Buñuel – this is no new *Los Olvidados* for the bicentennial. Social realism is rather subordinated to film form. Shadowy night shooting combines with rhythmic cross-cutting: as Alfredo finally kisses the gay boy he so desires and fears in the nightclub, his mother prepares bloodily for the cannibal ritual, and the incompetent policemen continue their fitful investigation. The expert visuals are matched by the sound design. As the bereaved family, stricken with grief and hunger, moon about their squalid home, they are accompanied by ticking clocks and dripping taps. This is surely a sign that time (and water) are running out for the hard-pressed citizens of the megalopolis, who now number some 25 million. Late in the film, mirrors and knives glow ominously in the candlelight. It's a handsome *mise-en-scène* that owes something to that cosmopolitan reinventor of horror – who also eludes the established tradition of Mexican auteurship – Guillermo del Toro.

Mexicans sometimes complain with reason that the violence in their country is overstated abroad. And it is indeed the case that the murder rate in Brazil, little cited, is twice as high as in Mexico. Yet as any casual visitor can attest, the most relentless publicists of Mexican horror are the local press, competing to splash over their front pages the latest deeds of the drug cartels ('Decapitated!' is one not untypical headline). As a proficient genre movie, albeit an unusually innovative one, *We Are What We Are* cannot be reduced to an allegory of such intractable social problems. But a warning note is still sounded in the film's final credits. The name of Alan Chávez, who played hot-headed son Julián, is followed by a cross. Aged just eighteen, he was shot dead in a gun battle with police outside a shopping mall. There could surely be no clearer and crueler sign of what Carlos Bonfil calls the collapse of Mexican society – and of its brutally direct mirroring in Mexican cinema.

Sight & Sound (December 2010)

Leap Year (*Año bisiesto*, Michael Rowe, 2010)

Mexico City, the present. Laura, an immigrant from Oaxaca, is a young journalist who lives alone and works at home in her flat. Ever so often she picks up men in nightclubs and brings them back for casual sex. She is also occasionally visited by her younger brother, Raúl. One of Laura's pick-ups is called Arturo, a would-be actor. The two begin a sado-masochistic relationship, whose violence increases in intensity. Laura finally asks Arturo to mutilate and kill her with a knife during sex. She makes the necessary preparations for the act to take place on the 29th of February, the fourth anniversary of her father's death. As she awaits Arturo, Raúl arrives unexpectedly, upset because he has split up with his girlfriend. Laura comforts him and he spends the night at her flat. The next day Laura tears off the page for February from her calendar.

Leap Year, the first feature from Australian-Mexican writer-director Michael Rowe, is quite literally a chamber piece. After an opening sequence set in a desolate supermarket, the camera never ventures out of the gloomy apartment of protagonist Laura, a depressed journalist who works from home. In the opening minutes Laura's world is expertly sketched: returning to deep pools of darkness in the hall, she undresses in her bedroom (gloomy magenta walls), fields a phone call from her mother, washes up the dishes and watches the apparently happy couple in the flat opposite while indulging in a bout of businesslike masturbation.

Leap Year is clearly acute, then, in presenting something rarely seen on screen: the private pleasures and minor eccentricities of those who live alone. Loveless Laura (bravely played by newcomer Mónica del Carmen) picks her nose and pees, smokes and spies on her neighbours, incinerates troublesome ants with her fag ends and crosses off days on her calendar as if she were in prison. But Rowe's film is also skilled in recreating the rhythms of loveless sex, which seems hardly distinguishable from Laura's equally joyless labour at the computer. Bringing back a hook-up from an (unseen) nightclub ('So you're a designer?'), she is greeted only by a cockroach creeping across the darkened floor of her flat. And these anonymous guys have barely evolved above insect-level themselves: one sneaks out at dawn (Laura feigns sleep), another calls his wife just as soon as he's cum (he gestures to Laura to keep quiet). Meanwhile Laura's work colleagues, accessible only by telephone and unseen once more, seem no more reliable than her one-night stands. Employed with conspicuous irony by a magazine called 'Your Business' (articles include '30 Tips to Survive the Economic Crisis'), the hard-pressed Laura loses her job when her editor asks her to carry out an interview with an entrepreneur who turns out to be an imposter. In this bleak vision of modern Mexico City, where single women have gained autonomy but not humanity, it's a toss-up as to which is more alienating and enervating: work or sex.

Halfway through a film that is apparently as marooned in stasis as Laura herself, things take an unexpected turn. Laura's only named lover (Arturo, played by veteran Gustavo Sánchez Parra) seems, amazingly, to take some interest in his partner, kindly enquiring how long she has lived in the capital (the mestiza-featured young woman has indeed emigrated from distant provincial Oaxaca). Yet this nascent domesticity (Arturo will thank Laura for the offer of a drink and spend evenings with her watching TV on the couch) is combined with an overt sadism that hitherto was only hinted at. While this arrangement is clearly consensual (Laura passionately requests to be harmed), the graphic evidence the film displays of, say, being pissed on or burnt by cigarettes is deeply distressing. Although the director assures us in interview that Laura is traumatized by her past (the leap year of the title marks the fourth anniversary of her father's death), this psychological rationale is barely established in the film itself. Rather it appears, more worryingly, that Laura craves violence simply to shock herself into some semblance of life, some form of feeling. Even the cheesy love song that plays over the closing credits (no music is permitted during the film itself) is memorably depressing, its lyrics boasting 'We are alone – both of us know it'.

In spite, or perhaps because, of such pervasive miserabilism, both lead actors are impressively committed to *Leap Year*. Del Carmen is naked and vulnerable much of the time, while an aroused Sánchez Parra offers evidence that at least one of the sex acts in the film was not faked. And both are graduates of a less graphic and more established Mexican director, Alejandro González Iñárritu: she had a supporting part in *Babel*, he in *Amores perros*. The minimalist *mise-en-scène* thus stands or falls on their generous and convincing performances. But it also relies on atmospherically gloomy cinematography (*Leap Year* was shot with a lightweight Red One digital camera). The lengthy takes and static shots so typical of Latin American festival fare are here successfully animated by the play of light and dark on faces and bodies, physiognomies that are mercifully distant from those of the willowy blondes that tend to be cast as the stars in Mexican film and television.

A graduate of one of Mexico's official national film schools (the Centro de Capacitación Cinematográfica), Michael Rowe is clearly devoted to his adopted homeland, in spite of the protracted difficulties he had in finding funding for his project there. He even allows his protagonist Laura, apparently doomed from the start, a ray of hope: at the end of the film she turns over a new leaf, literally, on her calendar. As the recent winner at Cannes of the Caméra d'Or award for first features, Rowe is surely assured, like his character, of a future that is brighter than his past.

Sight & Sound (December 2010)

Part IV

Tales of Insecurity

7

Film Fictions of Violence:
Hell (*El infierno*, Luis Estrada, 2010), *Saving Private Pérez* (*Salvando al soldado Pérez*, Beto Gómez, 2011), *Miss Bala* (Gerardo Naranjo, 2011)

Maps and Mirrors

A convenient point of entry into recent fictional representations of violence in Mexico is the special issue of *Revista de Estudios Hispánicos* from October 2008 entitled 'Narcogeografías'. In her introduction to the collection of essays she edited, María Fernanda Lander explores the cultural 'mapping' of Latin America as a drug-making region, commenting on the role of cartography in constructing cultural images in the distinct, but related, media of popular music, cinema and the novel (2008: 505–11).

Lander notes some paradoxes in her model of the 'map', which refers in part to actual plans drawn up by law enforcement bureaux. While based on a supposed correspondence between reality and representation, the map in fact restricts reality, depicting it in a way that makes it not only comprehensible, but also subject to manipulation (2008: 505). For Lander, narco-geography maps call into being the existence of two worlds (the US and its others) which they claim only to document (2008: 506), thus inadvertently revealing the origin of the violence experienced in those spaces (2008: 507). The 'culture' of drug trafficking is inseparable from the maps that define these narco-geographies (2008: 508), which Lander identifies with Baudrillard's notion of hyperreality, a simulacrum without a stable referent: not only what can be reproduced, but that which is always already reproduced (2008: 507).

In the first article of the collection, Miguel A. Cabañas addresses in a similar vein what he calls the global 'narcocorrido' and transnational identities, discussing the distinct form of a popular music genre, which depicts the life of drug-traffickers in the US–Mexico border regions. Cabañas treats the genre's association with criminality, comments on its symbolic links to marginality and explores its popularization and censure in the US and Mexico (2008: 519). He also reflects on the intermingling of global cultural images of illegality, drug-traffickers and immigrants within this distinctively Mexican cultural form.

While Lander chooses the map as her critical tool, Cabañas employs the mirror. The 'narcocorrido' thus functions as a reflection of frontier violence and a way of narrating the global order and its interaction with the illegality fomented by the US 'war on drugs'. The popularity of such songs (widely featured in films) is explained in part by their frequent censorship, analogous to the criminalization of the drugs themselves, which are destined for consumption in the same US and Europe that demonize their producers. Both processes of illegalization, for Cabañas, respond to an ideology that criminalizes certain people and places while promoting the social control of working people and the poor (2008: 519). The 'narcocorrido' is thus said to vindicate the agency of the working classes, singing the 'epic' of criminalized communities and rewriting globalization from the margins (2008: 520).

In the second article on Mexico, Gabriela Polit-Dueñas writes 'On Reading about Violence, Drug Dealers and Interpreting a Field of Literary Production Amidst the Din of Gunfire: Culiacán – Sinaloa, 2007' (2008: 559–82). Striking here is the personal engagement of the narrative, which begins, as the title suggests, with the author writing to the accompaniment of gunshots (albeit, here, recorded from drug dealers' celebrations of New Year's Eve) (2008: 559). The article, which narrates in part the author's experience in a space racked by violence, also explores the challenge of understanding the literary depiction of drug trafficking, as seen from within the perilous northern town cited in the title.

Beyond this very particular process of witnessing, however, Polit-Dueñas also makes some theoretical commentaries on the role of fiction in extremis. Thus she writes: 'A literary representation of violence necessarily implies an ethical approach which either reifies or questions the aestheticization of certain practices and their agents. A work of fiction, in its intent to represent the external world, constitutes an important site to decipher how violence works at the symbolic level' (2008: 576–7). Or, again, she comments hopefully: 'Literature can thus contribute to a discussion on the phenomenological approach to reality' (2008: 567). However, she acknowledges the problems inherent in taxonomy:

To classify this group of books as novels on narco-trafficking, before undertaking a careful close reading of each of them, can invert the order of things and put the cart before the horse. In representing and contributing to the understanding of the nature of violence in the local culture of narco-trafficking, each author offers up his own position on it, and discloses his view on the role of literature. (2008: 567)

Polit-Dueñas's welcome concept of the cultural 'field' as the space of intersections between texts, producers and institutions (originally derived of course from Bourdieu) is also used by Persephone Braham in her monograph *Crimes against the State, Crimes against Persons: Detective Fiction in Cuba and Mexico*. As with Cabañas in the case of transnational song, Braham is concerned here with cross-border relations. Thus she writes in her introduction: 'The detective novel came late to Hispanic letters, and one of its defining characteristics has been a concern with foreign paradigms of modernity and ultimately the failure of liberalism . . . in a Hispanic context' (2004: ix).

But unlike Lander and Cabañas, for whom US maps and mirrors seem to determine the narco-geographies they claim only to chart or reflect, Braham argues that Latin American fictions do not engage in 'parody or subversive colonial mimicry of metropolitan models . . . While Cuban and Mexican detective writers borrow freely from Anglo-European traditions, they refigure the character of delinquency, the nature of victimization, and the process of detection itself.' (2004: x) Here she returns to her genre's specific position in the field: 'the very marginality [of the detective novel] has allowed it to evolve into a tool of social criticism'.

This marginality has a particular charge in the case of Mexico. After the Tlatelolco student massacre of 1968 and in the light of the continuing 'oppressive official discourse of Mexicanness', detective-fiction writers 'reject cerebralism' and the 'scarred bodies [of their protagonists] become visible testimony to the abuses of power' (2004: xi). This popular genre is thus uniquely able to question Mexico's myths of authority and identity in the way proposed by Bourdieu in the case of France: 'the international student movement of 1968 [is] evidence of a struggle over cultural consumption [attempting to erase] borders between those with "high educational capital" and the rest of society'. The writers studied by Braham are thus 'seeking to democratize the terms of this cultural capital' (2004: xi).

A similar vindication of a despised artistic genre, attempted this time by appeal to Jesús Martín Barbero (who is, as we saw in the previous chapter, a key sociologist of TV fiction in Latin America), is made by O. Hugo Benavides in his monograph *Drugs, Thugs, and*

Divas: Telenovelas and Narco-Dramas in Latin America. Benavides argues, with some credulity, that 'melodrama might be the most successful and culturally authentic revolution . . . since the 1960s' (2008: 2). But he coincides with Braham's analysis of the literary field when he writes that 'a greater democratization of the media . . . met with harsh judgment from academics, intellectuals, and film critics' (2008: 2) and that 'Telenovelas and narco-dramas allow a form of "emotional democracy" that nurtures their popularity and at the same time reifies the social distance between "real art" (which is what the elite consumes) and the melodrama as the main form of popular entertainment' (2008: 11).

Moreover, the main narrative drivers of the genre (familial relationships and social excess, both of which are prone to violence) are not random but are used rather 'to understand and express the complexity and opacity that the new social relations embody' (2008: 11). In general, then, 'through its critique of . . . the safeguarding of sexual and social mores, the telenovela . . . provides a new assessment of the colonial legacies and desires that permeate contemporary Latin America [and] a sense of redemption and revelation' (2008: 12).

When he treats the drug-trafficking sub-genre of melodrama ('Being Narco', 2008: 111), Benavides finds in this 'continental sensibility' (like the previous scholars in their work on song and fiction) a 'border narrative' that is typical of a 'hybrid culture' (2008: 112). Rescuing television fiction from the attacks of elite cinephiles, he goes on to suggest that it was not 'the collapse of Mexico's [cinematic] golden age' that led to the popularity of similarly themed TV serials, but rather the fact that the latter offered 'a greater opportunity for the "other" Mexican and Latin American to see themselves as protagonists for the first time' (2008: 116). This 'narco-sensibility' is said to mark the creation of 'a new morality or cosmology' in which the central place of violence is not gratuitous but serves rather to express 'a new way to relate to the world . . . a survivor mentality' (2008: 121). Indulgently sympathetic to his chosen genre (like the previous scholars, once more) Benavides dismisses the misogyny of these serials, claiming they serve as a 'melodramatic parody of patriarchy' (2008: 125) and suggests that 'the veneration of violence in narco-drama' serves to 'define one's space and distance from the violent and oppressive state' (2008: 128). He even claims that 'narco-drama might be violent, but it is infinitely more humane and realistic than any anti-drug campaign or judicial process for massacred women in the area' (2008: 128).

Now, even though they fail to mention the father of modern sociology, all of these critics are writing broadly in a tradition of Durkheimian functionalism. Their argument is that it is the law that creates the crime and the criminal in the service of preserving the current norms of social order. As a scholar of media 'crime stories' writes in the wake of Durkheim:

> Rituals of processing and punishing crime are functional in construct-ing a society's morality, teaching its members to abide by certain rules, and promoting cohesion among members by making it public when individuals have violated shared moral values (Grabe, 1999: 155).

It should be remembered, however, that for Durkheim punishment is not only functional but also expressive, just as violence is phenom-enological for the cultural critics cited above.

What is striking in the Mexican case is, of course, that the roles of heroes and villains have been inverted with consumers (and aca-demic scholars) of narco song, print fiction and television identifying with the perpetrators of crime and against the supposed forces of law and order, which are held to be playthings of the US criminal agencies and global capital and/or irredeemably corrupted by collusion with the criminals they claim to police. There is thus a pervasive sense of what Rossana Reguillo, the sociologist of violence to whom I appeal in my next and final chapter, calls 'paralegalism', a void or vacuum in legitimate government that narco-geography or -sensibility rushes in to fill.

In the rest of this chapter I will examine three varied examples of a medium not treated by the scholars above: the recent fiction feature films *Hell* (*El infierno*, Luis Estrada), *Saving Private Pérez* (*Salvando al soldado Pérez*, Beto Gómez), and *Miss Bala* (Gerardo Naranjo), which were all released in 2010 or 2011. The questions raised by my opening literature review, then, would include: To what extent can Mexican cinema be seen as a map or mirror of a distinct order of violence? How do Bourdieu's questions of the cultural field and edu-cational capital relate to these films and their reception at home and abroad? And is it possible or plausible for those films to be read, in Martín Barbero's terms, as a kind of social democratization of or through the emotions? I shall pay attention to the role of genre in production and reception here, appealing above all to local, rather than transnational, responses to these films.

These responses call attention to a final question that is rarely voiced by foreign-based academics: how is it that sympathy can be directed towards and expected for fictional figures whose real-life equivalents are so widely feared and detested in modern Mexico? But first we must examine the state of the Mexican cinematic field at the end of the first decade of the new millennium, as seen through industrial and critical accounts which are very different from each other.

Two Movie Surveys

The Mexican film ecology in 2010 and 2011, as revealed by IMCINE's invaluable bilingual statistical yearbooks, is somewhat contradictory. Indeed, the former edition begins by acknowledging that the film industry must be seen in 'a broader audiovisual framework' and not 'isolat[ed] from the structural changes now confronted by all sectors involved in the creation of content in view of local and global convergence' (IMCINE, 2010: 9). Admirably broad in its technological range, the yearbook tells us, for example, that of the sixty-nine movies produced in 2010 (85 per cent of which received government funding) the most downloaded was one of my case studies: Luis Estrada's black comedy *Hell* (2010: 11).

In spite of an influenza outbreak, which led some screens to close at certain points of the year, box office revenue and attendance levels reached their highest point for a decade, helped by the growth of 3-D projection (2010: 14). Viewers of local films declined, however, by 1 percentage point to 6.1 per cent on the previous year, even as the number of Mexican features on release increased slightly (2010: 17). While US movies scooped 90 per cent of the theatrical audience, it is notable that Latin American film is statistically insignificant, registering 0 per cent on IMCINE's charts (2010: 16). Cross-border cultural traffic thus works with only one hegemonic partner (conversely the US is also the world territory which saw most Mexican features screened in its theatres [2010: 113]).

Movie-watching has its distinct calendar and cartography, which are also nationally inflected. Thus July was the month in which the greatest number of seats were sold, but September (the time of the 'patriotic' holidays) was the month when most Mexican features were shown and seen (in 2010, 38 per cent of the annual total, influenced once more by the disproportionate success of the single title of *Hell*) (2010: 18). While fantasy, animation and adventure were by far the genres most favoured by Mexican audiences (2010: 21), auteurist local film-makers preferred an unpopular specialism: 'drama' accounted for a full 50 per cent of local releases (and just 38 per cent of the local box office) (2010: 22).

The top two local films by number of viewers were romantic comedy Alejandro Springall's *It's Not You, It's Me (No eres tú, soy yo*, released on 351 prints with 2.9 million admissions) and *Hell* (316 prints and 2.1 million) (2010: 30). By comparison, however, the top film of the year was Pixar's *Toy Story 3* with 1,104 prints and an astonishing 14.8 million viewers (2010: 29). It would appear that Mexican film-makers have, like those in so many other countries, retreated upmarket to serious drama, abandoning commercial genres to US products, except in the case of comedy, where national references are still prized by local audiences.

The movie map of Mexico is also as distinctive as the narco-geographies mentioned earlier in this chapter. The theatrical audience is concentrated in central and northern states boasting the largest cities (Guadalajara's Jalisco and Monterrey's Nuevo León), along with Mexico City and Mexico State, which together comprise a full third of total viewers (2010: 33). Curiously, however, it was another state that saw the highest rate of attendance for domestic films: Michoacán (one of many racked by drug-related violence), where the single title of *Hell* once more accounted for nearly half of the total box office (2010: 35).

Turning from distribution and exhibition to production once more, IMCINE tells us that with an average of seventy features a year, Mexican cinema has reached levels 'unprecedented . . . for decades' (2010: 50). Contrary to the globalization hypothesis, few of these titles are co-productions; indeed, IMCINE suggests that the rule remains 'internal co-production' between Mexican commercial companies and the state agencies (2010: 53). Curiously, the main co-producer (with 29 per cent of the small number made) is neither the US nor a fellow Latin American country but rather the former colonial power, Spain (2010: 54).

Two further factors are important in production. 'Career directors' (those who have managed to make four or more features) now have to wait less time to produce a new film (an average of just three years) (2010: 55). And TV series, now mainly directed by film veterans, have recently experienced 'technological convergence' with the feature film sector, boasting newly elaborate screenplays, prestigious casts and 'mature' themes far from traditional telenovela (2010: 59).

Valuable evidence for audience tastes comes from the informal (or illegal) DVD market. Vendors tell IMCINE researchers that they make their own trailers excerpting 'obscene language or fun stuff' (*Hell*, which heavily features both of these enticing elements was once more the top seller, shifting fifty to eighty copies a day in each street stall) (2010: 93). Actors known from television also help sell pirate DVD titles in a crowded market (2010: 94).

Strikingly the list of films most screened abroad, where the criteria that count are festival prizes and perceived 'quality', bears no relation at all to those consumed by local audiences at home, either in theatres or on DVD (2010: 112). In its survey of audience preferences, IMCINE discovers that Mexicans prefer their own films to be comedies (although here the public is thinking of the Golden Age period, not present-day releases), even as they identify a comic sub-genre (the *fichera* or sex comedy) as the kind of movie that they most dislike (2010: 122). Of the large minority that has negative views of Mexican cinema, the main reasons are said to be 'something missing', vulgar language, violence and low production values (2010: 123).

Clearly, however, there is some conflict here. For example, when asked, 28 per cent of informants offered *Amores perros* as the recent film they would recommend to others; but the same title was cited by 22 per cent as the one they would not recommend (2010: 125). Likewise, the 48 per cent who admit to actually seeing Mexican films in theatres say they do so because they like the subject matter and want to support local movies; the 52 per cent who claim not to see Mexican movies offer 'poor quality' and 'not liking them' as explanations (2010: 130).

An initial hypothesis would seem to be, then, that there is a gap in the market for local films that treat Mexican themes (which are not of course catered for by the dominant superhero and animated movies of Hollywood), just so long as those Mexican features can boast high production values and avoid the stigma of poor quality with which audiences tend still to associate their local cinema. As we shall see, this is indeed the case with the three features I examine in this chapter. However, their radically different levels of bad language and graphic violence, which, we have seen, are key points of contention for local audiences, suggest that my three case studies may well be reaching different demographics within the Mexican population.

The yearbook for 2011 shows little change to that of 2010, except that comedy *Saving Private Pérez* (my second case study) takes over the position held by *Hell* in the previous year. *Saving* comes in as the second biggest-grossing domestic film after highest rated *Don Gato* (the Mexican animated feature based on *Top Cat*, the Hanna-Barbera TV cartoon, which remains inexplicably popular in Mexico). *Saving* was released on 312 copies and reached a theatrical audience of 2,036,000 (equivalent figures for *Miss Bala*, my third case study, at number nine in the list of local box office successes, are 100 prints and a healthy 405,000 spectators) (2011a: 32).

With IMCINE now offering breakdowns by region, the cartography of the putative narco-film genre also becomes clearer. Viewers in the capital were relatively uninterested in Beto Gómez's comedy, placing it number four in their top ten; cinema-goers in the North (the region in which much of the film is set) pushed it to number one (2011a: 38). *Saving* also played well across the full range of windows beyond theatres. It was number three in official DVD rentals (*Hell* from the previous year remained number one) and the only domestic film in the Blu-ray charts (2011a: 144). *Saving* was one of just seven local features available in all territories where pirate DVD sales were monitored (2011a: 158) and was the second most downloaded and the fourth most frequently streamed, with its trailer the third most played on YouTube (2011a: 165, 167, 173). Surprisingly for an art movie, *Miss Bala* was also widely available in all these formats.

Crucially, IMCINE now provides a spectator profile for theatre attendance in 2011. Sixty-four per cent of the audience are between eighteen and thirty-three (as are the buyers of pirate DVDs) and 67 per cent of spectators are of the middle or upper class (the figure for pirate DVD purchasers is 55 per cent) (2011a: 193, 195). It would thus appear to be the case that my chosen films, so far ahead of the field of local production (the great majority of which failed to find any significant audience – if, indeed, they received a theatrical release), coincided with widespread public preferences and the broad segments of the population who consume domestic features through the several different forms of distribution available.

What is surprising, however, is that the three movies have so little in common apart from their shared subject matter. The black comedy *Hell*, the swaggering farce *Saving Private Pérez*, and the disconcerting auteur movie *Miss Bala* may all treat drug trafficking and violence, but (as Polit-Dueñas suggested of narco-novels) it would be putting the cart before the horse to lump the three films together as a new narco-cinema genre before examining them more minutely.

Before moving on to close readings of the films, however, I would like to give an account of a very different survey of Mexican movie production in 2010, which Carlos Bonfil, esteemed critic of leftist daily *La Jornada*, wrote for respected cultural journal *Letras Libres* (2010a).

Bonfil begins by distancing himself from the 'invariably optimistic official discourse' that he presumably associates with government bodies such as IMCINE. But his first proposal is not critical but industrial: a new regulation of the market so that it would no longer favour large transnational enterprises at the expense of small and medium-size local businesses. Looking back to 1994 and the signing of NAFTA, Bonfil writes that the lack of provision for a cultural exception in a free trade area dominated by the US has meant the dismantling of the Mexican movie industry under cover of making it more competitive at an international level and, supposedly, more profitable.

The modernization of theatres (recently equipped with digital projection and sound) has thus gone hand in hand with the liberalization
of ticket prices, now excluded from the 'basket' of basic goods on
which the cost of living is based, and the loss of a screen quota for
the exhibition of local films. This last has declined from 30 per cent
in 1993, to 10 per cent in 1997 to its virtual elimination now. Old
theatres, supposedly shabby and unproductive, have been replaced
by new screens in shopping malls located in wealthy areas; and with
the rising costs of tickets, parking and confectionary, attendance has
become a 'privilege' of the middle class, with working people restricted
to consumption on booming pirate DVD.

Returning to the past, Bonfil writes that the swamping of the
market by Hollywood films had led local production to fall to just
ten features in 1998. But he is not reassured by the recent renaissance
in production. Commercial factors have 'perverse' and 'counter-
productive' cultural effects: Mexican movies are thought by Mexicans themselves to be obsolete in their themes and style; and an unjust
distribution of box office income (with just 15 per cent going to
producers) is a disincentive to the making of local films.

Young film-makers are thus discouraged, forced to choose between
two strategies: making commercial movies that are considered safe
bets by the public authorities that distribute funds and create financial
incentives or attempting more challenging and original projects that
will be recognized in international festivals but will founder on the
local commercial circuit (I noted in the first chapter of this book that
one young film-maker, Jesús Mario Lozano, had said the same thing).
Thus, although production and tax breaks have increased, local features are reduced to one or two weeks of exhibition and are pro-
grammed in distant locations and at unpropitious hours and dates.
Moreover, such films that are seen are judged in quantitative terms,
not in accordance with their quality.

Bonfil's answer is cultural protectionism: the renegotiation of the
terms of NAFTA and the return of the screen quota. Once more, the
industrial is also cultural here. Such measures are held to prevent
Mexican production from aligning itself with the dominant US model
which 'erodes the identity and creativity of Mexican artists' ('la
erosión de la identidad y creatividad del artista mexicano'). Local
cinema, writes Bonfil, is not in good health when it goes unappreciated by its local audience; but nor can film be deprived of its cultural
and educational vocation and reduced to the status of mass
entertainment.

Scornful of art cinema, Vicente Fox (first President belonging to
the rightist PAN) had called in 2004, Bonfil says, for the eventual

suppression of the three public institutions which make up Mexico's cinema infrastructure: the film institute IMCINE, the major studios of Churubusco, and the best film school, the CCC, all of which were held to be unproductive. Although such a threat now seems to have passed, Mexican cinema is now facing a natural death, trapped in a vicious circle where the only projects that prosper and find an audience are those stripped of all originality and critique. Independent cinema is marginalized and the Mexican film industry reduced to a 'maquiladora', a plant for manufacturing goods designed by and for transnational companies.

In spite of this pessimistic panorama, Bonfil ends by praising a number of young film-makers who continually renew their artistic proposals, ignore the rampant anti-intellectualism that discredits their works, and surmount the financial hurdles put in front of them. Such directors of fiction and documentary (the best known on Bonfil's list is Carlos Reygadas) herald a 'renovation' of the Mexican film scene, presumably against all the odds.

Bonfil's vigorous defence of cultural exception and distinction is not unusual for those who occupy his relatively privileged position in the cultural field where subjective dispositions (a taste for artistic innovation) coincide with objective conditions (an identification with a minority audience in film, as in journalism). But it is striking still to compare the differences between his pessimistic panorama and the more hopeful vision of IMCINE. Most striking is Bonfil's focus on film as a unique, and gravely threatened, repository of cultural identity. IMCINE, on the other hand, takes for granted the convergence of media at a local and transnational level, seeing even pirate video as a valuable (albeit unmonetized) mode of distribution for local features. IMCINE also carefully charts the complex crossover between cinema, television, DVD and internet, media to which the cinephile Bonfil fails to refer.

While IMCINE's quantitative report remains professionally detached from questions of quality and offers no value judgements, Bonfil takes for granted the two economies of cultural production familiar since Bourdieu's study of nineteenth-century Paris (1996). Thus on the one hand we have the independence and originality of the true artist (like Reygadas), who may go unrecognized in his own time by the mass public, and on the other we have the crowd-pleasing populist who has no acknowledged aesthetic project (Bonfil generously gives no examples of the commercial film-makers he abhors). Unlike Bourdieu, however (for whom the avant-garde derived its prestige from its independence from all patrons, including the state), Bonfil allows his artists to rely on the modest bounty of government sponsors, even as they rail against public philistinism. What Bonfil does not address, however, is the problem of popular taste. He laments the fact that current production does not connect with the Mexican public. Yet surely he cannot hope that the demanding auteurs he lists at the end of his piece can ever find a large local audience, even if the improved conditions of distribution and exhibition that he advocates were to come into effect?

What would seem to be absent, yet necessary, in Bonfil's scenario would thus be the hypothetical films to which I also referred at the end of my account of IMCINE's report: fiction features of some artistic interest that, combining the cultural and the commercial, manage to appeal to a wide public. I will suggest in the close readings that follow that my three case studies, appealing as they do to a narco subject matter that is uniquely urgent to Mexican spectators, come close in their very different ways to squaring that near impossible circle.

Hell: Chronology and Cartography

Luis Estrada's third feature, released in the 'patriotic month' of September, aims to keep the movie calendar for Mexico just as it offers itself as the last in a trilogy of national allegories by its director (*Herod's Law* [*La ley de Herodes*] was from 1999 and *A Wonderful World* [*Un mundo maravilloso*] from 2006). Thus the first thing we see is the official logo of the (Bi)Centennial, white on red: 'México 2010' (Figure 9), followed by an alphabet soup of those public funding bodies, institutions and financial incentives (IMCINE, CONACULTA, FOPROCINE, Estudios Churubusco and Article 226) that for Bonfil were so threatened by the first PAN President (Estrada, however, attended not the CCC but CUEC, the other prestigious state-funded film school).

Having established his (collective) chronology through this signposting (the 2010 logo is also present on the film's poster), Estrada sketches out a narco-geography appropriate for a hybrid culture. Like the 'narcocorrido', it is conspicuously based on US–Mexico border relations. Thus to an ominous reverb guitar we see a prologue in which El Benny, sympathetic and eternally optimistic as played by skilled pro Damián Alcázar, leaves mother and sister for the US, only to return twenty years later when his handcuffs are removed at the border. The guard, in somewhat incoherent English, warns him: 'Welcome back to Mexico. Don't come back'. Benny will practise code-switching even at home, sprinkling his speech with anglicisms

Figure 9 *Hell* (Luis Estrada, 2010)

('So sorry') when addressing *compadres* who understand no more English than the single word 'business', which they take to refer to the only trade in town.

The credit sequence proper shows a bus trip to a song of the border by the US–based Los Lobos named, emblematically, 'México-Americano'. But the landscape we see is symbolic rather than actual. Benny passes a Santa Muerte chapel and fields strewn with trash along the (imaginary) Route 2010. He is robbed in turn by armed guards patrolling on the bus and by soldiers who strip-search him off it. After his long-suffering, sainted mother receives him with profanity on her modest ranch, he arrives in his hometown. Its place name is now unsubtly defaced on the road sign to make 'San Miguel (N) Arcángel'.

The prodigal is greeted by a dead body lying in the street (soon stripped of its valuables) and the dilapidated town looks as ruinous as any war zone (anticipating Iraq in *Saving*). His godfather offers some over-explicit dialogue, citing the ills of crisis, unemployment and deadly violence that have resulted in 'more deaths than the Revolution'. Benny next visits the bar cum brothel named with typically heavy irony 'Salón México', the workplace of his widowed sister-in-law (the improbably beautiful Elizabeth Cervantes, also a star of Azteca's *In the Sewers* [*Drenaje profundo*], treated in the next chapter). He subsequently gets to know her son, his fourteen-year-old nephew, as foul-mouthed as his mother, who is named Benjamín after him. Loyal to the familial relationships that are also central to telenovela, an emotional Benny swears on his brother's grave to look after the widow and her son.

As the above synopsis of the opening sequences suggests, *Hell* offers a map of Mexico that is comprehensible, but also limiting and subject to manipulation. And by focusing on familiar clichés, Estrada puts in play from the start the hyperreal, that which is always already reproduced. As a crazy distorting mirror, in which no one is spared (the poor are as venal as the rich, only less proficient in their crimes), the film markedly fails to vindicate the agency of the working classes or sing the 'epic' of criminalized communities, even if it does rewrite transnational globalization from the margins.

The local capos, the Reyes, serve as a typically grotesque parody of the Holy Family, named as they are José, María and Jesús. It is a leisurely thirty-six minutes before the supplicant Benny first enters their lavish ranch ('Rinconcito del Cielo' ['Little Corner of Heaven']) with its gold-framed photos of the narco capos with presidents and popes; and fifty-one minutes before a jaunty accordion introduces Benny's initiation into 'business' with the first scenes of graphic violence. Ghostly lit in a yellow night, a man sells out his twin brother for 1,000 pesos. One of the pair is shot down in the street as he flees, panicking, before a car; another has his tongue and hands severed. Benny, our identification character, faints clear away here.

A ghoulish montage follows – of violence, drugs, drink and sex – that culminates with the disposing of a body in a tub of acid (real-life 'narco pozoleros' are yet more baroque) and the placing of a sombrero bearing the slogan 'Viva México' on another unlucky victim. In a violently contrasting scene at a primary school named 'Heroes of the Bicentennial' (the 'patriotic gift' of the Reyes to their town), the unholy family poses before a mural of Hidalgo, Morelos and other renowned historical figures as the kids sing the national anthem (unlike the adults who are evidently unfamiliar with the words).

Clearly Mexico here has failed to achieve foreign paradigms of modernity. Yet, resolutely autochthonous, the film also neglects to offer colonial mimicry of metropolitan models. *Hell* refigures the character of delinquency (by making it indistinguishable from the workings of the state), transforms the nature of victimization (by granting the initially powerless Benny our only sympathetic perspective), and wholly negates the process of detection (by having even Daniel Giménez Cacho's apparently honest Commander of Federal Police prove to be just as corrupt as the notorious local force). Drawing on farce and telenovela, Estrada thus rejects cerebralism, employing the increasingly mutilated bodies of his actors as visible testimony to the abuses of power in his country. The question remains, however, as to whether such popular and populist film-making, which, like the detective novel, occupies a relatively marginally position in the cultural field and appeals to the qualities prized in pirate DVDs (vulgar language and fun stuff), is able to evolve into a tool of social criticism.

Surprisingly, perhaps, Estrada's film is highly aestheticized. Indeed, although it failed to gain admission to major foreign festivals, it won Ariels (Mexican Oscars) in the technical categories of editing, art direction, make-up, sound and special effects, as well as the more sought-after awards for Best Film, Director and Actor. Dull and dusty exteriors, bleached out in the sun, are matched by an ominously shadowed bare and brown decor inside. Popular attractions (including such well-known and respected actors as María Rojo who plays the narco matriarch) are thus matched by artistic distinction in a way calculated to attract both the young and the middle or upper classes who now make up the majority of cinema-goers. We remember that they are generally ill-disposed to a local cinema that they have come to associate with low production values.

The problem is whether Estrada's proficient aestheticization of narco practices and their agents encourages or prohibits discussion of a phenomenological approach to that reality, one in which subject (Benny) and object (San Miguel (N)Arcángel) are understood to be mutually constituting and inseparable. There is no doubt, however, that we are made to observe at length (the film is well over two hours) the gradual changes in the stranger in this newly strange land, as he matures from fainting neophyte to seasoned, but still sympathetic, assassin. Clearly this is a new, and frightening, way to relate to the world.

Perhaps, then, this transparent social excess can be read as a kind of 'emotional democracy' that serves to understand and express the complexity and opacity of nightmarish social relations. For example, in amongst the parody and grotesquerie, there are scenes that play as moments of genuine emotion. Thus José Reyes soundly beats his son Jesús when the latter states that the hated gringos are the cartel's best customers. But the parents' intense grief over the secretly gay son (butchered in an inn with his naked lover) seems sincere. And although materialism and violence are universal (when, newly wealthy, Benny gives his mother a TV set, she asks for his Rolex too), Benny's farewell to his namesake nephew (the young cause of the final blood-bath) is affecting.

There is little doubt that we are asked as spectators of *Hell* to reflect on such contradictions. Benny's brutal partner El Cochiloco (played by the excellent Joaquín Cosío), introducing his friend to his large brood of children, claims in what is something of a refrain in the film: 'One thing is one thing and another is another' ('Una cosa es una cosa y otra cosa es otra cosa'). The talismanic phrase is intended to keep in play conflicting realities (such as violent work and domesticated home life) through insistent disavowal. Yet it will not take long, as severed narco heads tumble from sacks, for spectacular violence to claim Cochiloco's children too, when they are slaughtered outside their cosy suburban chalet. At the end of this sequence Estrada fades to a funereal black.

Of course, with the possible exception of the everyman Benny, Estrada's characters are incapable themselves of such critical self-examination. María Rojo's mother is one moment keening over her son's corpse and the next congratulating her husband on summarily shooting the luckless police chief whom they hold to be responsible for their child's death. There is thus a fine line between comedy and tragedy. Indeed, at points the characters seem to willingly embrace their terrible fate. When Benny asks Cochiloco with some curiosity: 'Aren't you afraid of going to hell?', he replies (and by now we could expect no other answer): 'This *is* hell.' In somewhat similar fashion Estrada also has his characters repeat that 'the President is winning his war on crime, even if it doesn't seem like it' (a real-life statement by an unfortunate politician).

Narco-sensibility, in business as in politics (and the film barely distinguishes between the two) is thus a new kind of cosmology, if not morality, a way to relate to the world through a survivor mentality. But it is a mode of bare life whose horrors prove near interminable. Thus Benny's trials become increasingly hyperbolic: tortured by the Federal Police, he is buried alive and emerges from the cemetery like a ghostly revenant.

And his story just can't come to an end. In what seems like a final vendetta, Benny sprays the Reyes and their cronies with gunfire after they have given the ceremonial 'Grito' of Independence at the Bicentennial celebration in their town: blood flows freely over the golden Mexican eagle on the balcony where they stood. Estrada caps this allegorical image with an equally symbolic display of fireworks (reading, once more, 'México 2010') which bursts into flame and then pathetically dies away, only to cap that once more with yet another pair of endings. Young Benny (the protagonist's nephew) returns to the village at some later date (boasting an SUV with Arizona plates) to mourn at what are now three identical lavish tombs (those of his father, mother and uncle) and then to slaughter his old foes. The frame freezes on his handsome face, distorted into a fatal rictus as the bloodletting is set to continue.

Despite the crudity and relentlessness of Estrada's satire (which spares no object), *Hell*, a rare and undeniable success, cunningly combines the cultural and the commercial. It is a challenging and original project (as Bonfil recommended for Mexican cinema) whose subject matter is, nonetheless, highly familiar. Elite critics were not unfriendly. The film was lionized in *Letras Libres* by critic Fernanda Solórzano (2010), who wrote that, contrary to its tagline, there was 'much to celebrate', in that eleven years earlier IMCINE had attempted to prevent the release of the first feature in Estrada's trilogy, while now the National Film Institute had itself part-funded a yet more corrosive satire at this most patriotically sensitive of times.

Bonfil himself (2010b) praised in *La Jornada* Estrada's 'skill' in directing actors and creating atmospheres, even as he lamented what he saw as the director's reliance on the obsolete models and coarse humour necessary to achieve commercial exhibition. As we shall now see, this question of the supposed conflict between cinema's cultural and educational vocation and its reality as mass entertainment is posed yet more acutely by the unrepentant 'narcomedy', *Saving Private Pérez*, which spurns *Hell*'s saturnine pessimism for an incongruously sunny take on the twin wars on drugs and in Iraq.

Saving Private Pérez: 'Narcomedy' and Catharsis

The DVD extras to Beto Gómez's popular comedy include an interview with purveyors of narcocorrido Los Tucanes de Tijuana (whose music is also featured in *Hell*). Their leader invokes cultural nationalism: the film deals with family and the struggle to survive – quintessential Mexican themes. *Saving* is entertaining, but also thought-provoking. The musician even raises the question of quality, calling it quite simply 'a good film'. Certainly *Saving*'s marketing was exemplary. A teaser viral video featured pseudo vérité footage of the fictional kidnapped brother as shown on the TV news; and an English-language trailer boasted extravagantly mispronounced names and a playful sound gag (at the end the American announcer, apparently kidnapped by the producers, asks plaintively: 'Can I go now?').

The film's first credit is for its independent production company: Lemon Films, with its distinctive logo, a Spielbergian child under a tree. Lemon is known for its box office-friendly retreading of genre films: *KM 31* (Rigoberto Castañeda, 2007) had been a commercially successful and professionally produced horror title. And just as that film was publicized by placing a model of a ghostly child on movie-theatre floors, so in this case Lemon sent out images of camels on carpets to announce their new local blockbuster. Confirming IMCINE's account of media convergence, the film's producer stressed the importance of social media such as Twitter in raising awareness of his feature in advance of its release (*Informador*, 2011). In spite of its narco subject matter, *Saving* also received public funding from violence-racked Coahuila State and from Fidecine, the national competitive fund for film investment.

The pre-credit sequence identifies its location as 'Sinaloa 1973' (we remember that by contrast *Hell* was studiously non-specific in its cartography). Two children run perilously barefoot through the northern desert, barely avoiding scorpions. They encounter a long-haired Yaqui Indian boy in Y-fronts who silently schools them in smashing bottles with a catapult. We cut to Los Angeles in 2003. The now adult Julián (played by a ponderously dignified Miguel Rodarte) strides with his posse through a hospital, pointed crocodile-skin shoes first. In his white suit and gold chains, the latter nestling in luxuriant chest hair, Julián is a parody narco boss. But his first word is 'Mamá'. The sick matriarch laments that the 'most powerful man in Mexico' has not come to the aid of his brother, a US soldier taken hostage in Iraq, and orders Julián to bring him home.

With a quick cut, the return to Julián's stockade is shown with hyperbolic, but po-faced precision, involving as it does in rapid succession a private jet, a helicopter and a fleet of black-windowed SUVs. We are deep in the US–Mexico border regions once more (cross-frontier traffic is constant in this bi-national family, as in the drug trade). But we are also back with the hyperreal: Julián is a simulacrum without a stable referent: the always already reproduced stereotypical narco hero.

But now bilateral cross-border traffic is displaced (and this is the film's main dramatic and comic trope) by a newly multipolar world. The question 'Where the fuck is Iraq?' becomes a running gag (the answers cite variously Saudi Arabia or Holland). However, before this exotic travel begins, the narco's home territory is presented at some length. There is a suave pink-suited flunkey (telenovela heartthrob Jaime Camil) who provides exposition in front of a hi-tech screen; and a tubby son (said to be 'the man of the house', when father is away on 'business'), who is first seen eating an overstuffed sandwich in a tent pitched in his capacious bedroom.

As in *Hell*, then, a male camaraderie and genealogy of (comic) violence is established from the start. Yet the setting, handsomely realized, is flagrantly hyperbolic. As Julián rides a golf cart through his ranch, he reviews his herd of elephants (their trumpeting returns on the soundtrack), outstares a noble white lion, and then emerges sexily in a figure-hugging swimsuit from a huge palm-frond-shaped pool. Although he is always striking a pose, Julián's perilous dignity is enhanced by Rodarte's controlled performance, which ensures some direction of sympathy to his character. Details of the *mise-en-scène* also bear the burden of this humour: the camera lingers for just a moment on a portrait in oils of the capo, posing as a centaur with his small son. In such details the director reveals his hand. He is crafting a mock epic of and for the criminalized communities. Any social criticism dissolves here into parodic exaggeration.

The depiction of violence, on the other hand, is muted throughout. In a further flashback to Sinaloa, 1974, the young Julián implausibly and bloodlessly dispatches with a slingshot the narco who killed his father. Later the terrified henchmen who have put Julián's son in danger meet rapid deaths that go unseen. Rather than glorying in violence, the film is more concerned to touch all the bases with its generic models, which go beyond Spielberg's *Saving Private Ryan* (1998), so showily cited in its title. Thus the gathering together of the varied rescue posse, a traditional trope, is allotted appropriate screentime. Chema is called from his ranch in Beverley Hills. Rosalío (Joaquín Cosío from *Hell*) is first seen dressed as a lethal lobster at a child's birthday party. Scary Pumita is sprung from prison and attempts in vain to escape Julián's private plane in mid-air. The Yaqui Indian Carmelo fights off rivals, amid much smashing of tomatoes. He is, stereotypically, Julián's best childhood friend and conscience, having exchanged drug-running for placid vegetable-gardening.

As the story develops at a leisurely pace (it takes thirty minutes to get to the Middle East), localist references vie with culture-clash internationalism. Thus the posse makes a solemn visit to the real-life Chapel of Jesús Malverde, the narcos' patron saint, in Culiacán, Sinaloa, before setting off for Istanbul in a private jet. Menacing soldiers and an over-friendly guide provide an opportunity for polyglot, subtitled dialogue, first in plausible Turkish and Russian and later in Arabic and English.

The comedy from here on is of incongruity, heavily directed to a local audience: the Mexicans wear their sombreros in the souk and liberally employ chilli sauce to make their guide's green gunk ('Babushka's recipe!') palatable. In sight gags, Julián broods handsomely on a camel or, again, the Indian dances determinedly on sand dunes in his Y-fronts. This comedy of cultural specificities depends, of course, on viewers' close familiarity with its references, inaccessible to foreign audiences. Pumita, a deadly hitman, boasts a conspicuous tattoo of Rigo Tovar, a romantic and tragic balladeer of the 1970s more likely to be favoured by middle-aged housewives than snake-hipped hitmen. With equal incongruity, the Russian guide's musical tastes include 'Soy rebelde' ('I'm a rebel'), a strikingly unrebellious number by Jeanette, a bland teen songstress also of the 1970s.

More generally, the perilous crossing of the US border, so familiar in Mexico, is here transposed to the equally treacherous frontier between Turkey and Iraq. The parallel is heightened by twin flashbacks as the posse drive through the desert. First, a narco tells the young Julián: 'In the US you'd be nothing; here you can be a man.' Secondly, Julián's brother, shown selling humble burritos at a food cart in LA while wearing a humiliating donkey-ear hat, retorts to his flashy sibling: 'People [in Mexico] don't respect you, they fear you.' Bilateral narco-geography is thus rewritten for a new, more complex terrain through the implicit parallels drawn between familiar and unfamiliar border territories.

In spite of this liberal use of stereotype and exaggeration (Julián's ponderous pose-striking and penchant for violet shirts [Figure 10]), production values are as high as in *Hell*. There is some handsome cinematography here, especially in scenes where the full moon looms over the desert (these scenes were shot in northern Mexico, but

Figure 10 *Saving Private Pérez* (Beto Gómez, 2011)

Istanbul plays itself). When, fifty minutes in, the Mexicans arrive in an impressively ruinous Karbala, Iraq, the art design is meticulous, with convincing details such as the battered portraits of Saddam Hussein hanging off the shattered walls of modest homes.

Moreover, *Saving*'s politics is more nuanced than one might expect. In the first action sequence, the Indian rescues a mother and child caught in the crossfire between insurgents and Americans. Later an Iraqi confronts Julián (in English), claiming 'None of us wanted war'. (The sentiment is deflated when, gesturing to Julián's medallion of the criminal Malverde, he adds 'May your saint protect you.') And Gómez barely stoops to subversive colonial mimicry of metropolitan models. Even though his film offers some wish fulfilment to Mexican audiences (Julián lectures the liberated US hostages: 'Listen, gringos; do as I say'), the American troops, no less than their Iraqi enemies, are by no means presented as buffoons or sadists, both of which would have been easier (and lazier) comic choices for the director.

In this family-targeted comedy, such a mixture of tones is typical. The *mise-en-scène* may be comic: the Mexicans at one point escape their kidnappers in an ice-cream van, riddled with American bullets. But the shoot-outs are as proficient and convincing as they are ridiculous, in spite of the lack of explicit carnage, and the vainglorious Mexicans are progressively humiliated: taking refuge in an oil pipeline, they emerge to stagger, black and dripping, through the burning desert and are later obliged to roll in the sand to avoid detection.

While (unlike in Spielberg's original) there is little blood and guts here, the humour serves to undermine the narco as a Mexican myth of authority and identity, even as it invokes national shibboleths. For example, the posse claim to have used 'chile de árbol' sauce, quite precisely, to get information from informants, saying it works better than torture by electric shock (even this scene is not directly shown). Once more such verbal humour is complemented by well-chosen sight gags: we see the empty sauce bottle lying abandoned in the desert sand. Or again, after the impressive climactic action sequences (an impossibly long leap through the air shooting all the while, a chase over rooftops, a fall from a helicopter), we are given a handsome shot of the brother winched to safety, his body silhouetted against a minaret at dusk, as the team's helicopter flies, black, into the golden sun.

This highly skilled aestheticization, unexpected in a farce, offers some reassurance to upper-class viewers, nervous perhaps at risking their educational capital by enjoying a low-status and all-too-Mexican genre movie. The strategy seemed to pay off. In *La Jornada* once more, Leonardo García Tsao (another of Mexico's most prestigious critics) wrote that while *Saving* is not as critical and incisive as *Hell*, it belongs to the same new genre of 'narcomedia' (2011). He also praises the high production values and location shooting, so different to earlier Mexican cinema when the film would have been shot on the back lot in Churubusco using flea-bitten camels and cardboard tanks. As a reaffirmation of life, he writes, laughter may be the only proper response to tragedy. The film is thus not irresponsible but stages rather what the Greeks taught us is called 'catharsis'. Male viewers at García Tsao's screening, he reports, not only cackle like hyenas, they even stamp their feet with laughter at climactic moments.

The film's final sequence, however, must have proved curiously ambivalent and disconcerting to such pleasure-seeking spectators. Safely back in Mexico, we see a wordless, slow-motion family barbecue, all set to a song ('Corazón negro' ['Black Heart']) specially written for Chavela Vargas, the gravel-voiced and much-respected veteran folk singer. The lyrics claim that the land that saw him grow celebrates his return. Gómez freezes the frame as Julián dances with his happy (and now healthy) mother, a marked contrast with the murderous freeze-frame with which Estrada finally ends *Hell*.

But a last laconic title notes that Julián died three months later in an ambush and his mother and brother have gone into hiding. Hence, if *Saving* expands or extends the border narrative that is typical of a hybrid culture in order to embrace new global tensions beyond US–Mexican relations, it also shows some evidence of an emotional democracy based on familial relationships. The laconic final title perhaps encourages viewers to understand and express the complexity and opacity of the new social relations that have been repressed throughout the body of the film, which has disavowed crowd-pleasing foul language and spectacular violence.

Rather than celebrating the narco-sensibility of the 'survivor mentality', then, *Saving* could be read, finally, as part of a traditional ritual of processing and punishing crime à la Durkheim: we know that Julián will not be around to enjoy the pleasures and profits of either his crimes or his good deeds. Ironically, however, this film that so clearly rewrites globalization from the margins failed, like *Hell* before it, to find significant distribution abroad, either in festivals or theatres. That expansion into the international market was left to my third case study: the narco art-movie *Miss Bala*.

Miss Bala: Fashion Victims

After the hyperreal stereotypes of *Hell* and *Saving*, *Miss Bala* offers a new spin on the narco theme: beauty queens meet drug barons.

Gerardo Naranjo (with Estrada and García, one of those 'career directors' whom IMCINE says are increasingly prolific) has a flashy track record for an arthouse auteur: in *Drama/Mex* (2006), glossy models emote in beach-houses in scenic Acapulco; in *I'm Gonna Explode* (2008), as we saw in chapter 5, teens run wild with cars and guns in historic Guanajuato. While *Hell* was publicly funded and *Saving* bankrolled by the private producer Lemon, *Miss Bala* is a (rare) co-production between Fox International Productions (the specialist division of a US major) and Canana (Diego Luna and Gael García Bernal's boutique Mexican company). This commercial arrangement fits Naranjo's theme. Like the movie, the drug business is, as we have seen in my earlier case studies, transnational, dependent on cross-border collaboration. And travelling as his films do to disparate states of the Mexican republic, Naranjo can now lay claim in his *oeuvre* to an attempted national cartography.

Miss Bala's title boasts a pointed pun. While 'bala' of course means 'bullet', it also rhymes with 'Baja' (California), the state whose beauty pageant is hijacked by the local mafia in the film. And the script (for which Naranjo takes co-credit) is based on a collage of headlines ripped from the front pages. A real-life beauty queen (Miss Sinaloa, named, like Naranjo's character, Laura) was indeed charged with gang membership; an agent of the American Drug Enforcement Agency was killed by organized crime; and, as is well known, US weapon sales to Mexican cartels, also shown in the film, are massive and lucrative in spite of loud American complaints of drug-smuggling from south of the border.

But if troubling truth is indeed stranger than fiction, then cinema has, as we have seen, already been active in this area. Naranjo, however, rejects the clichéd figure of the crime boss in his white suit and gold chains so central to *Hell* and *Saving*. His opening scenes are thus very different to those of Estrada and García in both form and content. In his first shot, the camera pans over glamorous pictures pinned on a bedroom wall, including one of tragic icon Marilyn. A motto reads (in English) 'Fashion Victim'. But for the future Miss Bala/Baja the cliché will prove literally true. The quest for glamour (gratified for narcos and audience alike in *Saving*'s lush *mise en scène*) will be repeatedly frustrated here.

One early sequence stands out. After a failed audition for the pageant, the initially unglamorous Laura (played by impressive newcomer Stephanie Sigman) is taken by a friend to a seedy nightclub. Naranjo (or his director of photography, the Hungarian Mátyás Erdély) chooses to shoot in depth, respecting the complexity of this unusual space. While Laura waits placidly in the bathroom, inspecting herself in the mirror, behind her and to the left we glimpse a surreal sight: gunmen drop silently down the wall into a corridor, in preparation for a massacre. Belatedly becoming aware of this invasion, Laura sinks to the floor and retreats into a corner. A drug baron (later she will learn that he is called 'Lino'), shown only from the waist down, comes into shot on the left and listlessly tosses a roll of bills down to her.

This first sight of the unprepossessing Lino, in which he is faceless, is vital. Unlike the directors of earlier films discussed, Naranjo allows not the slightest identification with, much less celebration of, the drug barons. And by scoring the whole nightclub sequence to annoyingly repetitive *norteño* dance music, the low-key drama is disconcertingly heightened. After this initial chance encounter (captured in just one lengthy take) there will be no escape for Laura from the tentacles of all-too-organized crime. While Benny is slowly initiated into the 'business' he comes to embrace and Julián is a fully formed criminal right from the start, Laura is the passive victim of random circumstance. In the very banality of her predicament, then, Naranjo conclusively rejects the aestheticization of narco practices and their agents, showing the true working classes (Laura's family run a small laundry business) to be wholly deprived of agency, let alone epic heroism.

With a pace yet slower than *Hell*, *Miss Bala* shapes up against all expectations as a surprisingly thoughtful slow-motion thriller. There is unaccustomed solemnity in the rhythm of shooting and cutting, not to mention impressively underplayed performances from novices Sigman (a native of Sonora) as Laura and Noé Hernández as Lino (Hernández has a small role in *Hell*). In his extended press notes, Naranjo insists on the violence and inequality of life in Mexico, tracing with some poetic licence the narcos' ghoulish mutilation of their victims' bodies (illustrated daily on the front pages of newspapers) back to Aztec rituals that were equally gory (*Miss Bala*, 2011).

But his comments say more about a certain kind of Mexican self-image than they do about the film itself. In fact, unlike in *Hell*, but as in *Saving*, explicit violence is conspicuous by its absence in most of *Miss Bala*. And it is only after some seventy minutes of screentime that Naranjo will finally allow us an action set-piece: an operatic inferno filmed on the city street where Laura, hapless as ever, is caught in the crossfire between cartel and police. If 'narco-sensibility' can be identified here with a new morality or cosmology, then it is one in which the central place of violence is indeed gratuitous, expressing no way to relate to the world other than Laura's stunned anaesthesia.

Figure 11 *Miss Bala* (Gerardo Naranjo, 2011)

As the film develops, moreover, we see that it is in its deceptively simple technique, not its high-profile spin on a well-known subject, that *Miss Bala*'s real originality lies. Surprisingly perhaps, Laura is consistently shot from behind, her dark hair hanging down her back. The audience is thus encouraged to adopt the point of view of this stranger in a strange world, a familiar enough strategy. But with our vision partially obscured by Laura's head, the viewer is as disorientated as the increasingly shell-shocked character who, time and again, wanders or blunders into mayhem (Figure 11). Naranjo has noted in the press book once more (*Miss Bala*, 2011) the lack of close-ups in his film, which deny us easy psychological proximity. But perhaps even more important is his frequent use of shallow focus: when two characters are shot together, more often than not one person's image will be blurred. This is a society whose citizens are isolated from one another even when they share the same space. Naranjo's coolly cerebral shooting style thus evolves into a tacit tool of social criticism.

Likewise *Miss Bala* favours dreamy steadycam shots that are difficult to interpret. For example, in one early sequence the camera floats woozily over the heads of would-be contestants at the Miss Baja contest, suggesting that something strange is in the air. And, indeed, as Laura drifts ever further into drug territory, her (and our) sights become yet more surreal. Thus when the criminals induce her to transport money across the border, a lengthy sequence shows great wads of bills being solemnly taped to her slim waist. But if this is, like *Hell* and *Saving* before it, a 'border narrative', then, unlike them, it is one in which 'other' Mexicans see themselves not as protagonists, but as powerless walk-ons, mere extras in someone else's drama.

For example, even after she is crowned queen (the drug cartels control the beauty business), Laura is dumped at night outside town. She attempts to make her way across the desert dressed in high heels, chandelier earrings and a satiny pageant dress, an image as incongruous as any in *Saving*. Much later Laura will be led into an equally bizarre scenario: a luxury hotel, where guests sit placidly in a courtyard oblivious to the violence outside. Here she has an assignation with an elderly general, all part of the job for beauty queens. The scene is shot by Naranjo, however, through the billowing clouds of the hotel room humidifier, lending a surreal visual quality to an already sordid situation. And the odd couple's tryst will soon be interrupted by a squadron of federal police in their black masks, eerily reminiscent of Darth Vader. If, then, *Miss Bala* serves as a map or mirror to narco-geography, it is one in which visibility is strictly – brutally – limited.

Naranjo's nightmarish vision is reminiscent of Julio Cortázar's well-known short story 'Casa tomada' (literally 'taken house') in which a home is gradually invaded by unknown and unseen forces, obliging the complacent inhabitants to fall back and finally flee their living quarters (Cortázar, 2012). Once taken as an allegory of political repression (suggesting that the bourgeoisie sat idly by during the rise of dictatorships in Latin America), now the story could well apply to the insidious growth of the drug cartels.

Indeed, in Naranjo's chilling account, narcos, far from being luxurious like *Hell's* Reyes or glamorous like *Saving's* Julián, seem stubbornly everyday, their activities barely distinguishable from the domestic life of the nation. Typically, Laura is given a homely *nom de guerre* by her comrades-in-arms, even though they betray not the slightest tenderness towards her. It is 'Canelita' ('little cinnamon'), a name more appropriate for a pet (a small dog of the same name was indeed fatally wounded by police shooting in Ciudad Juárez) (*Juárez-Dialoga*, 2011). When Laura manages briefly to escape back to her modest home, it is soon afterwards taken over by gang members who spread out a prodigious display of weapons on the domestic floor. The house (like Laura herself and, Naranjo would suggest, all of Mexico) is well and truly taken. Any possible 'emotional democracy' of familial relationships has long since bled away.

At another point, Naranjo cuts from the wounded narco warriors being ferried home in a truck, who are conspicuously unattractive, to glamorous beauty contestants rehearsing on stage a Bob Fosse-style number in tights and hats. It is a kind of contrastive editing that, given the film's premise, is surprisingly rare in *Miss Bala* and never used for cheap shock value or facile irony. Rather it points to a key insight: that it is increasingly hard to distinguish between contestants and casualties. While it would be a stretch to say that the merciless beauty business is as cut-throat as drug-running, the former is shown to be wholly complicit with the latter. There is thus no cultural or commercial activity that is immune to narco influence.

Naranjo here undercuts the most pervasive and seductive female myth in Latin America. Unlike Benny's implausibly beautiful prostitute-cum-sister-in-law in *Hell*, Laura is the anti-Ugly Betty. Model-tall and skinny from the start, she would seem to be ready for a Betty-style makeover. Like Betty, once more in the various versions of the transnational franchise, Laura's hidden beauty will be revealed by the end of the story: she is professionally made up and coiffed before staggering out on stage to win the longed-for contest. But unlike Betty (who gained promotion and married her boss in the telenovela) this new look brings Laura no personal or professional success. On the contrary, Laura will be brutally fucked in a truck by ugly drug baron Lino; and she remains throughout the film an accidental, and increasingly traumatized, tourist in the foreign territory of organized crime.

During the pageant Laura is asked if her dream is money or fame. Struck dumb by her trials, she can answer only with tears. The oleaginous MC praises her 'genuine emotion' as she stumbles offstage. It is a rare and bitter moment of humour, equalled only when Laura, finally paraded as a criminal on TV, is condemned for bringing the supposed good name of the beauty pageant business (so superficial and corrupt) into disrepute. It is no accident that in the press book Naranjo, clearly sceptical of IMCINE's 'technological convergence' and an adherent of cultural exception, attacks the 'manipulation' of Mexico effected by television and claims that 'movies . . . operate on a higher level' (*Miss Bala*, 2011).

In spite of the many bizarre moments in his film, Naranjo also speaks in the press book (*Miss Bala* 2011) of the social accuracy of his depiction and his desire to educate foreigners in what is happening in his country, even though he also (in a somewhat contradictory move) denies that *Miss Bala* is a 'denunciation' of current conditions. His film is certainly a bracing change from the images of narcos in popular film as Robin Hoods or comic heroes, although, as we have seen, even those images are more complex than they at first appear.

In interview (if not within the film itself), Naranjo offers a social aetiology for the narcos, claiming erroneously that his home country suffers the greatest inequality of income in the world (even within the OECD, the club of rich nations to which Mexico has now gained admission, Mexico is second to Chile in inequality) (*Economist*, 2012). Absolute poverty has thus fallen in the Mexico that is now a middle-income country, helped by initiatives such as a government conditional cash-transfer programme that has been adopted as a model as far away as New York (Rosenberg, 2011). *The Economist* wrote (2011) that the true cartels holding Mexico to ransom are not the drug gangs but the monopolies in areas such as telephony (controlled by Carlos Slim, at that time the world's richest man) that charge ordinary Mexicans inflated fees for their services. As we saw earlier, those same ordinary Mexicans prefer their local films to be comedies; and it is no surprise that an art movie, destined for a relatively small audience, should give such a resolutely downbeat version of the narco-narrative, one which offers so little obvious aesthetic or narrative pleasure.

Nonetheless, Naranjo succeeds in directing sympathy towards his hapless and hopeless protagonist. Laura will finally be set free by the police who are in league with the cartel, but she is still dumped on a desolate street. The sound design is again innovative here: we hear only a roar of white noise, which is impossible to interpret. This last sequence is a reminder that, in spite of its claims to reflect contemporary Mexico, *Miss Bala* cannot be reduced to realism. Naranjo's film offers no facile psychological analysis of the criminals whose unglamorous daily lives it documents. But it also offers no easy remedy for the nightmarish social conditions to which it attests.

No Mere Maquiladora

Miss Bala, unlike my previous case studies, would seem to embrace cultural distinction, offering a stripped-down aesthetic that proved highly acceptable to international art-movie circuits: it premiered in Cannes and was also shown theatrically in the US and Europe. Yet (as noted earlier) it gained a domestic audience of almost half a million in theatres. It is not clear that Naranjo's film fulfils the 'educational vocation' that Bonfil prescribes for film: *Miss Bala* seems more likely to provoke stunned paralysis in its spectators than any learning process. But if the mass entertainment of *Hell* and *Saving*, democratizing cultural capital, proved more questioning of Mexico's myths of authority and identity than might have been expected, the avowedly high-culture *Miss Bala* seems also to have struck a chord with local cinema audiences, many of whom are newly upmarket. At the very least, all three films reveal that the new genre of 'narcomedy' or narco-drama has produced challenging and original projects through which Mexican artists have reworked their identity and creativity.

Adapting Polit-Dueñas's question around literature, we might ask if any cinematic representation of violence necessarily implies an ethical approach beyond the aestheticization so clear in the high production values of these features. Perhaps García Tsao's proposal of catharsis is helpful here: to mime horror can be to exorcize rather than endorse it, depending on specific contexts of production and reception. Certainly these films could be seen as phenomenological in that they stress the interaction between witnesses, whether naive, complicit or brutalized, and a new and nightmarish reality. And tellingly they position themselves at all levels in the cultural 'field', with *Hell* staking out the middle ground between *Saving*'s populist comedy and *Miss Bala*'s relatively elite art movie. There is thus some sense of an increasing democratization of the media, especially given the friendly response of some critics to this wide range of genres and tones. Perhaps Mexican cinema, newly diverse here, deserves itself to be called a 'hybrid culture'.

The veneration of violence in much narco-sensibility is barely present in any of the films. *Hell* is relentlessly hostile to its savage narcos, although the indiscrimination of its critique renders its social criticism ineffectual. *Saving* disavows violence by refusing to show the carnage that would plausibly by employed by its sympathetic hero, also a somewhat problematic choice. *Miss Bala*, most radically, renders violence dull and everyday, even as its stresses its horror. The role of women in the first two films is clearly problematic, identified as the spectators are with their respective male protagonists; but *Miss Bala* also deprives us of female agency, as its heroine is a passive victim of circumstance. Conversely, the colonial mimicry of metropolitan models seems to disappear here: Mexico has evolved a coherent, if complex and contradictory, indigenous genre.

The struggle over cultural consumption is thus bracketed, as it were, in a film narco trilogy that sidesteps questions of cultural capital and challenges Mexico's myths of authority and identity with varying degrees of crudity. Certainly the common, unique theme of violence can be read throughout these films in Durkheimian functionalist terms as an expressive force or collective ritual that is as socially constructive as it is divisive.

As a map or mirror of a distinct order of violence, the films relate problematically to lived experience in Mexico, which will of course vary so much according to social class and geographical location. Yet their popular success, reaching a collective audience of some four and a half million domestic spectators in just two years, suggests that there is at play here a kind of social democratization of or through the emotions, one in which localism is a key attraction for national audiences even as it serves as a barrier to entry for foreigners, in theatres or festivals.

While the direction of sympathy to narcos remains troubling in *Hell* and *Saving*, even these films have managed to challenge the stigma of poor quality under which Mexican cinema labours at home. And, finally, the success of all three (while limited in the context of production as a whole) challenges both the appeal to cultural protectionism by some critics and their claim that the local industry is merely a 'maquiladora', assembling product for the foreign market. These fiction features thus combine the cultural and the commercial in a newly multipolar world. Paradoxically, perhaps, their success is due to the fact that they target a distinctly Mexican audience for whom their common theme has a special and sadly urgent relevance.

8

TV Histories of Violence: *In the Sewers* (*Drenaje profundo*, Azteca, 2010), *Cries of Death and Freedom* (*Gritos de muerte y libertad*, Televisa, 2010)

Out of the Underworld

Violence or insecurity seem to be everywhere in contemporary Mexican media; and we have seen that they are key themes in cinema across a wide range of genres. However, there are good grounds for the hypothesis that television fiction is a more immediate and cogent medium than feature film for reflection on the subject. After all, the electronic medium has a much faster turnaround than does cinema, where a project may well take years to come to fruition. It is thus no surprise that TV fiction anticipates themes treated only later on film. Indeed, Televisa's unremarkable series of one-off dramas, *The Rose of Guadalupe* (*La rosa de Guadalupe*, mentioned in chapters 5 and 6) broadcast an episode on a beauty queen caught in the clutches of the narcos ('Miss Narco') on 3 August 2010, well before Naranjo brought *Miss Bala* to movie theatres. Moreover, consumed as it is by a much wider demographic than feature film, with its increasingly pricey tickets, television fiction also takes up its place within the home, a more intimate and charged space than the theatre. We should not be surprised, then, to see the theme of violence addressed within the context of the everyday in a TV environment that is as ubiquitous as it is continuous.

What I argue in this last chapter, however, is that just as the topic of violence needs to be addressed in Mexican film across a variety of unlikely genres (farce, satire and art movie), so its representation in television fiction should be analysed in perhaps unexpected places. Here, then, I examine two big-budget serials or mini-series made in the symbolically loaded year of the Bicentennial of Independence and Centennial of the Revolution: an expert genre piece (pitched somewhere between crime and horror) which, it will be argued, addresses Mexico's violent past as well as its bloody present; and a prestige costume drama on the Independence struggle, which, beyond celebration, suggests that violence is at the very origin of the state. The twin histories of violence they suggest are curiously complementary, with the flashy contemporary show reaching back to a tragic moment of recent history (the student massacre at Tlatelolco and the dirty war against dissidents) and the respectable period-piece, in spite (or because) of its avowedly nationalistic ambitions, casting an unavoidably sombre light on Mexico today.

Such oblique reference to violence, filtered as it is through established but exceptional televisual genres (of action and heritage, respectively), requires a theoretical model of the subject adequate to its complexity and one which goes beyond empiricism or sensationalism. Such an approach is offered by sociologist Rossana Reguillo, who has provided perhaps the most complex and consistent approach to the subject. In a 2008 essay on the multiple frontiers of violence, Reguillo attacks what she calls the supposed exteriority of violence and its positioning in a kind of underworld, metaphorically identified as the kingdom of death governed by Hades. In this context the role of the scholar is thus clear:

> para pensar las violencias de una manera analíticamente eficaz, hay que sacarlas de los 'mundos inferiores' y del mundo de los muertos y de los infiernos, para pensarlas más bien en su habitual presencia en el mundo. Arrancarse del infra-mundo no es sólo la tarea de los individuos sometidos por Hades, sino la tarea fundamental de un pensamiento que no acepta el artilugio de la lejanía, la excepcionalidad y la exterioridad de las violencias. (2008: 207)

> (To think violences in an analytically efficacious manner, it is necessary to take them out of the 'underworlds', from the world of the dead and of hell, to think them in their everyday presence in the world. Pulling oneself out of the infra-world is not only a task for those subjected to Hades, it is also a fundamental task for a mode of thought that is not taken in by the trick of the supposedly distant, exceptional and exterior nature of violences.)

Insisting on 'violences' in the plural (rather than a monolithic, unproblematized singular), Reguillo goes on to identify three 'dimensions' to the topic: imposition (the infliction of damage on the self or others), intentionality or rationality (the logic and objectives of such impositions), and causality (the explanatory 'stories' or 'keys' to motivation beyond hypothesis or deduction) (2008: 208). This triple focus will enable a critique of the common-sense notion that 'violence' (in the uncontested singular) is 'extra-muros': a force that is inexplicable and even supernatural.

Reguillo thus attempts to place youth violences, associated with drug-trafficking, in a structural context where their 'spectacularization' has created both an increased collective reflection on and a greater perception of the theme (2008: 209). Two social trends are vital here: the dissolution of social bonds and increased real-time access to violent events that appear to have no ordering 'narrative'. But it is precisely this perceived ubiquity of violences that makes their explanation in terms of historical specificity more urgent. And if poverty and exclusion feed the phenomenon, it is also nourished by less evident factors such as the challenge to legality and the crisis in legitimation of the established order. Reguillo proposes three more analytical 'keys' here: the erosion of imaginaries of the future; the increase in structural and subjective precariousness; and the loss of legitimacy in politics. Having laid out the theoretical territory, she then offers a moving ethnographic study of 'Fredi', a young criminal who crossed multiple borders in Latin America and the US in the course of his brutal and brutalized narco career. Going beyond biography, this case study (like, I would argue, the very different fictional TV narratives I discuss in this book) reveals the articulation of individual stories within narratives of narco violences (2008: 219).

Reguillo stresses in this context the 'transcoding' of rules and mechanisms, which read differently in different contexts and territories, but take on their general meaning in the lingua franca of a 'violence' that, she writes, all are able to decipher. It is no surprise, then, that she rejects the moralizing or psychologist reading that appeals to the supposed lack of traditional values or family breakdown (2008: 220). Yet, making no simple apology for her young subjects, she also rejects a direct relation between poverty or exclusion and violence (2008: 221). Rather, the power of the narcos (beyond that of life and death) is to break down and transform distinct social orders. This power is expressed, Reguillo writes in a theatrical or filmic metaphor, in terms not of discrete 'scenes' but rather 'escenificaciones' ('stagings' or 'set-pieces') which fill the void in the established order and generate their own symbols, symbols which cannot be explained through the simple opposition of legality and illegality. These diverse scenarios thus resist reductive explanations: normative, epidemiological or authoritarian.

Reguillo proposes a final concept here – that of 'paralegality'–
which emerges as a parallel order to the Law in the frontier zone
opened up by violences. In the face of the decay of the political, contemporary unease thus finds its most eloquent expression in violence.
Yet subjects like Fredi embody a history of de-appropriations of the
self and a constant struggle for re-inscription. As she concludes:

> las violencias no se ubican en un más allá, restringido a un espacio-
> otro, a una heterotopía salvaje y lejana, vinculada a la barbarie por
> contraposición a la civilización; ellas están aquí, ahora, presentes en
> un espacio complejo cuya recurrencia pone en evidencia, cuando
> menos, la falacia de pensarlas como brotes excepcionales que sacudirían
> de vez en vez el paisaje armónico y pacífico de una pretendida nor-
> malidad 'normal'. Las violencias juveniles se instalan justo en el vacío
> de legitimidad y la ausencia percibida de un proyecto colectivo porta-
> dor de sentido. Desde ahí, desafían la legalidad. Pero al hacerlo con-
> frontan una ausencia, no una presencia. Y, sin embargo, a esta ausencia
> de legitimidad se responde con dosis redobladas de legalidad, en una
> espiral punitiva que termina por alimentar las violencias. (2008: 222)

> (Violences are not placed in a 'beyond', limited to another space, a
> distant and savage heterotopia, which is linked to barbarism as opposed
> to civilization; they are here, now, present in a complex space whose
> recurrence makes manifest, at the very least, the fallacy of thinking
> them as exceptional outbreaks which would send periodic shudders
> through the harmonious and peaceful landscape of a supposed 'normal'
> normality. Youth violences take up their place precisely in the vacuum
> of legitimacy and the perceived absence of a collective meaningful
> project. It is from that place that they challenge legality. But in doing
> so, they come up against not a presence but an absence. Nonetheless
> the response to this absence of legitimacy consists of redoubled doses
> of legality, in a punitive spiral that finally feeds violences.)

We will test this complex hypothesis later in a TV narrative that is
literally set in that 'underworld' to which Reguillo claims an unex-
amined 'violence' is relegated: Azteca's *In the Sewers* (*Drenaje profundo*) takes place in part in the sewers of Mexico City. But first we
must sketch the relation of our chosen theme to the TV environment
in 2010, the year that also boasted the historical serial *Cries of Death
and Freedom* (*Gritos de muerte y libertad*).

Two TV surveys

The 'Highlights del Media Performance 2010' (*sic*), produced by
IBOPE (the audience rating service equivalent in Latin America to

Nielsen in the US or Sofres in Spain), provides some interesting data. The report sets the scene grandly by praising the increased (and it argues irreversible) process of commercial competition and political democratization that Mexico has experienced in recent years, a process which has made the role of the media in society ever more important (2010: 2). Likewise, the consumption of media by Mexicans is increasing and diversifying. Average daily TV watching per viewer has risen to a record four hours and forty-five minutes, twenty-three minutes more than ten years earlier (2010: 3). Content has also changed considerably during the same period. National channels dedicated an hour and a half longer to fiction series in 2010 than they did in 2000, with one-off dramas rising by fifty-two minutes per week, as magazine and sport programming declined. This last trend was in spite of the fact that this was the year of the Football (Soccer) World Cup. There would thus seem to be some positive correlation between social change (deregulation, democratization), media consumption (an increase in TV viewing hours in spite of new competition from the internet), and innovations in formats (the rise of series drama and the decline of talk and sport shows).

IBOPE's yearbook for 2009, the most recent available in its complete form to non-corporate client readers at the time of writing, gives more detail. In 2009, 33.7 per cent of households had a computer at home (up from just 7.2 per cent in 1998), while 98.8 per cent had at least one television (2009: 8). Significant here, however, is the substantial rise in access to pay TV: from 14.2 per cent in 1998 to 32.2 per cent in 2009. Clearly viewers were no longer satisfied with the free-to-air offer of duopoly Televisa and Azteca. The new Mexican viewers were, nationally, more likely to have two sets than one (40.2 per cent to 36.7 per cent) and to watch TV in the main bedroom rather than in the living room (37.4 per cent to 33.6 per cent) (2009: 9). Prime-time viewing peaked for the hour of 9 to 10 p.m. on weekdays (2009: 21). In spite of changes in viewing habits, the year's fifteen top-rated fiction shows seem nonetheless remarkably traditional: thirteen are from Televisa (ten telenovelas, one sport broadcast, one reality show and one quiz) and just two from rival Azteca (both sporting events) (2009: 25). By far the biggest viewing days were for special non-fiction programmes on the influenza outbreak of 2009, which (at 43 per cent share) eclipsed such previous prominent events as the attacks on New York in 2001 or the contested declaration of Felipe Calderón as President Elect in 2006 (2009: 29).

It is not surprising, then, that 'the year of influenza' is one of the media case studies of IBOPE's annual. The outbreak considerably increased the total number of viewers, especially amongst children and the young (2009: 67). And with almost 84 million pesos spent on health education spots by the government, 88.8 per cent of the audience was reached at least once, with the average viewer seeing no fewer than 14.6 commercials on the theme (2009: 74). IBOPE's second case study, on 'daily activities in Mexico', includes the interesting information that while women favour free-to-air TV over men (69 per cent to 64 per cent), the opposite is true of pay TV (21 per cent to 24 per cent) (2009: 82). A final case study here is on 'Generation Y' (defined as those born between 1977 and 1997). Of interest in this context is that while younger people's consumption of cinema and internet is significantly higher than that of their elders, they still make time to enjoy free-to-air TV at the same stratospheric rates as other Mexicans (2009: 97). Identified as taste-makers (in Spanish 'campeones' or 'champions'), this sociable generation convinces others to adopt their preferences in areas such as cellphones, consumer electronics and clothing (2009: 100).

Commercially oriented, IBOPE has, of course, only a glancing interest in TV content. For that (and for the relation to violence, strangely absent in IBOPE's survey) we must turn to a yearbook from transnational academic organization OBITEL. This annual account of Iberoamerican television fiction embraces eleven countries and, in its 2011 edition (which treats content aired in the previous year), also focuses on the twin themes of 'quality' and 'transmedia' (OBITEL, 2011).

In the comparative section of the report, the OBITEL collective note the continuing strength of fiction production in Mexico, one of the 'big three' in their universe. But they also refer to organized crime as the key theme in both fictional and reality programming:

> the topic of organized crime was an important narrative pillar for fiction in Mexico, since the panorama of social violence caused by the battle against drug-trafficking (undertaken by the government) was retaken by the Mexican telenovelas with two objectives: to legitimize the government actions and to make the widespread violence context [sic] seem natural. In spite of its violent contents, no telenovela was taken off the airwaves [unlike in other Latin American countries]. Another element to emphasize in the Mexican context is the open interference of the most important TV stations of the country, Televisa and TV Azteca, in social politics. Through the Iniciativa México co-production, these companies aimed at showing themselves as social paladins, capable of filling the power vacuums left by government. The programme, a Sunday reality show, promoted financial and visibility support to the work of Mexican civil organizations. (2011: 53)

The dedicated chapter on Mexico, written by a team led by Guillermo Orozco (whose work on reception I cited in chapter 5), restates this theme, stating at the start: 'television . . . injected a lot more violence into its fiction programmes in order to legitimize its use by the state and the army as the only strategy to obtain peace in the war scenario announced and repeated in [*sic*] all screens by the President himself' (2011: 279). While total hours of fiction decreased relative to non-fiction or reality programming (a claim which would appear to contradict the trend of IBOPE's data from the previous year), the format of the series (as opposed to telenovela) increased its share in 2010 (2011: 280). Nonetheless the demographic profile of the audience for the top-rated shows revealed no change on previous years: women over forty with a medium-low socioeconomic status predominate (2011: 295). (The only exception here is precisely one of my case studies, the historical epic *Cries of Death and Freedom*, whose 41 per cent male public is unrivalled and whose 17.6 per cent ABC+ rating makes it the second most favoured by the upper middle class.)

The special section on 'quality' in Mexican television calls attention to the dual and ambiguous role of the state, which is at once a 'watchdog' claiming to monitor commercial channels in the service of an ill-defined and mutable 'public interest' and a producer and exhibitor of content through minority channels of public television (2011: 304). (OBITEL monitors in its survey cultural channels OnceTV and Conaculta but not commercial innovator Cadena 3.) Moreover, 'quality TV' has long been identified in Mexico with educational programming. Only since 2009, writes Orozco, has it been proposed that quality could also relate to fiction, a prestige status that the survey restricts to the (few) titles produced by little-seen public channels (2011: 306). Audiences themselves, no longer passive, have their own definitions of quality. The transmedia survey in the yearbook focuses on postings on Televisa's own site for the year's most popular telenovela. It comments that although most viewers loved the serial's 'beautiful ending' and expressed their sorrow at their enforced separation from the characters in the future, '18 per cent of those who left a message on Tvolucion expressed some type of critical comment towards the telenovela or its actors; either detailing a lack of coherence or credibility, its pink [i.e. overly romantic] tone or the bad performances' (2011: 301). Clearly even traditional audiences (the show in question was a remake) were now becoming more critical or found it easier to voice their complaints with the monopolistic offer of Televisa.

However, the main theme of the national survey is the 'integration' of violence (no longer confined to the news) into fiction; and the claim that in both series and telenovelas we are now shown a violence (or more properly 'violences') carried out by both criminal gangs and the government (2011: 281). For Orozco et al. such TV violence is at once more 'spectacular' and more 'routine' than it once was, justified in the fiction narratives through the networks' pervasive editorializing on the subject in news coverage. The authors also call attention to my own two test cases, describing them in similar terms in spite of their transparently different genres and settings:

> [Fictions are] all framed in official discourse which proclaims that everything is done 'to rid the streets of crime'. Along these lines, the series *Drenaje profundo* [*In the Sewers*] (TV Azteca) presented an 'incorruptible' police force that was dismantling and punishing criminal groups with the 'long arm of the law'. This series was filmed in the facilities of the Federal Preventive Police, letting the audience see the technological and administrative capacity of the police force. (2011: 281)

And again:

> When showing this violence, television productions remove its sense of violation and abuse of rights of third parties. The violence on screen 'is not punished', not questioned, not discussed, it is only answered with more violence. Or even worse, it is justified as part of a historical struggle, as it happened with the series *Cries of Death and Freedom* (Televisa) that was conducted by the Televisa news management and not by the fiction production area of the same company . . . In the 13 chapters, 13 relevant moments of the Independence of Mexico were portrayed, and it was even affirmed that every 'war casualty' is a product of the quest for freedom and peace. This message is fully related to the current situation of insecurity and demagogy on this matter that Mexico lives [*sic*]. Perhaps, due to this situation it was propitious that in its premiere for the first time a spot was transmitted in which Televisa itself 'thanks the Mexican army' for its struggle against drug-trafficking. (2011: 282)

A further but complementary addition to what the survey sees here as an 'erosion of the culture of law' is the rise of series that appeal to popular religion and superstition in order to restore social order for a vulnerable populace that has lost faith in the authorities. These include the aforementioned *The Rose of Guadalupe* (2011: 282).

Now clearly this analysis is reminiscent, in a slightly different register, of Reguillo's thesis, according to which an absence of established legitimacy feeds a punitive spiral of paralegality and repression, not to mention a flight into the supernatural or infernal. Yet it seems to me that the institutional complicity of networks (both Azteca and Televisa) with a government that itself depends in turn on favourable coverage by the media duopoly does not exhaust the meaning of the complex TV texts made and exhibited by those broadcasters. Indeed, Orozco et al.'s brief account of *In the Sewers* suggests that the research team is unfamiliar with the show's labyrinthine plot and slippery political address.

The all-pervasiveness of television, which is attested by IBOPE's survey, matches the ubiquity of violence on and off Mexican screens. But the rise of the series format in an environment dominated until recently by telenovela would seem to be especially significant here, signalling not just a renovation of an archaic offer but also a new demand from an audience that now has access to perhaps more sophisticated foreign fare on pay TV. I would thus suggest that the innovative and successful series of 2010 (*In the Sewers* was the very first series shown by its network; *Cries* was placed at number ten in the whole year, with a rating of 12.9 and share of 20.5) deserve closer and more sympathetic attention for their production, reception and, most importantly, textual detail.

In the Sewers: Production and Reception

> Cuenta la historia de Ulises, un obstinado investigador de una agencia policiaca de elite, especializada en resolver crímenes de diversa índole: asesinatos, desapariciones, accidentes, robos, o emergencias de gran alcance en las que en ocasiones es puesta en peligro la estabilidad de la ciudad más grande del mundo. Es también la historia de una vieja conspiración, y de la ruptura del equilibrio entre dos mundos: uno visible y otro oculto en las entrañas de la ciudad. (Azteca, 2010)

> (The story is about Ulises, a dogged investigator in an elite police force that specializes in solving a wide range of crimes: murders, disappearances, accidents, thefts or large-scale emergencies in which the well-being of the largest city in the world is endangered. It is also the story of an old conspiracy and of a breach in the balance between two worlds: one visible and the other in the bowels of the city.)

The tagline for Azteca's first US-style series (as opposed to traditional indigenous telenovela) is 'No one knows what lies beneath' ('Nadie sabe qué hay abajo'). However the official website, from which I take the teasing synopsis above, is rather predictable. The 'news' section presents the (all-Mexican) project, introduces the cast, and promotes, in turn, the premiere screening and the 'VIP' showing of the final

Figure 12   *In the Sewers* (TV Azteca, 2010)

episode (three lucky winners from the audience effusively recount their gratitude at gaining access to this event). Actors also made themselves available for video-chat with fans. The latter were encouraged by Azteca with some success to vote the show the best 'series' of the year (*In the Sewers* took second place after Cadena 3's *The Aparicio Women* and came in ahead of Televisa's *Women Murderers* at number four) (*20 minutos*, 2010). Yet the series' ideology appears, initially at least, disturbingly similar to Reguillo's account of repressive state violence that is simply reactive to a political vacuum. On the one hand, the site asks 'Who defends street kids?' ('¿Quién defiende a los niños de la calle?', taking up a social theme from episode 3), while on the other it shows the glamorous principles posing with formidably armed, black-masked Federal Police agents as they descend from official helicopters (Figure 12).

Other aspects of the site promote memory management on behalf of a complex narrative that will prove unusually demanding on audiences, especially when double episodes were aired until midnight on a single night, as opposed to the telenovela's reassuringly familiar rhythm of one episode five evenings a week. Thus the characters are presented in helpfully direct ways: Ulises is the protagonist and inspector, Rita a housewife and inspector, Yamel is based underground, Milosz (a mysterious magnate) is bad, Igor (his chemist) is good, and, in a huge spoiler, Diego is a 'young rebel experimental subject in eternal youth' ('joven rebelde experimento de la eterna juventud'). Photo galleries on the site remind viewers how, step-by-step, loose ends link up to form the resolution of the mystery plot. Elsewhere they document action set-pieces or call attention to the distinctive artwork of the series in its sepulchral palette of blue and black and its credit sequence of mysteriously billowing fluids.

Videos include the stylish lightning-cut teaser trailers or offer enigmatic taglines for each character: Rita says 'life is like a missing bullet' ('La vida es como una bala perdida'), Yamel has 'a body aged twenty-seven and a soul aged sixty-five' ('Cuerpo de 27 años, alma de 65'), Diego is 'afraid only of not being afraid of anything' ('Le temo a no temerle a nada'). Offering access behind the scenes (and stressing the series' 'quality' production values), further video shows how a spectacular metro accident from the opening episode was shot in real metro-cars and offers, helpfully, to 'decipher' the show. Such mechanisms are intended to lower the substantial barriers to entry to a fictional world that is very different to that of the telenovelas with which viewers were hitherto familiar on Azteca, a channel which was, as we saw, a lagging rival to Televisa in the traditional fiction stakes. And *In the Sewers* serialized narrative required greater cognitive investment from the audience than either the telenovela genre, with its lumbering slow-paced plots, or the one-off drama, with its briskly told stories that begin again with each episode.

External websites give a broader context to the show's production process. After the press launch, centrist daily *El Universal* noted, unexceptionably, that Azteca was seeking success with the show, its first US-style series, said to be based on veteran procedural franchise *CSI* (CBS, 2000–) (Madrigal, 2010c). In the same article Roberto González and Benjamín Salinas, credited as the series' 'creators', cited rather a documentary on the divers who work in Mexico City's vast and troubled sewage system as their creative inspiration. Film veteran Elizabeth Cervantes (recently a prostitute in Estrada's *Hell*), who plays female lead Rita, claimed to be surprised by the quality of the script and the nature of her character: an upright police officer and single mother who risks her life for the 'social order' and the 'common good'. Later the same paper stressed the national nature of the show, citing another producer who said that, having been 'bombarded' with US product, Mexico was now exporting shows such as his own (*In the Sewers* was bought by multinational MGM) (Arellano M., 2011a). As before, national (even nationalist) TV rhetoric combined with praise for the local forces of law and order: the show shows 'the good side of the police' ('el lado bueno de la policía'). Cervantes, once more, recounted how she was moved when, shooting in an authentic police station, she saw inscribed on the walls the names of officers who had fallen in the struggle against narcos (Madrigal, 2010d).

Other members of the cast tell a different story. One says quite bluntly that the reason for the series' high budget, enormous production and large cast is that it is the project of the son of Ricardo Salinas Pliego (Durand, 2010). The latter, one of the richest men in the world, is the CEO of TV Azteca, as well as many other companies, including telephony operator Iusacell (whose products were prominently placed in the series). The younger Salinas's only previous project had been a bizarre Nordic mythology-themed quiz show. In collaboration once more with buddy González, he went on to make a further series, with the armed forces: *The Female Lieutenant* (*La teniente*) (Arellano M., 2011b).

In spite of this nepotism and apparent collusion with authorities whose reputation in Mexico is at best mixed, *In the Sewers* proved a critical success. Álvaro Cueva, the best-known and most prolific journalist in the field of television fiction, wrote a rave review in his newspaper column, 'The Well of Repressed Desires' ('El pozo de los deseos reprimidos', 2011). Cueva judges that this first real series from Azteca is infinitely superior to most local production, well up to US standards. He praises the suspense of the action (again a first for Mexico) and the new image of Mexico City it shows (with locations like the metro and sewers far from the picturesque quarters of Coyoacán, Roma or Condesa that normally appear on TV). Oddly, he calls this image 'attractive' and (anticipating international sales) looks forward to foreigners' positive reactions to the series. The direction of actors and action, the art design and special effects are all internationally competitive. And this original and modern story (here Cuevas cites approvingly the frequent appearance of those mobile phones) has the virtue of not being bought in Bogotá or Buenos Aires. His only concern is the scheduling: how will Azteca 7's viewers, unused to local production, cope with two premiered episodes each Monday at 10 p.m.?

Viewers' responses did indeed seem mixed. Although, as we saw, committed fans made sure *In the Sewers* came second in the votes for best series of the year, more casual viewers were hostile. In the weeks after the show bowed, Network 54, an aggregator of press material and fan forums, carried many negative comments, which ironically enough centred on some of the perceived strengths of the series (Network 54, 2010). Thus forumers attacked the action sequences (the helicopters and metro accident) as poorly done and the realistic use of swearwords (no doubt seen by the producers as 'modern') as inappropriate or offensive. One claimed that the series was just an ode to the Salinas Group of companies with its highlighting of Iusacell, the Azteca soccer stadium (not in fact owned by the TV channel) and a fictional reporter whose microphone carries the TV channel's logo. Scheduling proved a moot point too. One forumer says that the best thing about the show is that it is only on once a week; while another watches *In the Sewers* on Mondays, but then switches over to catch the immediate retransmission of the hard-core telenovela that plays against Azteca's series at the same time. Another fan complains that, after endless promos of the show, the first episode actually bowed fifteen minutes late (thus no doubt sabotaging the channel-switching strategies of those flexible viewers whose tastes embraced both newly dark series and old-fashioned 'pink' serials).

Fans seem unconcerned by the level of violence in *In the Sewers*, which is surely much higher than the telenovelas that Azteca viewers would have come to expect, even in a 10 p.m. slot when viewing figures start to slide and even for the many Mexicans who now watch TV in bed. Given that ratings were respectable but not remarkable (six or seven is par for the course for the channel), it seems likely that Azteca was here aiming for the male and upmarket demographic normally neglected by rival Televisa (*Cries of Death and Freedom* was of course a special case) and who would respond to innovations in format that they may well have become familiar with on pay TV. Certainly *In the Sewers* product placements coincide with the interests of the 'opinion formers' of Generation Y, whose tastes in, say, telephony are assiduously courted by advertisers.

We can now go on to offer a close content analysis of *In the Sewers*. This will examine the linked hypotheses of the rise of extramuros paralegality and the erosion of the culture of law that Reguillo and Orozco et al. see in that routine spectacularization of violence(s) that *In the Sewers* would appear to stage with such conspicuous expertise.

In the Sewers: Close Reading

An extreme close-up of a drain and dripping tap. In a public bathroom, a bald, bearded man adjusts what appears to be a bomb in a briefcase. Spotted on blurry black and white close-circuit TV, he enters the subway, pursued by the police. Taking a train, he positions himself next to a child in the car. Suddenly he is shot by a police officer, and his own gun goes off, killing the driver and sending the train careering out of control. We cut to a station where an anonymous traveller is reading the newspaper: the headline refers to 'the Milosz Laboratory'. Suddenly the screen, with a crash, flares to white and the pulsing fluids of the credits begin.

This expert action sequence, the first scene of the first episode of *In the Sewers*, clearly serves its narrative function as a hook or tease, drawing in the audience from the start. Technically its feature-film production values and look, evocative (and locally recognizable) authentic locations, nervous hand-held camerawork and quick-cutting style reinforce the visceral charge of the scene. Shots of maimed bodies after the crash (or explosion, it is not clear which) are reminiscent of the London Underground bombings of 2005 (Mexico has not suffered such an outrage). Surely we could not be closer to Reguillo's anomalous 'exteriority' of violence than here? And the rest of the episode will continue this evocation of a (literal) underworld (subway and sewer system) which is also a metaphorical kingdom of death.

Thus returning to the station, emblematically named Ulises (a stern Juan Pablo Medina) sets off on an unwilling voyage: pursuing a man into the subway, he careens down a pipe into the vast sewer tunnel. Wounded and unconscious, he awakes bound and gagged in a grimy, white-tiled room, where he is drugged and fed by a mysterious young dreadlocked woman (Yamel will prove to be one of the 'miraculous' underground dwellers). The episode ends with Ulises' partner Rita taking a helicopter to the site where he was lost, as magnate Milosz orders the floodgates opened to drown the police officer and keep the secrets of the deep. In this equally expert catch or tag, Ulises disappears under the roaring waters.

Distant (although troublingly close to the city surface), exceptional (although a rarely considered part of everyday life), the sewer with its evocatively named 'black waters' ('aguas negras' means 'raw sewage') is Reguillo's Kingdom of Hades, with the mysterious Milosz as omnipotent governor. This space (fictional, actual) would be easy to read in psychic terms as the repressed or abject element which threatens to return with unexpected violence. In episode 2, the now released, but traumatized Ulises, sexily taking a shower with his girlfriend, will suffer fantasy flashbacks evoked by the running water and open plughole. It seems likely that such 'spectacularization' (never before seen in Mexican TV fiction) is likely to heighten a troubled and troubling perception of (ill-defined and anomalous) violence but not increased collective reflection on the topic. To use Reguillo's three dimensions, violence is here 'imposed' (whether by terrorists, capitalists or police), but, in accordance with the mystery genre, in which clues must be scattered through a full twenty episodes, it is (initially at least) deprived of rationality and causality, inexplicable and even supernatural: soon, we learn, the little girl on the metro and the young woman who tended to Ulises have remained frozen in time for some thirty years.

This spectacular and inexplicable violence manifests in the series as Reguillo's twin themes of the dissolution of social bonds and increased real-time access to violent events that appear to have no ordering 'narrative'. Thus episode hooks (seeking to lure young male viewers away from Televisa's reassuringly romantic telenovela) suggest a social breakdown in symbolically charged spaces: a soccer player, having injected himself with green serum, collapses in the stadium, flesh boiling beneath the skin (episode 2); a homeless man, searching a rubbish dump, comes across a pair of boots, with the severed feet still inside them (episode 3); a wealthy businessman is found dead in his drained swimming pool, his body teaming with rats (episode 4). Later episodes stage set-pieces of violence in the boxing ring (a fighter attacks the press and audience), a supermarket (a mother disappears in a blackout), and a fancy restaurant (a father leaves his family at the table to shoot himself in the mouth in the bathroom). Clearly there is (in one of Reguillo's 'keys' once more) an increase in the structural and subjective precariousness that pervades everyday life. Moreover (as in the real world once more), real-time access to violent events is shown in the show through the recurring figure of the Azteca TV 'journalist' (she insists she is not a reporter), who is ambiguously allied with the Federal Police officers.

Many of the procedural cases of the week refer to spectacular narco-violences: bulldozers dig up victims' bodies from under a tree; an unexpected interlude has Ulises go undercover as a recovering addict in a kind of rehab-cum-training camp; or again, he poses as a photographer at the lavish *quinceañera* party (all purple and green) of a mob boss's daughter. But violent imposition would also appear to come from the government: the most disturbing hook shows the massacre of inhabitants of a shanty town by uniformed gunmen who look (the sole survivor tells Ulises) just like you. Extra-muros locations, apparently appropriate to such horror, include the real-life 'Island of Dolls' in touristic Xochimilco, where a child discovers an actual severed head hanging from the trees amongst the toy body parts. As in Reguillo's case studies, individual stories would seem to be collapsed within narratives of narco-violences, wholly anomalous and idiosyncratic border crossings between the threatened land of the living and the irruptive realm of the dead. In another apparently exploitative plotline (referring to the most watched event of recent Mexican media history), crowds are shown desperately waiting in line for a flu vaccine that will prove to have deadly side effects.

However, in TV fiction as in ethnographic life stories, such narrative rules and mechanisms are 'transcoded', reading differently in different contexts. I would thus suggest that *In the Sewers*, for all its spectacular set-pieces, proposes that there are not one but many violences and that they deserve (as Reguillo recommends) to be dragged into the light of social, historical and political practices. Thus in spite of its title we can see from the plot summary above that, after the first dramatic (and expensive) episode, little time is actually spent in the sewers, with the Federal Police concentrating, in traditional procedural style, on over-ground crimes which are more terrestrial than infernal. The opening metro bombing is no inexplicable act of terror, but rather the revenge of a worker whose son was injured and fired by the authorities (when a manager claims 'We are all suffering from the [financial] crisis', Rita replies sardonically, 'Some more than others').

In such cases of the week, the series shows its politically progressive hand: Rita notes that a young lesbian confined by her rich parents to an asylum was 'perfectly normal: she just liked other women'; the man whose boots (and feet) were found on the dump (emblematically named 'Cristos') was a radical who gave up his job to care for street kids in a ruinous church (another of the series' evocative urban locations); the mute special-needs man who, it turns out, kidnapped the woman from the supermarket, was mutilated by his own abusive mother. It is not for nothing that Ulises' girlfriend is a therapist, thus providing access to damaged souls like the burns victim who will be abducted by organ traffickers at a singles bar. In the diverse and perverse Mexico City of the series (from abandoned buildings to the handsome Roma or Condesa *colonias* familiar from telenovelas), there are thus many distinct frontiers of violence and they are shown to have (psychic or more commonly social) intentions and reasons. Strikingly, such dramas are not attributed in moralizing style to lack of traditional values or family breakdown: feisty Rita is a devoted single parent; noble, troubled Ulises is childless and unmarried; and his girlfriend is the daughter of Milosz, the old-school patriarch who is the villain of the piece.

The frame tale of the series, slowly developing, confirms this historicizing reading. The underground group members are not perpetrators but victims. As survivors of Milosz's medical experiment, their eternal youth is bought at the cost of addiction to the green serum (an allusion to the ravages of heroin and AIDS is clear here). And halfway through the series there is an unsettling leap into flashback. Episode 9 begins with documentary footage of student protest in 1968. In what is clearly a reference to the Tlatelolco massacre, we see Yamel attempting to flee the bloody square, only to be kidnapped and brutalized with many others by the authorities in the sewers. Escaping to the surface in the next episode, having 'disappeared' for three years, the student radical group find that their families are not anxious to take them back in a time of dirty war. Finally they find seclusion underground once more, cared for this time by ethical scientist (and foil of one-time friend Milosz) Igor.

Surely this radical plot-turn (familiar characters of the present day are neglected for two full hours) was unexpected to viewers who tuned in for a genre piece (indeed, some expected the show to be about vampires). Hidden, but unchanged, old, but apparently youthful, the underground people are transparent metaphors for a historical trauma that Mexico has struggled so long to work through. And their message is clearly that a repressive political past persists into the present, with potentially harrowing effects.

While the plot spirals into conspiracy theories (even Milosz, the archetypal Mexican magnate, is subject to a US businessman who will finally depose him), the show performs an analysis of Mexico's past that parallels Reguillo's account of the present. It is not the narcos but the authoritarian PRI regime that enforces 'paralegal' violence; and the loss of faith in legality (the idealistic students' revolt) is clearly justified within the world of the show. That paralegal regime is contrasted with a more democratic polity (one ex-guerrilla is now shown to be a law-abiding deputy). But even that polity is not without its flaws: the massacre of shanty dwellers was ordered by a corrupt junior politician in league with real-estate developers.

In spite of Orozco's complaints about the series, then, the Federal Police are never shown to use violence here, unless it is absolutely necessary (Rita shoots dead another would-be metro bomber). The series is (like its actors in interview) clearly supportive of the Federal Police in their duties; but it does not propose force as a universal panacea. Much less does it (in Reguillo's terms) deliver a 'redoubled dose' of punitive violence that will provoke a spiral. *In the Sewers* seeks rather, within its evident industrial and generic restrictions, to fill the perceived void in the established order by generating its own symbols and set-pieces (the underground heroes and their exploits). While the reliance of the above ground *mise-en-scène* on military uniforms, locations and hardware (the constant shots of the principals supported by black-masked extras) may seem troublingly normative or authoritarian, the show's labyrinthine narrative resists reductive explanations. And the attractive but harassed officers are more than matched by the eternally young sexy student rebels.

The series ends, disconcertingly and inconclusively, with the band of now sickly sewer-dwellers, relocated to a shanty town on a hill high above the city, looking out over the distant megalopolis as they wait for supplies of the serum to run out. It is an ending that stresses the wounds of history and rejects the retreat into the supernatural so common in other Mexican series. The underground monsters have been humanized (at a cost), led out of the dark to take up their position, however marginal, in the world. It is the same task that Reguillo recommended to the scholar of violences.

Cries of Death and Freedom: Production and Reception

> La historia de hombres y mujeres que cambiaron nuestra historia. Desde los albores de la Independencia con el movimiento de Miguel Hidalgo hasta su consumación por Agustín de Iturbide. La más ambiciosa producción de Televisa que retrata, en cada uno de sus trece momentos, el sinuoso camino de la Independencia de México. (DVD blurb)

> (The story of men and women who changed our history. From the dawn of Independence with Miguel Hidalgo's movement to its completion with Agustín de Iturbide. Televisa's most ambitious production portrays, in thirteen historical moments, Mexico's tortuous path to Independence.)

The tagline for Televisa's most prestigious fiction production is: 'The series where history counts' ('La serie donde la historia cuenta' [Figure 13]). Yet the promotional materials give a necessarily mixed account of the nature of that history and what it counts for. Extras on the DVD promise revelations from behind the scenes ('Detrás de las cámaras'). Executive producer Leopoldo Gómez, Vice-President of the company's news division, recounts that the project was initially for fifty-two short pieces on Mexican history for the Bicentennial and Centennial year (only one, on Zapata, was shot). Subsequently the team chose to narrow their focus and extend their length to thirteen thirty-minute episodes, shown at 10 p.m. from Monday to Friday and climaxing on 16 September, Independence Day (because of the ratings success, mentioned earlier, the first five episodes were rapidly repeated in a 'marathon' session). As dominant (albeit controversial) broadcaster, then,

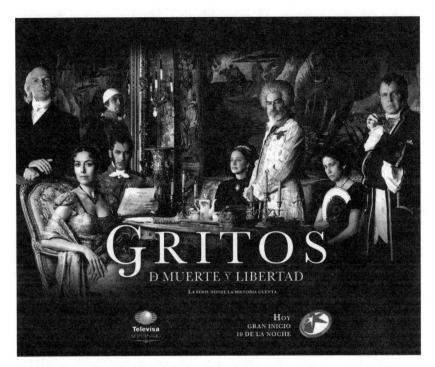

Figure 13 *Cries of Death and Freedom* (Televisa, 2010)

Televisa attempted to keep the calendar for a divided nation. And, uniquely, alloting responsibility for a drama series to the news division raised expectations of barely mediated actuality: Gómez cites his team's experience in dealing with current events as a qualification for the project, in spite of the lengthy and extensive tradition of Televisa's fiction units. The fact that Leopoldo's brother Bernardo was given a co-credit as Executive Producer may also have helped midwife the channel's most ambitious project: Bernardo is Executive Vice-President of the whole Televisa Group, and the right-hand man of its CEO, billionaire scion Emilio Azcárraga Jean.

Of the two directors, Gerardo Tort makes a fine distinction: the show aims not for 'veracity' but 'verisimilitude' (the final titles will also say that the production team took 'creative liberties' with historical fact for which they alone are responsible). The diction of the dialogue will thus be appropriate, yet accessible, not sounding as if it were spoken 'yesterday'. Likewise the music (curated by Lynn Fainchtein, of *Amores perros* fame, and composed by the Argentine scorers of *The Aparicio Women*) keeps a delicate balance between current and period styles.

On the other hand, Mafer Suárez, the series' second director, cites national pride here: the production values of *Cries* are 'up to the level' of any series in world television. The DVD 'making of' goes on to offer, as is common in such prestige projects, a blizzard of statistics as proof of quality (a characteristic which, we remember, was the theme of OBITEL's survey of Ibero-American TV fiction for 2010). The wardrobe department thus made 8,000 costumes, all historically sourced and realistically distressed, while the special effects provided 4,000 rounds of gunfire. Suggesting that this series transcends the medium for which it was made and shown, we are told that the distinguished cast boasts stars from film as well as television (Daniel Giménez Cacho plays first Emperor Iturbide; Diego Luna first President Victoria) and, ecumenically, actors from both inside and outside the Televisa family. Such unusual factors of production are held to bolster the legitimacy of the *Cries'* much debated re-creation of the past, just as the high production values of *In the Sewers* were intended to uphold that series' polemical depiction of the present.

While attention is paid to state-of-the-art digital effects (the impressively realized brig ['bergantín'] in which Iturbide returns to Mexico; the innumerable cadavers at the battle of Monte de las Cruces, laid out beneath the wings of circling, digital vultures), we are also treated to a close account of the series' use of gory physical modelling – of fake mutilated bodies and even viscera strewn on the ground below. Extreme violence is thus oddly juxtaposed with the craft and refinement of the heritage genre: finely embroidered waistcoats and ornate historical locations, meticulously 'dressed' by the set designers. Indeed, as the series' title suggests, death would appear to take precedence over freedom in this narrative of what counts as national history. This contradiction could also be read in terms of gender address. *Cries* offered women viewers an exquisite version of the visual pleasures in costume and décor traditionally provided by the sub-genre of historical or 'bodice-ripping' telenovela, even as it gave male spectators the blood and guts of the war movie, rarely recreated on television (we have seen that, according to OBITEL, the series achieved an unprecedented share of men amongst its audience). Historical consultant Ursula Camba (granted a Ph.D. from the Colegio de México) also stresses the physical embodiment of story or history here: the great men and women were contradictory figures who 'sweated' and quarrelled with one another. The War of Independence was, she says, a fight amongst friends and brothers, as well as against the colonial oppressors.

As might be expected, press coverage was yet more contradictory than these promotional materials. Centrist daily *El Universal* carried reverent interviews with the actors that reinforced the producers' and directors' line. Thus Giménez Cacho was cited as saying that his Iturbide was not made of bronze but was rather a complex character; and that history could now be rethought without the ideological charge of previous TV productions made under the PRI (Silva G., 2010). Cultural quality and political impartiality are here made to join hands. Meanwhile movie actors Julio Bracho and Emilio Echevarría, who play General Allende and the Viceroy Iturrigaray respectively, were also quoted as praising the 'human' nature of their characters (the first was a womanizer, the second humbled when, stripped of his wigs and finery, he was imprisoned by his enemies). Enhancing the pedagogical prestige of the show, Bracho further claims that he learned new things about Mexican history from a production that 'sticks close' to reality ('apegada a la realidad') (*El Universal*, 2010a).

The conflict between nationalist legend and documented history was strongest, however, in perhaps the series' bloodiest reconstruction: the massacre of Royalists at the granary or Alhóndiga in Guanajuato by Hidalgo's informal troops. When viewers complained about the absence of El Pípila, a legendary hero of the conflict prominent in a previous hagiographic version by Televisa, the series' historical consultant replied that the figure (commemorated in a monolithic statue in the city) was merely a foundational myth, although he reveals much about the collective imaginary of Mexico (*El Universal*, 2010b).

An opinion piece after the full series had been aired proved equally disabused. In an article entitled 'Telenovela-ing Independence', Andrés Ramírez (2010) praised the actors, screenwriters and directors for avoiding cliché and the costume and production designers for their specialist skills. But he also noted the insistent marketing of the series in Televisa's promos, talk shows and even news bulletins; and the prominence of the credits of the Gómez brothers, the strong men of the network's big boss. He suggests that the show did indeed avoid falling into political interpretations, while telling the story from today's viewpoint ('la mirada de hoy'). Yet the gaps in the structure of the story and the brevity of the series' thirty-minute episodes (an uncommon format in Mexico) were combined with occasional excesses reminiscent of the channel's normal house style: 'telenovelesque' overly dramatic music and contrived dialogues. The journalist ends with a question he himself cannot answer: how do you make an epic without making it epic? Old certainties, of style or content, thus no longer hold when it comes to replaying familiar national narratives in a new and unsettling context.

Unsurprisingly, the leftist *La Jornada* is much more scathing, reading *Cries* as complicit with the PAN government's vision of the past. While a news report of the series' press launch repeats the producers' line that the show will reveal heroes 'as they really were' (Caballero, 2010), an interview with a historian who did not provide consultancy for the series is scathing. Ricardo Gamboa of the UNAM is quoted as complaining of the excessive violence of the series, focusing on the scene of the massacre in the Alhóndiga (Olivares Alonso, 2010). While acknowledging the many victims of the rebels, Gamboa claims that the historical event is presented here as resulting from the ignorance of the masses and is shown in an exaggerated manner, far from what it really was. Coinciding with sociologist Reguillo, he says that violence has causes and explanations and that here it is wholly lacking in context. The cause of this error, for Gamboa, is presentism: historical figures are depicted as our contemporaries, a technique which, he claims, oddly perhaps, reinforces the 'bronze' or official history of goodies and baddies.

The verdict of the expert is reinforced by a virulent opinion piece from regular columnist Luis Javier Garrido (2010), run under the headline 'Dishonour' ('La deshonra'). Here, Garrido takes Televisa's programming to be co-extensive with a PAN national government that is oligarchical and anti-national and took office only through electoral fraud (the 2006 elections were contested). *Cries*, dismissively referred to as a 'telenovela', is for Garrido an authentic insult to the Mexican people. Under cover of depicting contradictory characters, it presents historical figures who wanted to change the power structure (Hidalgo, Morelos, Guerrero) as cowards, lacking in ideas, and denying the people their right to rise up against their oppressors. Curiously, then, presentism is said to be both rightist and leftist in the same newspaper. By showing the past in terms of the present, the series may reinforce official liberal history, contributing to the cult of popular heroes. Alternatively, it may undermine that history, depicting the people's representatives as all too fallible.

As we have seen, the role of violence (or, more properly, 'violences') is crucial here. Were the excesses of the Independence struggle exceptional and external, an inexplicable anomaly more at home in Reguillo's Kingdom of the Dead than in any recognizable nineteenth-century Mexico? Or were they merely part of a habitual presence in the everyday world, albeit with their own specific forms of intentionality and rationality? For Orozco, we remember, every 'war casualty' in *Cries* is presented as an inevitable product of the quest for freedom and peace, a message supposedly related to the situation of insecurity and demagogy that Mexico is currently living through. Is it the case, then, that the series is a simple apology for government repression, in the past as in the present? We can now attempt an answer to these questions through a close reading of *Cries of Death and Freedom*, a unique fiction whose textual detail reduces reduction to either the epic or melodramatic modes that are invoked by its critics and defenders alike.

Cries of Death and Freedom: Close Reading

An expressionistic montage of tolling bells above and surging crowds in streets below, all shot with a dizzying camera. We cut to an unestablished underground location: a dark, infernal cell where a half-naked prisoner, wild-bearded and crazy, stammers to a new arrival, who is more modest in dress and performance style: 'Once you cross that door you are no longer anything' ('Una vez que cruzas esa puerta, ya no eres nada'). His doom-laden voice is one of a piece with the swelling orchestral soundtrack. We cut to the opening credits.

The first scene of the first episode of *Cries* (as surely as that in *In the Sewers*) plays the part of a hook or tease, attempting to reel in the reluctant viewer to a rare historical series on Televisa's self-styled mass audience 'Channel of the Stars'. Jailed lawyer Francisco Azcárate (showily played by Miguel Rodarte, soon to be baring his chest once more as the narco star of *Saving Private Pérez*) is only the first of the insurgent heroes reduced to the status of bare life: wild men barely surviving in the prisons and jungles of colonial Mexico. But the sequence also signals the series' status as a history of and through affect, communicating, as its producers and consultants intended, a sense of the intense bodily experience of time past.

Yet emotion (immediate, embodied) is combined unstably from the start with cognition (distanced, dispassionate). Lengthy titles inform us of the complex back-story: after the Napoleonic invasion of Spain, a small group of *criollos* (amongst them Azcárate) attempt to persuade the Viceroy to create an autonomous government. In disorientating flashback, we see the now bewigged and suited Azcárate making a reasoned argument to a sneering audience of Spaniards (effete aristocrats and clerics): now there is no legitimate king, he proclaims, the authority to propose a new provisional order must come from the people. In extended and handsomely dressed interior sequences, the somewhat timid proponents of autonomy, precursors of the more martial heroes of independence, voice their fears of reprisal and hopes for the Viceroy's support, while foppish Peninsular courtiers make clear their disapproval. Soon Emilio Echevarría's ineffectual Viceroy will himself be shut inside his lavish chambers, while the three noble lawyers are thrown into jail, where, bleeding and vomiting, they are tortured by dark-robed monks. Here the cinematography breaks into what will prove to be a typical technique for such moments: slow motion and superimposition of images signal the special status of violence in which time freezes and discrete episodes bleed together.

The final titles inform us that Mexicans' early quest for autonomy led merely to a *coup d'état* (the Spaniard Bataller, one of the few figures to recur in a number of episodes, is made to blow out a candle to signal the extinguishing of hope); but that others were to take up the cause of freedom. The problem is that this episode (like so many in the series) has an obscure or uncertain conclusion: we are told only that two of the three imprisoned *criollo*s died in mysterious circumstances.

Spectacular violence is of course inflicted here by the repressive colonial regime, and is thus, so far, hardly deprived of rationality and causality. Yet the prisons of the Inquisition, which feature in a number of episodes, are a Kingdom of Hades whose monarch is, during the Peninsular Wars, confusingly unclear. (Later when Hidalgo gives the eponymous cry or 'Grito' of Independence, it includes support for the ousted Spanish king, Fernando VII.) In the second episode, however, there is an unambiguous heroine. Josefa Domínguez conspires with insurgent leaders until her husband, the Corregidor of Querétaro, confines her to their home. In spite of the hagiographic treatment applied uniquely to female figures in the series (it will recur in episode nine with Leona Vicario), the grand narrative of history is here replaced by a micro-narrative of domesticity: Josefa is reduced to stamping on the floor to alert her allies to the discovery of their conspiracy. More interestingly perhaps (and as in *In the Sewers*) the family setting signals a dissolution of social bonds and an increase in structural and subjective precariousness that will come to pervade everyday life, a situation with clear implications for the present day.

Thus in episode three, the priest-rebel Hidalgo sups placidly with bourgeois hosts in Dolores, before instructing his troops to enter their house and steal their treasure. And the entire episode, including the climactic 'Grito', takes place over the night of 15–16 September and is shot in unnervingly thick shadow, inside and out. Surely emancipation has never looked so saturnine. The controversial fourth episode, on the massacre at Guanajuato, is yet more ambivalent. Spaniards and Royalists take refuge in the granary as Hidalgo's rag-tag rebels approach. Our point of view is that of the wealthy *criollo* family of Alamáns, who presciently refuse to leave their comfortable home.

The looting and slaughter in the Alhóndiga (bloodily convincing and extended) is thus not only prefaced by action shots of surging, anonymous peasants, wielding pitchforks and torches (no heroic Pípila here), but also heralded by shots and screams heard through the shuttered windows of the threatened domestic space. What Reguillo calls 'set-pieces' ('escenificaciones') of violence, elaborately staged and executed, are thus supplemented by more idiosyncratic and troubling border crossings between the land of the living and of the dead: the Alamáns send out from their barricaded home a faithful servant who fails to return; and they take in a bloody victim who is laid to rest on their richly brocaded sofa.

Hence, while the titles to each episode confidently suggest that chronology (from 1808 to 1824) is also teleology (from the 'first dream' of autonomy to the birth of the Republic), the script and *mise-en-scène* of the series are saying something quite different. Indeed, as *El Universal* remarked, flagrant gaps and discontinuities make the grand narrative unusually incoherent to those without specialist knowledge of the historical sources. Of course, any story of revolution will turn on newly created structures of legitimacy and authority that may prove perilous. My point is rather that *Cries* points surprisingly often to the absence of a meaningful, collective project, precisely the situation that for Reguillo gives rise, in the very different circumstances of the present, to narco 'paralegality'. Thus the frankly unsympathetic Hidalgo of episode three (who proclaims 'No war is won without shedding blood' ['No hay guerra que no se gane sin sangre']) is replaced by the suddenly repentant Hidalgo of episode five, who, fearing further massacres, refuses to march on Mexico City (here it is his ally and rival Allende who exclaims 'Wars are won with blood'). The fierce priest now kindly ministers to the graphically mutilated casualties left on the digitally supplemented battlefield.

In later episodes, the series returns obsessively to the bare life of the condemned man, first glimpsed in the opening episode. Two instalments (six and eight) are wholly devoted to the confinement and execution of hero-priests Hidalgo and Morelos, culminating in lengthy shots of their bullet-riddled bodies. A shaky POV shot even invites viewers to share the perspective of the former's dying moment, as he clutches a crucifix in his bloody fist. This spectacle of violence is at best dispiriting and at worst confusing. In episode ten, the Royalist bigwigs (including the cruel fey fop Bataller) are suddenly themselves in favour of independence, shocked as they are by Spain's new liberal Constitution; and by episode eleven matted-haired wild man Vicente Guerrero has left his lengthy jungle campaign to join forces with his preening former adversary, Iturbide.

It is useful here to appeal once more to Reguillo's 'dimensions' of 'violences'. *Cries* glories troublingly in imposition, showing with minute care the infliction of damage on self and others in what it presents as a civil war (remarkably, and somewhat confusingly, there is no difference in the accents employed by actors playing Spaniards and Mexicans). But the rationality of such damage (its logics and objectives) remains unclear (for example, is independence an enlightened or a conservative project?). The series is thus obliged to appeal to explanatory 'keys' that go beyond logical hypothesis or deduction, most evidently the recurrent stress on the body in its obdurate travail.

The problem is that such a key, while offering that emotive link so prized by the producers, cannot provide a source of legitimacy in politics or, indeed, ethics. The checkered careers of the national heroes – discontinuous and fragmented as they are presented here – are almost as brutalized and brutalizing as the biographies of Reguillo's young narcos. While the series is clear enough about its gender politics (devoting entire episodes to two unambiguous heroines who survive the turmoil unscathed), its attitude to the better-known male insurgents – newly 'humanized' and often destined for violent ends – is, as we have seen, slippery enough to enrage conservatives and liberals alike.

The final episode sees Giménez Cacho's vain ex-Emperor Iturbide summarily executed for the crime of returning to his native land from exile. Diego Luna's Guadalupe Victoria, the last of the series' wild men to make the journey from the jungle to the capital, confronts himself warily in a mirror, now dressed in the finery of the first President of the Republic. For once the final titles are modest, claiming only that Mexico was now beginning to tread paths of freedom that would not always prove smooth.

Far, then, from legitimizing the use of violence by the state and the army as the only strategy to obtain peace (the presentist alibi that Orozco attributed to Televisa's series), *Cries* stages rather a hesitant and self-reflexive representation of national history even as it reconstructs at great expense the salons and battlefields of the period. It encourages audiences (perhaps especially those rare upper middle-class viewers who favoured the show) to meditate on the centrality of an often inexplicable savagery to the origins of that state and that army. In spite of its overt patriotic ambitions, then, the textual detail of the series would suggest (with Reguillo) that violence is not to be exiled to a savage and distant heterotopia, that that other barbarous space is here and now and at the very roots of modern Mexico.

Paralegal Rebels

I have argued that my two case studies, apparently so different, are curiously complementary, criss-crossing the border as they do between over- and under-worlds. The contemporary show thus goes back to a dark moment of recent history (Tlatelolco and its consequences) and the costume drama proves surprisingly sombre even as it celebrates the Bicentennial of Independence, making us think about the role of violence or 'violences' in the creation of the current Republic.

Reguillo's terms are essential here for an analytical approach to such material which, as yet, has only received superficial and contradictory journalistic appraisal. The three 'dimensions' (of imposition, logics and causality); the two trends (the dissolution of social bonds and increased access to violent events that appear to have no ordering 'narrative'); and the three 'keys' (the erosion of the future; the increase in precariousness; and the loss of legitimacy), all are clearly demonstrated in their different ways by the two series. Most evident, however, in these high-budget prestige productions is the 'spectacularization' of violence, which clearly stems from a crisis in legitimation of the established order, whether that order is the PRI government that persecutes *In the Sewers* young students or the colonial or, indeed, revolutionary forces that *Cries* shows to wreak such havoc in their different ways on daily life in colonial Mexico. Reguillo's 'Fredi', the young criminal who crossed so many borders, is thus joined by his comrades in arms, the charismatic rebels in the two TV series.

In both cases, however, violence is 'transcoded', reading differently in the different contexts of televisual genres (action and heritage). Yet both series reject (with Reguillo once more) the scapegoating of the supposed lack of traditional values or family breakdown as the origin for the violence depicted so professionally. And they clearly show through their well-crafted 'stagings' or 'set-pieces' how violence can fill the void in the established order and generate its own symbols. Indeed, the back-story of *In the Sewers* (the 'eternal life syndrome') is an extreme example of a compelling and internally coherent yet frankly bizarre response to current conditions of insecurity.

'Paralegality' is shown here through the time-honoured dramatic device of poetic justice: finally, one of the magnate's victims will kill him by injecting him with the same serum with which he had experimented on her and her underground companions. The hesitant and discontinuous revolutionary struggle is also presented in *Cries* as an exercise in paralegality when the established order was breaking down, whether that paralegality is argued in the courts, the battlefields or, most bloodily, in the massacre of the Alhóndiga. The rebel heroes of both series engage in a constant struggle for re-inscription of their selves in an other-space that does not belong to them: the equally troubling Mexicos of the nineteenth and twenty-first centuries.

But I have also argued that these shows only find their full meaning within the TV environment of 2010, the year in which they were broadcast. Social change joined forces with changes in media consumption to produce innovations in formats that went beyond the traditional telenovela and seemed more in tune with key 'Generation Y' taste-makers. OBITEL's stress on 'quality' and 'transmedia' are vital here, as are producers' successful attempts to widen the demographic profile of the audience beyond older women of medium to low social status. Although 'quality' is identified in Mexico with educational programming (thus excluding by definition the generalist broadcasters I have focused on here), I would argue that TV pedagogy should be expanded to include the treatments of past and present addressed here in these two entertaining, but complex and ambivalent, fictions.

Close analysis of them reveals that, in spite of superficial appearances, they do not legitimize government actions or make widespread violence seem natural. Nor is violence unpunished or unquestioned, or answered only with more violence. The noble (too noble?) police officer Ulises never responds violently even when he learns the identity of the villain responsible for the deaths of his parents; the saturnine Hidalgo, suddenly repentant, pulls back from bloodshed even at the cost of losing the campaign against the Spanish. Messy, confusing and distressingly realistic on screen, violence is by no means justified as part of a historical struggle by a series which seems at ease only in praising the domesticated heroines of an insecure era. Nor does the 'erosion of the culture of law' inevitable in a revolutionary process lead to an appeal to popular religion and superstition: Hidalgo clutches a crucifix at the moment of execution but there is, of course, no miraculous intercession of the kind we find in popular series like *La rosa de Guadalupe*. The absence of established legitimacy is here a cause of reflection and concern, not a justification for murder.

Even professional TV critics sometimes seem unfamiliar with the detail of the texts they treat (and television studies, unlike cinema, raises an intractable practical problem of the sheer extensiveness of the primary material). It would thus appear to be the case, as *In the*

Sewers' tagline puts it, that 'No one knows what lies beneath'. Or to use the title of one review of *In the Sewers*, such television fiction is a 'well of repressed desires'. It seems unlikely that struggling Azteca knew or cared that their new action series, made by the son of the network's boss, would focus so closely on Tlatelolco, still a festering sore for many Mexicans; or that staid Televisa would have expected their heritage series to be quite so ambivalent and controversial. Indeed, *In the Sewers* showed that unusual spaces like the metro and sewers might be less disturbing than the more familiar and scenic Mexico City locations of Coyoacán, Roma or Condesa, when the latter are shot through with organized crime, conspiratorial business-men and subterranean dwellers who haunt the picturesque parks. It seems possible that national pride, which producers and critics alike invoked in the case of both series, might also be channelled through a questioning, rather than a celebration, of Mexico City and Mexican history. Certainly both series can be read in ways that are politically progressive.

The tagline of *Cries*, we remember, was 'the series where history counts'. But aiming not for 'veracity' but 'verisimilitude', the show acknowledged the necessary difficulties in representing historical events in a fiction format. In both series, high production values (a sign of 'quality') are oddly juxtaposed with extreme violence in a way that is surely intended to attract a wide and varied audience. Simi-larly, the complexity of characters in both shows (police officers who are troubled as well as noble; revolutionary heroes who are no longer 'made of bronze') render their 'ideological charge' ambivalent.

Yet the experience of watching the series at their full length makes it difficult to see them as mere apologies for government repression, whether in the past or in the present. This ambivalence is partly because *In the Sewers* and *Cries* stage histories through affect, with obscure or uncertain conclusions far from the confident predictions of the erstwhile grand narratives. Social bonds are shown to be fragile, subjective boundaries precarious and everyday life insecure. But if there is an absence of a meaningful, collective project (police and revo-lutionaries alike are beset by doubt), it is not clear that 'No war is won without shedding blood'. Hidalgo repents and Ulises becomes a care-giver – cradling his dying father in his arms in the last episode.

The spectacle of violence is thus dispiriting as well as (intermit-tently) exhilarating and the recurrent stress on the body (like the emphasis on affect) is politically and ethically confused. What both series reveal, however, is that, in spite of their increasing spectacular-ization, TV histories of violence make for surprisingly complex and self-aware national narratives in a contemporary Mexican context.

Jump Cut 5

The Prize (*El premio*, Paula Markovitch, 2011),
Windows to the Sea (*Ventanas al mar*, Jesús Mario
Lozano, 2012)

The Guadalajara International Film Festival is perhaps the most important in Latin America. With a wide selection of features, it is an invaluable weathervane for trends in the region. Yet there remains a status gap between an institution like the festival and distribution in the US and Europe, which results in important works remaining unseen outside their continent of origin. Such is the case for *The Prize* (*El Premio*), the first film by Paula Markovitch, which, after its victory in Guadalajara as best Mexican fiction film of 2011, lived up to its name and swept the boards at other Latin American festivals.

Pushing the envelope of what counts as 'Mexican' cinema, *The Prize* boasts an Argentine director (albeit resident in Mexico) and Argentine cast, crew and location: a bleak Atlantic shore where a young mother lives in a secluded seaside shack with her precocious daughter. *The Prize*'s minimal storyline (the child plays in the sand dunes, sometimes accompanied by a schoolmate or dog) is matched by the bare technique which is now a lingua franca for festival favourites. We are thus treated to extended, unbroken takes of the windswept infant heroine facing the unforgiving ocean. In keeping with the now familiar tenets of Bazinian realism and Deleuzian time-image, Markovitch clearly believes it is enough to place nature before the camera and respect the unfolding of action in space and time.

But, as we slowly learn, the hidden motive of the mother's exile is Argentina's 1980s dictatorship (we assume the mother is a leftist dissident). And the prize of the title is for an essay in praise of the military which the child, surreptitiously enrolled in a local school, is obliged by her teacher to pen. This premise of the child as unknowing witness to historical horror is well known in Spanish-language cinema. Since Erice's masterful *The Spirit of the Beehive*, there have been almost forty years of films from Spain on the theme. The year 2011 brought, in addition to *The Prize*, contributions to the genre from as far apart as Buenos Aires and rural Colombia.

Yet, however familiar it is to Spanish speakers, the political premise will likely remain mysterious to English-speaking audiences of *The Prize*, who lack guidance within the film itself. Markovitch veers latterly into melodrama, even providing a happy ending, albeit shown, characteristically, in extreme long shot. On the briefly peaceful shore, the tiny figures of mother and daughter are joined by an unknown man, presumably the father who has been missing throughout the film, feared murdered by the regime. *The Prize*'s bid for aesthetic distinction clearly succeeded for Ibero-American festival audiences (and juries). Its long takes, elliptical narrative and rigorous rejection of visual pleasure are not simply artistic choices but social ones as well, intended to exclude the general audience that favours less austere fare. Although its unaesthetic aesthetic coincides with the most rigorous strand of transnational art cinema from Iran to Hungary, the political reference which rang true to post-dictatorship Latin American festival-goers clearly travelled badly beyond the continent's borders, where audiences were deprived of the chance to see *The Prize*.

Jesús Mario Lozano's third feature *Windows to the Sea* (*Ventanas al mar*), shown in competition in Guadalajara this year, could hardly look more different. Shot in the lush location of Cozumel, an island off the coast of the Mayan Riviera, it boasts sexy stars, familiar to the local public from Mexican television, and a relatively ample budget, which, far from *The Prize*'s determined stasis, permits spectacular aerial and underwater shots of tropical forests and coral reefs. A glamorous young couple have come to stay at the boutique hotel of the title, which (like *The Prize*'s shack) faces the ocean, although this time it is not the relentlessly grey South Atlantic but an intensely turquoise Caribbean. Lozano shoots his actors' burnished flesh and gilded bodies with relish, often cutting in for tight, abstract close-ups of tangled fingers or meshed limbs. Male lead Raúl Méndez, who noted on Twitter that he starred in no fewer than three of the features selected for the current competition in Guadalajara, is perhaps best known in Mexico for *KM 31*, a rare horror film that won international distribution, and *The Weaker Sex* (*El sexo débil*), a telenovela on the decline of the Mexican macho male, whose title refers not to women but to men.

As this last example suggests, there will be trouble in paradise. Méndez's character hides a dark secret, as do the elderly Spanish couple he bumps into at the intimate hotel. The wife has been diagnosed with an infirmity which soon will strip her of her memory. Meanwhile the husband himself is clearly in decline (we first see him near-drowning in that inviting ocean). Far from simply lingering on sensual delight, *Windows to the Sea* thus becomes a moving meditation on ageing. The alarmingly paunchy Guillén (who not so long ago, it seems, played the leading man in Almodóvar's *Women on the Verge of a Nervous Breakdown*) makes a pathetic stab at jogging down the island's only road and, in the film's creepiest moment, he investigates his young neighbours' bed in their absence, sniffing the sheets and inspecting stray hairs. Similarly it is a shock to see Charo López, still famous as a pioneer of frank female sexuality in Spanish film, as an ailing grandma, at one point literally washed up by the sea.

If, then, *The Prize* tackles politics with art-movie reticence, *Windows to the Sea* addresses history with polished expertise, hiding its critique within the dazzling spectacle of sun and ocean. The older couple take a tour of the island's pre-Hispanic ruins (the guide ruminates on lost Indian deities); and surely Guillén and López are here as resonant a ruin as any Mayan temple, overgrown with tropical foliage. And crucially they are of Spanish origin, as were the conquistadors whose momentous conquest of Mexico began (as the guide once more reminds us) on this very island.

But of course history is never wholly lost. Rather (again as in Bazin or Deleuze) time is concretized in space, unfolded in movement. The Mayan maids, first shown pliantly providing tourists with fresh towels, later voice a mordant commentary on the guests they serve, spoken in their own (subtitled) language. Likewise Lozano's expertly smooth technique (the camera glides on tracks and soars on cranes) sometimes breaks up into the art movie that we glimpse lurking beneath the polished reflecting surfaces (there are many mirror shots).

Thus the pre-credits sequence shows a disorientating montage of beach fragments (drinks and hats, books and looks) to the accompaniment of an enigmatic poem in Spanish and Italian and the discordant strings of the elegantly disturbing soundtrack. It is not for nothing that Lozano directed his first film, *Just Like That* (*Así*), as a formalist puzzle, with each shot lasting exactly thirty-two seconds. And, in what is finally a mood piece, the storyline here is almost as minimalist as in *The Prize*: two couples meet up and simply set out to sea. Unlike Markovitch, Lozano does not even allow us the facile pleasure of a satisfying ending. *Windows to the Sea* is thus an expert example of what may well be a new genre: the art movie that does not see fit to turn its back on the general audience; or, what comes down to the same thing, the commercial feature that embraces artistic ambitions.

Lozano's last sequence returns appeals to voice-over once more in a text that speaks of a final farewell to memory. What these two exceptional films, so different and yet so similar, reveal, however, is that on the beach, that most fragile and fluid of locations, past and present cannot be so easily separated, each drifting as they do imperceptibly in and out of the other.

Film Quarterly (web exclusive, May 2012)

Conclusion:
Between Cinema and Television

In February 2011, on the inauguration of a year of Mexican cinema events in France, *Cahiers du Cinéma* published a special supplement on the country, edited by Charles Tesson. Such an occasion and publication might seem to be the opportunity for the celebration of 'cinéma mexicain' in the style lamented by Jesús Mario Lozano: that is, the subordination of Mexican film to external criteria of legitimation. And indeed, one piece on *nouvelles vagues* seems to interpret auteur films (notably those of festival favourite Carlos Reygadas) within the context of dominant French paradigms (*Cahiers du Cinéma*, 2011: 8).

However *Cahiers*' survey, aided by Mexican contributors such as Carlos Bonfil and Fernanda Solórzano (cited in this book), is surprisingly diverse. Although the emphasis is, unsurprisingly, on somewhat rigorous art movies (Pedro González-Rubio's *Alamar* and Michael Rowe's *Leap Year* are cited in the Introduction [2011: 3]), the panorama includes Luis Estrada's *Hell* (albeit described as a 'phenomenon') (2011: 6); profiles of two producers (including Canana, makers of *I'm Gonna Explode* and *Miss Bala*) (2011: 10); a veteran and now disenchanted director (Arturo Ripstein) (2011: 14); the Golden Age period, presented as 'popular tradition' (2011: 16); and a survey of 'cinéma fantastique' (2011: 20), a category taken to include both the horror and wrestling movies that are so essential to an understanding of Guillermo del Toro. In spite of the use of inevitable clichés ('Under the volcano', 'So far from heaven . . .'), the survey strikingly avoids both the patronizing tone and sheer factual error that Nancy Berthier (2007) has discerned in previous years of *Cahiers*' coverage of Spain and Latin America. The increased visibility of Mexican features at international festivals, aptly described as 'sites of passage' (de Valck, 2008), may also have led to greater knowledge of Mexican cinema's historical legacy.

We should be wary, however, of claims to exceptionalism, whatever their source. *Chilango* magazine's humorous guide to local living in Mexico City ('Manual del buen chilango') includes such allegedly distinctive cinematic practices as speaking on mobile phones in movie theatres and leaving an empty seat between oneself and neighbouring patrons. The riotous laughter that, according to the magazine, greets any use of a swearword on screen may well be distinctive, however (*Chilango*, 2011: 25).

Perhaps, then, even as interest within Mexico itself remains restricted or contested, the diversity and particularity of Mexican cinema are now making themselves better known abroad. Television, of course, remains another case. Telenovela is much studied across Latin America; and there has been some interest academically in global television formats (Oren and Shahaf, 2012). I myself have examined in this book two successful series (*Rebel* and *Women Murderers*) that were the result of border crossings. Yet, as throughout the world, television fiction in Mexico remains mainly local in its attractions and references (it seems unlikely that, for all their glossy visuals, *In the Sewers* and *Cries of Death and Freedom* would arouse much interest abroad).

Moreover, TV remains more sensitive than cinema to social change in individual countries. Julián Hernández provocatively places glossy art-movie homoeroticism within the context of a grungy Mexico City or pre-Columbian pyramids for an appreciative niche audience that ranges from Mexico City to Berlin. *The Aparicio Women*, on the other hand, exploits the conventions of telenovela to promote an openly political lesbian agenda (the climactic same-sex marriage in the town hall), which is, nevertheless, by no means devoid of visual and narrative pleasure and reached millions of faithful fans from Mexico to the US and Spain.

Given the increased access to TV drama, via the internet and DVD box sets, it would seem that it is not so much distribution that hinders the wider appreciation of such series but rather critical prejudice. As Raúl Miranda López writes of his corpus of Televisa feature films, some of which 'break with their own norms of production' ('rompen con sus propios esquemas de producción' [2006: 10]), it is not easy to elaborate forms of reflection on mass media fictions that need to be examined within their own 'universe' (2006: 11). Miranda López thus appeals, as I do, to sociological sources for an awareness of how the cultural representations of television are vital contributors to a national symbolic market and discursive 'training' ('formación' [2006: 11]). And, he would acknowledge (as I have argued throughout this book) that cultural tastes are by no means innocent, but are always socially produced.

The market share of Mexican feature film in its own territory may have been just 6.76 per cent in 2011 (IMCINE, 2011a: 16). But, as I suggested in the penultimate chapter, accomplished examples of genres as diverse as satire, farce and auteur movie have been able to address with some critical and commercial success the most urgent of issues facing Mexico today, namely drug-related violence. Hence, while duopolies of distribution in both film and television have clearly placed restrictions on creativity, it is by no means unknown for new and innovative projects to come to fruition in both media. If more collaboration were to take place between practitioners in the two fields it would surely be to the benefit of both. To take just one promising example, not treated in this book, Gerardo Naranjo directed episodes of *I'm Your Fan* (*Soy tu fan*, 2010–12), a romantic dramedy made by Canana for cultural TV channel Once.

In the light of such changing phenomena (not to mention growing awareness of the new cultural distinction of television drama in many countries), critics and scholars might also widen their horizons to embrace the aesthetics and economics of the two media and to employ approaches that draw on both the humanities and the social sciences. It may well be the case that Mexican festival films, like those elsewhere in Latin America and beyond, are becoming increasingly austere and avant-garde, destined for an audience in art galleries and other non-traditional exhibition spaces rather than in theatres. But, as I suggested in chapter 7, popular genre film has (like TV drama) been moving upmarket, featuring impressively improved production values. While, in spite of such evidence of convergence, the space between cinema and television is likely to remain conflictive in Mexico, that conflict may prove to be, as I have attempted to show in this book, an unexpectedly productive one.

Appendix:
Interviews with Five
Media Professionals

The Director: Jesús Mario Lozano

Jesús Mario Lozano is a director and screenwriter. Among his feature films are *Así* (2005, accepted for the Venice Film Festival among others) and *Más allá de mí* and *Windows on the Sea/Ventanas al mar* (2008 and 2012 respectively, both premiered at the International Film Festival of Guadalajara). He holds a Ph.D. in Philosophy at the European Graduate School and his doctoral thesis was published in book form under the title *Aesthethicon* [sic]: *Theatrical Acts at the Limit of Philosophy*. He has also taught at the School of Visual Arts at the Universidad Autónoma de Nuevo León.

How did you get to make your first feature?

Before coming to cinema, I might say that I had two great passions that I'd combined since adolescence: theatre and philosophy. On the one hand, I joined the theatre as an actor, although stage fright quickly led me to direct. On the other hand, I was studying philosophy and started teaching for a while, even joining the faculty of the School of Philosophy at the University where I worked. But the two worlds had no connection. I felt that I was two different people with different schedules and even wardrobes; and still inside myself I felt dissatisfaction in both roles. In philosophy, I was exhausted by continuing 'abstraction', and felt the need for the 'live flesh' of the theatre; but on the other hand, in my work as a theatre director I needed to 'abstract' myself somewhat, to freeze the relentless joyful immediacy of the stage event. I longed to be able to intervene in time, to return obsessively to the act itself.

One day I decided to combine the two universes; and that's how my first feature began, or at least how I understand the process now. In *Así*, there was a philosophical premise that simultaneously integrated actorly fiction, physical bodies and the scenic moment in a 'cinematic abstraction'. In fact, when I finished filming I doubted that what I had actually made was a movie.

You trained as a theatre director at the Central School of Speech and Drama in London and have directed many plays. How has your theatrical experience influenced you in your film directing?

I think that it has influenced me in how I work with actors, and the fact that I like to rehearse. It amazes me to witness the 'event of being' in the actors (the *Dasein*, as a German acting coach would say) and then figure out how to portray this with the camera. Moreover, critics constantly said in their reviews of the plays I directed that they were very cinematic. Sometimes I think it was the other way around, that (even before I was one) it was the film director who influenced the theatre director.

You've also written journalism on the visual arts. Do you see any connection between the art world and your film work? And how do you see the Mexican press in the context of cinema?

Sometimes I feel that the film medium is still defined implicitly and explicitly by the tyranny of the Aristotelian narrative. Even those who 'rebel' against it take it as a clear reference point; and, after so many years, it's amazing that it still dominates today's cinema. Hence in the art world it's refreshing to me that there is no crazed obsession with 'stories' and that there are still explorations of other types of aesthetic or philosophical issues that sometimes interest me more than 'storytelling'. What might be important is a colour, a movement or a philosophical premise that does not have to go through the dictatorship of the Aristotelian narrative (or anti-Aristotelian narrative, which, of course, comes down to the same thing).

And as far as the Mexican press is concerned, it seems to me that there are very few brave writers who are still attempting to explore different ideas about what cinema is, beyond giving star ratings to movies; but fortunately they do exist, and whether or not they like my work, their existence is essential.

You have a doctorate in continental philosophy. Has your training in theoretical, mostly French, thought had some influence on your practice of cinema?

I think it's influenced me as a person, in my internal debates, in what I think, what I believe; and I guess that has somehow shaped my cinematic practice.

In fact, my teacher and dear friend Avital Ronell introduced me to Jacques Derrida, who was always very kind to me. One time when I was invited to his home in Paris, I told him about *Así*, the movie I was about to shoot. I dared to say that it was a 'deconstruction' of the Aristotelian structure, since in reality each of its thirty-two-second fragments could change place throughout the film, thus forming 'other stories' while using the same scenes. (I was planning on releasing the film in five different theatres with varying arrangements of the fragments but in the end the distributor did not agree to it.) I wanted to demonstrate that the illusion of 'the story' was actually located in the audience that took the existence of a plot for granted, but that in the film itself the 'narrative' was extremely fragile. During the shoot I took care that there were no temporal cues defining the day on which each scene took place, so as to be able to play later with the order in which they were chronologically organized. Derrida was interested in the idea and said he wanted to see the finished film, but sadly he died before the premiere.

You also worked as a university professor. Is there any connection between the worlds of the university and of cinema in Mexico?

In Mexico I think they are very separate islands, unfortunately. In the university there is some study (albeit rather little) of Mexican cinema, but seen from afar, with a certain suspicion, and vice versa; that is to say, film-makers also regard academics with deep suspicion. I think that everything is arranged so that the two islands remain separate enough not to interfere with their own particular agendas. However, I really believe that a close connection could be a way to forge a Mexican cinema that is more self-critical and assertive. But we must be willing to break with many prejudices before we reach that stage.

In my case I had to leave the university because academic managers did not look kindly on the fact that a Doctor of Philosophy made movies. They asked me to decide between being 'a serious scholar' (belonging to CONACYT [National Council of Science and Technology], SNI [National Researchers System] etc.) or being a film-maker, so I preferred to retire.

Do you watch any television series? Do the worlds of cinema and television have some contact or there is a gulf between the two?

There are extraordinary television series that I admire and follow, sometimes much more daring cinematically than what we see in theatres. I'm also very aware of what is happening on the internet. The problem in Mexico is that the genre of telenovela dominates almost everything. I think telenovela's clear promotion of an extreme conservatism is catastrophic for the country (and for the genre itself). People talk about a gulf between the world of telenovelas and Mexican cinema, but in reality their proximity is greater than one imagines. A mutual complicity is evident and it should not be otherwise. While I feel that more and more interesting TV projects are emerging that propose another way of doing things, they are still rather few in number.

You lived and worked for a long time in Monterrey. How do you see the relationship between regionalism and the centralism of Mexico City in the world of Mexican cinema?

Eisenstein wrote in his memoirs that Monterrey was an awful place in which there was 'nothing to do' and he was right to some extent. For a long time I tried to make films there without having to rely on the nation's capital. Not so much because I loved the city of Monterrey but because I believe that there are 'other cinemas' in the country that must exist and are crushed by a centralist hegemony that is really stifling. At that time I wanted to make the cinema of the place where I'm from – a 'geo-cinema' responding to the hot climate, to the mountains, to the aridity.

In one of your articles you criticized the cultural dependency of Mexican cinema, whereby legitimation continues to derive from the US or Europe. Given the relative success of Mexican cinema in the last decade, do you still defend this anti-'xenophilic' position?

I think so, although I fear I sound a bit dated. What I don't like is that in this country we have a cinema that is submissive to a handful of 'deciders' who are in Hollywood or directing some of the most prestigious film festivals in Europe. It's one thing for certain films to win awards in an international competition or to be selected for a particular festival – that I celebrate and applaud; but what I find ridiculous is that our national policies on exhibition or financial support for production should be legitimized by such awards or selections, when in many cases they promote racist, exotic or downright colonialist stereotypes of Mexican culture that nobody seems to notice. This is something now so 'naturalized' that it is accepted as if it were the way of the world and that's what I still do not agree with.

I recently discussed this with colleagues from other countries and this predicament is not exclusive to Mexico but is also very common in other national cinemas.

In your own practice, what are your priorities as a screenwriter? How do you see the creative difference between your writing and directing roles?

At the same time that I'm writing I'm already planning how I'm going to direct the film. Because of this, the initial 'scripts' I write are sometimes very personal, four-dimensional scribbles made up of colours and traces, newspaper clippings, photos and even smells. But then I translate these scribbles into standard scripts as required for competitions and for financing. Although I must say that this standardization does not come without a high cost and I know what awaits me: hours and hours with actors and colleagues trying to un-write it and retrieve that chaotic universe from which the script emerged (this is my priority as a director).

Hence sometimes I have mixed feelings about the script: while it can be an extraordinary creative force, it can also turn into a financial enforcer, a relentless policeman of time and of what can or cannot be done, something that is to be avoided at all costs. So far I've always written my own scripts, so I'm not familiar with the experience of working with a screenwriter; but, to be honest, this possibility does attract.

Your films have a very elaborate soundtrack. How do you understand the relationship between music and image?

Sometimes I already have the music for some scenes of the film even before the shoot and what I do is tease out the image that the music bears within itself. At other times the music is composed later, though starting from musical elements that have already been there since the time of the shoot.

In *Ventanas al mar*, because of the subject matter of the film, the soundtrack derives from a study of the music of the colonial period in Mexico and I think in the final composition you can clearly hear the motifs of this musical tradition. The composer was Fred Saboonchi, who also composed the music of *Así*. He is an extraordinary Iranian-born Swedish composer whom I admire and with whom I have achieved an intense collaboration, although strangely I have not had the pleasure of meeting him in person: everything has been by virtual exchange. When we talked on Skype we decided not to use the camera. It was too distracting to see the unknown face of someone whom I knew in the extreme and absolute intimacy of his compositions.

Your first feature employs a formalist montage with shots of an arbitrary length of thirty-two seconds. What is your practice of editing and how do you see the relationship between shooting and cutting?

In *Así*, I wanted the editing to be 'performative', that is to say it should make the audience feel the claustrophobia of the protagonist, the relativity of time and the arbitrary cuts that life imposes on you. Through the formality of the editing I tried to reflect (and make people feel) the deepest part of [main character] 'Iván': a soul structured in mathematical units of thirty-two seconds.

I also tried to do something 'performative' in *Más allá de mí*, my second film. But there I wanted an editing style that would intentionally distance us from the characters, that made us feel their disconnect from themselves. The shots were like little postcards in which nothing much happened. I wanted the audience to feel the sensation of these young people caught up in their emotional problems as the war (against the narcos) was going on right in front of them. I used a shooting style that made the characters look as if they were in a sitcom, except with no shot/reverse shot, no jokes, no laugh-track. The result was very strange.

What is the most serious problem facing Mexican cinema?

The biggest problem, from my point of view, is the temptation to try to meet the expectations of subject matter and style that are stereotypically demanded of Mexican cinema (as dictated by the market).

And what is its greatest strength?

Faced with the serious problems this country confronts, I think its forte is the urgent need and willingness of society to think differently.

The Festival Director: Daniela Michel

Daniela Michel is the Founding Director of the Morelia International Film Festival (FICM), an annual event launched in 2003 to support and promote a new generation of Mexican film-makers. Michel has also served as a juror for the Rockefeller Foundation's Media Arts Fellowships, the Fulbright García-Robles Film Fellowships, and the J. William Fulbright Prize for International Understanding, as well as for film festivals, including the Sundance Film Festival, the Cannes Film Festival, IDFA (International Documentary Festival Amsterdam), the San Francisco Film Festival, the Transylvania Film Festival and the San Sebastián International Film Festival.

How were you trained? And how did you get to be artistic director and founder of the FICM?

I studied directing in the CCC [state film school in Mexico City] at a time when the teachers themselves were not at all optimistic about the future of Mexican cinema. In this daunting context, I got out of film school and graduated with a BA in English Language and Literature from the Faculty of Arts of the UNAM [National Autonomous University]. In 1994, when the production of feature films was at a really low level and the short film was what was keeping the spirit of young film-makers alive, I founded, together with a colleague, Enrique Ortega, the Festival of Mexican Short Film in the Cineteca Nacional, as a free initiative that was independent of government institutions. Due to the continuing growth of the Festival and the interest in participating shown by young film-makers, who included Fernando Eimbcke, Julián Hernández, Michel Franco, Ernesto Contreras and Rigoberto Perezcano, among many others, it became clear that we needed to rethink the size of an event that was put on with a budget of less than $10,000 and in extremely modest conditions.

I had the good fortune of meeting Alejandro Ramírez Magaña, CEO of Cinépolis, and Cuauhtémoc Cárdenas Batel, and I suggested that together we should found the International Film Festival of Morelia (FICM), which initially featured a Mexican short-film competition section, along with a Mexican documentary section, which was Alejandro Ramírez's initiative. The city of Morelia has a unique cultural legacy several centuries old and is logistically ideal for organizing a festival. Furthermore, the corporate offices of Cinépolis, the largest exhibition chain in Latin America and fourth largest in the world, are also housed in this beautiful city.

The FICM had its origin as a short-film festival and this is still one of the main activities of the Festival. What is the importance of shorts in the current production scene?

The short is the free territory of cinema. It is where young people still have no commitments and no agenda to fulfil, and it is becoming ever cheaper to make a short. I am very interested in seeing what young people are thinking, what someone in Chiapas is filming as opposed to someone in Tijuana. I've learned a great deal about Mexico thanks to the works that I review very carefully every year, as we receive nearly 500 entries from around the country.

There has been a boom in documentary film in Mexico and this genre is also central to the FICM. What is the relationship like between fiction films and documentaries?

From the first year of the FICM in 2003 we realized that the documentary was about to enter an extraordinary period in Mexico and that's why we added it to the competitive section. At that time young film-makers were not yet producing enough debuts or second films, so the competition for fiction features began only in 2007, the fifth year of the festival. The line between fiction film and documentary is increasingly tenuous and that can be seen in many of the works submitted to us.

You have mentioned on occasion the 'minimalism' of current Mexican features. How do you see the relationship between these auteur or art films and Mexican commercial or genre movies, which are not normally seen at the FICM?

A considerable proportion of the fiction features that we receive as submissions to the FICM, which only accepts directors' first and second films, is made up of contemplative films that are made most often without professional actors. However I think that in Mexico there is a great diversity of projects. Carlos Reygadas is a major influence in Mexico, but there are also genre films, comedies, etc. Film production in Mexico is eclectic, as is that of world cinema.

The FICM has had a partnership for many years with the Critics' Week at Cannes. What is the relationship between Mexican cinema and international festivals?

I think that after the success of *Amores perros* at Cannes in 2000 Mexican cinema was repositioned at international festivals and the path was cleared for a new generation of Mexican film-makers. The exhibition of Mexican cinema in some of the most important festivals of the world has revitalized the industry in our country. The prestige that Mexican cinema now enjoys has promoted co-productions and even motivated the Mexican public to see locally made films.

The FICM has a special interest in production in the state of Michoacán, where Morelia is located. How do you view the centralism of Mexico City in the Mexican film scene?

For the FICM it is essential to promote work done in Michoacán, both by new film-makers producing today and through retrospectives showing the work of cinematographers, directors and actors and actresses who come from this state and have left a mark on the history of Mexican cinema. Since its inception, the FICM has included works from different states of Mexico and has demonstrated versatility in the topics treated by its chosen films.

The FICM is a non-profit association. But it has a close relationship with Cinépolis, the large exhibitor, as Alejandro Ramírez is both President of the Festival and CEO of Cinépolis. What are the current conditions of distribution and exhibition in Mexico like?

Obviously, Hollywood movies dominate cinema exhibition in Mexico to some extent. However, thanks to initiatives by exhibitors, distributors and production companies, it has also been possible to build a circuit for independent film and art cinema. Some small producers, such as Mantarraya, Canana and Ambulante [a documentary film festival], have managed to bring a selection of international contemporary film production to the Mexican audience and have extended distribution platforms (for online distribution and via cable television).

The festival circuit is becoming ever more widespread and successful. Do you think that it is replacing traditional theatres in the distribution of art films?

I think it's important to differentiate between art-film distribution (and the spaces dedicated to this type of screening) and festivals. Actually, the festivals in Mexico have specific profiles and are very different from one another. In Morelia, the mission is to promote the projects of young Mexican film-makers. The selection of international premieres frames and complements the competition section, but it's not a priority. Moreover, Cinépolis recently inaugurated its Sala de Arte ['Art House'] brand in more than twenty multiplexes around the country, which will be permanent spaces for the exhibition of independent films. Their programme includes titles that participated in Ambulante and the FICM.

You have a lot of experience in print and television journalism. How do you see critics in the context of Mexican cinema?

I think we badly need a film criticism that is more serious, more profound and more knowledgeable about the nature of cinema.

Do you watch any television fiction? Do the worlds of cinema and television have any contact or is there a gulf between them?

The truth is that I barely watch television, although I do know that there has been an attempt to produce quality series.

It is sometimes assumed that there is a generation gap between current and previous film-makers. How do you see the relationship between contemporary Mexican cinema and its predecessors?

In fact, I think that the most relevant reference points for current Mexican cinema are not national predecessors, but contemporary international cinema, and so-called 'slow cinema'. On the other hand, the reality of our country influences the diversity of thematic, narrative and aesthetic projects in local film. The rise of the documentary has favoured the production of fiction and vice versa. I think we live in a very vital moment for national cinema. I don't think there is a generation gap, just different views on the aesthetics of the moving image and on the aim of cinema in the current social and political context.

What is the most serious problem facing Mexican cinema?

There are several serious problems.

And what is its greatest strength?

The talent of the new directors.

The Exhibitor: Alejandro Ramírez

Alejandro Ramírez is the Chief Executive Officer of Cinépolis, the largest movie theatre company in Latin America, with a presence in Mexico, Brazil, Colombia, Peru, Central America, India and the United States. He has served as Mexico's Deputy Permanent Representative to the OECD and as Technical Secretary of the Social Cabinet of the Government of Mexico. He has worked for the World Bank and the United Nations Development Programme in the areas of poverty and human development. He co-authored 'Poverty, Human Development and Indigenous People in Latin America'. He is Chairman of the Morelia International Film Festival and Vice-Chair of Mexicanos Primero, an initiative to raise the quality of public education in Mexico. He was named a Young Global Leader by the World Economic Forum in 2005 and co-chaired the WEF's Annual Meeting in 2012. He is currently Chair of the B29, the G20's Business Summit.

What kind of training did you have? And how did you get to be CEO of the largest theatrical exhibitor in Latin America and the fourth largest in the world?

I grew up all my life very close to the family business because my home was right next to the cinema, which I visited several times a week. In 1996 I joined as COO. In 2004 I became Deputy CEO and in 2006 was appointed CEO.

Cinépolis has been innovative in improving the circumstances of exhibition in Mexico and ensuring loyalty through schemes such as VIP Lounges, Club Cinépolis and Movie Birthdays. What have been the effects of these changes that you've made?

In each market where Cinépolis operates, a strongly competitive situation exists. The exhibition sector has been modernized and customers are becoming more sophisticated. These challenges mean that exhibition companies are constantly thinking about how we can innovate to offer value-added services to our customers and thus gain their trust and loyalty. In the case of Cinépolis, we have been successful in achieving this process of securing customer loyalty through innovation. Today we are the largest operator of VIP or premium-type movie theatres in the world and our customer-base in Club Cinépolis is over a million members. The main effect of these changes is that we can rely on a remarkable customer-base that is loyal to our brand week in, week out.

The international expansion of Cinépolis is remarkable, especially in difficult markets like India and the US. How do you see this process of globalization in the Mexican context?

Cinépolis's international expansion began more than ten years ago with Central America. Our move into that area served as a platform to explore territories that were more distant but also more profitable in terms of growth. Such are the cases of Brazil, India, Colombia and Peru. Cinépolis will focus its international expansion efforts in all these territories in the coming years. The US case is unique because it is a much more competitive market and now has a rather high saturation of screens. That's why our expansion into the United States is limited to our VIP brand and specific markets like California and Florida. Our intention is to review our strategy frequently to determine where there is potential for growth.

How do you view the relationship between exhibitors and the production sector in Mexico? In your opinion, is it conflictive or rather collaborative?

The relationship of the exhibition industry in Mexico with the production sector is a relationship that naturally has its agreements and disagreements. To understand this relationship it's important to note that the exhibition industry in Mexico is one of the most modern in the world and that the supply of screens in the country has tripled in the last fifteen years. The possibilities offered by this exhibition infrastructure are enormous. Not for nothing Mexico is today considered one of the ten most important territories for the Hollywood studios, and in the case of many [US] films it is the number one international territory.

On the other hand, the production sector has not seen its best performance in the last ten years. The participation of Mexican movies as a percentage of the total box office has failed to exceed 10 per cent. And although the number of productions has grown significantly and the amount of resources that the government provides for production is the largest in history, Mexican movies generally have not managed to connect with the public's preferences. Significantly, the most successful Mexican film of all time is still *El crimen del padre Amaro* (*The Crime of Father Amaro*), which premiered in 2002, while in most countries every year or every second year a new movie breaks box-office records for local production.

To the extent that Mexican films achieve better box office and audience results and position themselves better in relation to public taste, to that extent the relationship with the exhibition sector will be collaborative rather than conflictive.

What have been, and what will be, the effects of the digitization of movie theatres in Mexico?

Digitization is the most important technological transformation that the exhibition industry worldwide has undergone in more than one hundred years of its existence. It is a transformation that significantly improves the experience of going to the movies because it ensures consistent and optimal quality for the viewer.

Additionally, digitization substantially reduces the costs of film distribution. During the transition period required to get back the multimillion-dollar investment involved in this transformation, these costs will not be affected significantly. It will be towards the end of that period, in ten years or so, that distributors will be able to enjoy these savings.

You have been pioneers in the transmission of special live events in theatres. Is there much potential for expansion of this type of exhibition? Or will it always be marginal, compared to the traditional screening of feature films?

One of the side effects of digitization is the ability to transmit a variety of non-traditional content or alternative content in cinemas. The growth of this type of content is not yet clear, but the possibilities are extensive. To date, we have experimented in Cinépolis with sports events, live and in 3D, such as matches of the World [Soccer] Cup in South Africa, pre-recorded 3D operas, operas broadcast live, pop and rock concerts, plays, WWE wrestling, NBA basketball games, and so on. Expectations are that customers will become increasingly frequent consumers of this type of programming in movie theatres and alternative content will shift from marginal to substantial.

Cinépolis has a charity, the Foundation. What are the social objectives of this charity? What do they have to do with the business objectives of the company?

The Foundation has three main components: visual health, education through film, and community action. Through our flagship programme, 'Del Amor Nace la Vista' ['Sight Comes from Love'] (which has a close relation to the exhibition business, as sight is the main sense used to enjoy a movie), we have carried out more than 12,000 cataract surgeries throughout Mexico since 2006, focusing on low-income populations. Furthermore, in terms of education through film, we are currently organizing the International Human Rights Film Festival, which this year will be in its fifth edition. Additionally, there is a constant search to promote various film festivals that contribute to the variety of cinematic offer in commercial cinemas. Finally, in terms of community action, every year we organize film screenings for children without access to theatres in rural and urban areas through the programme 'Vamos Todos a Cinépolis' ['We All Go to Cinépolis'], which is the longest lasting social responsibility programme in the company. Each year more than 100,000 children enjoy these free performances in Cinépolis theatres.

You already have a 'Sala de Arte' ['Art House'] brand with a network of screens in Mexico City and some regional cities. How do you see the relationship between auteur or art cinema and commercial or genre movies in Mexico in the context of the exhibition?

The Sala de Arte project emerged as the answer to a very clear need for the Mexican public to have spaces devoted to alternative or auteur cinema. The twenty-one cinemas in eleven cities that today offer the Sala de Arte concept seek to create a relationship of trust with their audience through a careful and selective programming of films that address this particular niche. In Cinépolis we are convinced that diverse film projects, whether commercial or niche, can coexist in commercial cinemas in a healthy and productive manner.

How do you view Mexican critics and the press in the context of cinema?

No doubt critics and film media in Mexico are as sophisticated as in any other country that loves movies. In Mexico we have great critics who contribute through their writing to the analysis and discussion of diverse cinematic projects.

Cinépolis originated in Morelia, Michoacán. How do you see the relationship between regionalism and the centralism of Mexico City in the world of Mexican cinema?

Mexico City remains the epicentre of the movie world in Mexico. The premiers in the country take Mexico City as their starting point and success in this market often determines success in other cities. However, both Guadalajara and Monterrey, like many other large and medium-sized cities, have grown significantly as film markets.

You are both President of the Morelia International Film Festival and CEO of Cinépolis. How do you view the relationship between distribution and exhibition in festivals and their traditional form in theatres? And what are the differences between the image of Mexican cinema abroad (seen through festivals) and the one Mexicans have of their own films (seen in theatres)?

Festivals are spaces of very important expression and coexistence as they allow the interaction of the creative community in its various forms, whether feature film, documentary or short film, with industry professionals, talent and the general public. For Cinépolis it is very important to be the founder of several successful festivals in Mexico such as the FICM and Ambulante documentary festival, and also to be associated with prestigious festivals such as the International Film Festival of Guadalajara or the International Film Festival of the Cineteca [Mexico City].

Do you watch any television fiction? Do the worlds of cinema and television have any contact or there is a gulf between them?
[No answer]

Do you agree that there is a rise of documentary in Mexico? What possibilities does this genre have of being shown in your theatres?

The documentary genre is probably where we have achieved the best results in recent years, not only in commercial terms but also in terms of quality and artistic merit. In Mexico there are great documentary film-makers who have addressed issues of great social relevance or intimate matters in a highly penetrating way. The phenomena of *Presunto culpable* (*Presumed Guilty*, 2008) and *¡De panzazo!* (2012) have contributed to the rise of the documentary, but good documentaries have been made in Mexico for some time. We hope that there will be many more documentaries that are important and attractive to the Mexican public, which will find their space in commercial cinemas in a successful fashion.

What is the most serious problem facing Mexican cinema?

Probably the biggest problem is a disconnect between the stories of Mexican films and what the Mexican public wants to see. It is remarkable that with the significant amount of resources the government has channelled into film production, we still cannot get a higher proportion of films to achieve commercial success. Obviously there are all kinds of film projects, but those with a commercial orientation are failing to connect with the mass audience that they are attempting to address.

And what is its greatest strength?

Mexico is a country where cinema is a form of entertainment that is a part of popular culture. Every weekend Mexican families turn to the cinemas to have fun, be together and have a good time. Among Latin American countries, Mexico is the one with the highest frequency of cinema visits as measured by total attendees per year divided by total population. This figure is 1.8 for Mexico, while for the other Latin American countries it is less than one. This great market of Mexican cinema consumers is the strongest point of the film industry.

The Producer: Roberto Fiesco

Roberto Fiesco is a prize-winning producer and film director. Among his more than forty projects are all three features directed by Julián Hernández (premiered and awarded at the Berlin Film Festival), *The Magician* (*El mago*, Jaime Aparicio, 2004), *Attack on the Cinema* (*Asalto al cine*, Iria Gómez Cocheiro, 2011), *Used Parts* (*Partes usadas*, Aarón Fernández, 2007) and *The Reasons of the Heart* (*Las razones del corazón*, Arturo Ripstein, 2011).

What was your training like in [official university film school] CUEC? And how did you get to produce your first feature film?

My training was primarily as a director. While CUEC provides a comprehensive education that includes the whole range of cinema skills (from writing the script to laboratory processes), the main emphasis is on the training of directors, and in that context I made during my school years various short films, both fiction and documentary. Two of these (*Falling* [*Caer*] and *Impure Acts* [*Actos impuros*]) would be my first to be exhibited outside film school and even made the circuit of small national and international festivals.

According to this academic model [of CUEC], all of us students were, in addition to being screenwriters and directors, the producers and managers of our own shorts. But I can say that I started to produce more formally after becoming fascinated by the work made at the school by Julián Hernández, who belonged to the generation above mine in CUEC, and with whom I established almost immediately a relationship full of personal and cinephile affinities that have led us to collaborate ever since the first films that we made together.

When he was about to undertake his thesis, which would become the medium-length *There Was a Time when Dreams Gave Way to Long Sleepless Nights (17 Notes for a Film)* (*Hubo un tiempo en que los sueños dieron paso a largas noches de insomnio (17 apuntes para una película)*), he suggested that we should co-direct. However, as it was a very small crew on the shoot (no more than just six people), we decided that it was best that I produce and he concentrate on directing. It was a very tough shoot, not just because of the limited financial and human resources, but because the school refused to let us shoot in black and white because of the terrible results that were obtained in those days with the laboratory that developed the film. This forced us to change the colour stock we'd been assigned for the [black and white] film we wanted and denied us the opportunity of having the normal post-production under the aegis of CUEC. It was also the first time that gay characters appeared in a frank manner in a work of this period, a fact that, no doubt, was not viewed with much sympathy. Nor were the unconventional approach to narrative structure and a commitment to form (static shots, the extension of film time, non-chronological structure, etc.) that went against the trend of other works at that time.

I found production work fascinating, in any case, and it was from this first shoot that I discovered my professional vocation, which would be confirmed by another shoot that was yet tougher, but also much more satisfying, [Hernández's first feature] *A Thousand Clouds of Peace* (*Mil nubes de paz . . .* , 2003).

You have produced and directed many short films. What is the importance of shorts in the current production scene?

I love working on shorts and even view myself as a director only in that format; and I deplore the idea of seeing shorts as a calling card or as a requirement for the direction of a future feature film. I believe shorts are in themselves an independent space full of formal and thematic possibilities with no commercial hindrance, which makes them even more tempting and stimulating. In the recent history of Mexican cinema you can see the wealth of ideas there are in shorts (and most recently in the documentary) as opposed to what happens in the field of fiction features. Unfortunately, shorts' lack of possibilities for distribution and marketing (restricted as they are to festivals and to a lesser extent to television) prevent a better understanding of their variety and possibilities, in addition to the fact that there now exists an excessive 'easiness' owing to the accessibility of modern audiovisual recording equipment, which no longer requires a minimum of rigour on the part of the film-maker. Currently shorts do not enjoy the good health that they did fifteen or twenty years ago (despite the considerable increase in volume), but they will always be that 'free territory of film' which we advocated in those days.

You also carry out radio journalism on the subject of film in a talk show called *Cinesecuencias*. How do you see film criticism in the context of Mexican cinema?

Criticism in Mexico, with remarkable (truly remarkable) exceptions, is a discipline threatened by extinction. Firstly, critics no longer have the reach and influence over potential viewers that they had in the past. I mean a conscientious criticism, one in which a profound knowledge of film history, film theory and various analytical perspectives on film language was evident in writings by notable critics of yesteryear that have gone down in history. Even the literary quality of such critics could have an aesthetic dimension that was comparable to the film work. Today there are very few print, television or radio media that support the presence of such critics, and the few that exist are true 'cultural islands'. What does proliferate now are bloggers or wordsmiths in digital media, with little knowledge of criticism, but with no limits on their freedom of expression, because it is now believed that anyone can sound off on cinema.

Where does funding come from for your projects? How do you see the state agencies in the context of production (IMCINE, CONACULTA, FOPROCINE, Article 226)?

The Mexican state established a protectionist policy towards the cinema dating from the 1970s, which allowed for the emergence of important new film-makers, but also brought with it flaws in the production, distribution and exhibition of our films, which are dragging us down even decades later.

We have imposed on the government the obligation to fund us without generating (except in very few cases) new forms of production that allow us to continue shooting movies with no commercial potential per se. No doubt, the intention of the financial support is good, albeit still insufficient for the growing demand. And democratization, namely the inclusion of film-makers rather than officials in decision-making when it comes to allocating support for production and the transparency with which IMCINE is organized today, these two factors protect us, almost always, from the arbitrary models of favouritism and dictates that were the daily bread of previous administrations, thus ensuring that the Institute is an exceptional government organization in these times of the conservative right.

The most innovative structure is the stimulus law, Article 226, which has increased the volume of production in the country exponentially. However, it favours films with a commercial bent that are to the taste of the companies that sponsor the scheme through their taxes. The lack of clear regulations in the past, or the lack, simply, of reliable auditing, also sparked widespread corruption and the allocation of significant resources to dilettantes who in many cases did not even finish their movies or filmed them badly and in a state of complete ignorance.

The existence and importance of government support are undeniable, but I think that, in terms of production, funding should be much more aligned to the kind of auteur cinema that is virtually impossible to make without a minimum of state support.

Your films have been very successful in foreign festivals such as Berlin and Sundance. How do you view the relationship between this form of distribution and exhibition and the traditional form in theatres? And how do you view the relationship between the image of Mexican cinema abroad and the image Mexicans have of their own movies?

Certainly I've been very lucky to be able to exhibit some of the works I have produced in the first rank of festivals. It's curious how the movies that achieve this kind of distinction and indicate internationally the apparent good health of our cinema (it's enough to cite the case of Cannes in 2012 [where Carlos Reygadas won as Best Director]) experience a disconnect with the local box office, and many times – I would say without exaggeration, almost always – find possibilities of distribution abroad that they do not enjoy in our own country. Screenings at foreign festivals, or prizes that are won there, are not an attraction for the Mexican audience, which mainly considers local cinema as just another genre, as if listings identified films on release as thrillers, animated films, horror movies, romantic comedies and Mexican films, not caring that the last category could belong to any of the previously mentioned genres. This perception seems widespread and is supported by the overwhelming power of American cinema and its distributors, which dominate almost all of our screens; to this can be added the complete institutional failure of the fight against piracy – all of which paints a bleak picture for those movies that seem to find an audience only abroad.

Do you watch any television fiction? Do the worlds of cinema and television have some contact or is there a gulf between them?

In practice I watch very little TV because I have no time at all, and I prefer when I do have time to go to the movies. I am a romantic of the movie theatre. In Mexico, the emerging industry of television series, or of telenovelas, which are now also using that name, has been nourished by elements from cinema in order to build not only its crews (both technical and artistic) but also its formal values, and no doubt the medium has been enriched by this. Most filmmakers in our country today make a living from television and advertising.

The movies you have made with Julián Hernández have strong gay themes. Do you think that this connection has helped or hindered the reception of these films?

I think the films had an unprecedented content when they were made. They addressed sexuality by avoiding the conventional blandness of previous cinema and there was none of the guilt-ridden or jeering factors that had accompanied the depiction of homosexuality for decades. Furthermore, legislation regarding the rights of the LGBT community and the rejection of discrimination in those same laws, first in the capital and then in the rest of the country, has run parallel to the making of our films. This makes me feel proud because from our embattled position we all helped support these changes through the visibility and validation that the films achieved, especially in their exhibition abroad. However, the label of 'gay cinema' (along with prevailing homophobia) has always denied the exceptional values that these movies have as films. Few have stopped to make a serious analysis of their structures, the complex construction of their shots, etc. Previously this used to make me really angry, but now I've stopped fighting it and I prefer that Julián and I go on making films without asking anyone's permission and with the sole purpose of continuing to believe that film is an act of faith, a deeply honest one, or it is not film at all.

Recently you produced a film with the veteran Arturo Ripstein. As it is sometimes suggested that there is a generation gap between current and previous film-makers, how do you see the relationship between contemporary Mexican cinema and its predecessors?

I feel enormous respect for the cinema of the past. In fact, I'm dedicated to movies because for years I fed voraciously on images from that period and I keep learning every time I see a film by Gavaldón, Rodríguez, Zacarías, the 'Indio' Fernández, Gómez Muriel, Bolaños, Cazals, Burns, Laiter and so many others that built and still build my imagination, as they did that of so many others. We respond to a tradition and are heirs to a way of telling stories and investigating the language of film. It is our duty to know the work of distinguished veterans, but I am constantly reminded of the deep lack of knowledge about them and even the contempt in which they are held, particularly by contemporary film-makers whose models rarely have anything to do with their own tradition. I don't want to sound chauvinistic, because I am also aware of the need, and indeed the duty, of drinking deeply from other sources of film. I think only that we are uneducated in so many ways and that our level of reading and respect is minimal.

I consider my experience with Ripstein to be fundamental and highly formative. He directed movies before my parents even met. Having the privilege of learning from tradition at his side was invaluable because of his enormous generosity, his ability to listen, his highly personal and brilliant conception of film-making, and his passion for a craft that has gone through all possible production set-ups, from the most indie to the most commercial. I have tried to get close in every possible way to those other generations still living, always with satisfactory results, and sometimes, unfortunately, with much more encouraging results than with younger film-makers.

How do you understand your practice as a producer? Does it include some element of creative contribution to the film?

In addition to the administrative role that is inherent to my job, I take great interest first of all in the writing process, which I try to accompany from the time when it is just an idea until it becomes a script. When the project reaches a later stage, I make a deep structural analysis of the text and make many observations and suggestions that, in most cases, are taken into account by the writer-director. I actively participate in the precise choice of the creative team of the film, depending on the type of project, and even the genre in question, and in the casting and locations. I attach great importance to the latter two processes, perhaps because of my own background working in small crews, but also because visual values almost always translate into dramatic and production values. I oversee movies until the completion of all post-production processes and I have input into the final cut, sound design and even the advertising. The development of the poster and advertising materials seems to me one of the most exciting moments of the process, unlike the marketing. On a few occasions I have given notes on directing, but only if I find myself with a conventional and unimaginative film-maker, which has been exceptionally unusual.

Has your experience as a director influenced your work as a producer?

Certainly, I think it has made me a producer who is more sensitive to the specific problems of the director, to the deep insecurities that he has to face on a day-to-day basis, and it forces me to become an ally and not a constant and authoritarian enemy, which is how many consider the role of the producer. I have always been on the side of the film-maker, sometimes to the detriment of the demands which shape projects financially, and I try to create an atmosphere of creative freedom in all departments. I have a definition of production which sounds really tacky: 'realizing the dreams of others'. And when I direct myself, it's clear to me that that is what I expect from my producers, though I know, on the other hand, that I'm a nightmare for them.

How do you see the relationship between the auteur or art cinema to which you have devoted yourself and commercial or genre movies in Mexico?

There is a dichotomy between the two. I definitely prefer the first, and I have tried to engage myself only in projects for which I feel deep ideological, emotional and formal affinities, projects that almost always have to do with a certain auteurist vocation and avant-garde innovations or discourse and which clearly have little to do with genre movies. In other countries there is not such a vast difference as here. And our dissimilarities have serious consequences for exhibition and even the size of the financial support for different kinds of films. However, the need to build an industry leads us to ally ourselves and ponder the success of others in either of the two fields (namely box office or festivals), and often to work together and try to have input on our cultural policies. This will ultimately be to the benefit of all creators.

You recently directed a feature documentary, *Disrupted* (*Quebranto*, 2012). Do you agree that there is a rise of documentary in Mexico?

I would even say that the best movies we are shooting now are documentaries and not fiction films. We are much closer to the reality of their mode of storytelling. Unfortunately we have not found appropriate ways for these mirrors of reality to be seen by a mass audience. We can't count on the support of television or the film-exhibition chains, so most documentaries are condemned to an unjust invisibility, which is even sadder given the amount of time invested in their making, which is sometimes more than in fiction films. If we add to this the fact that some people do not even consider documentaries to be 'films', we are just piling up difficulties that stop us getting to grips with them.

What is the most serious problem facing Mexican cinema?

Distribution and exhibition. The volume of production has increased significantly thanks to government policies (in particular, fiscal stimulus), but the dubious commitment by our film distributors and the zero interest from exhibitors (and the gringo majors favoured by the North American Free Trade Agreement) in establishing a clear policy of support that respects minimally what is described in the Cinema Law and reserves screentime for Mexican cinema, all these things impede our development. There is an absolutely inequitable distribution of each peso that comes into the box office, where the most favoured person is the exhibitor. And today we are fighting a new battle: the Virtual Print Fee which has increased costs for distributors and further reduces the already slim chances of recovering investment.

And what is its greatest strength?

The other kind of cinema, the non-commercial kind, which is being promoted at festivals outside of Mexico, which emphasizes constant experimentation and is full of honest voices and innovative and forceful projects in shorts, fiction features and documentaries. I'm sure such films will always exist for the better health of our cinema.

The TV Screenwriter: Leticia López Margalli

Leticia López Margalli began screenwriting in television in 1999, when she was selected by Bernardo Romero to work as scriptwriter for *Life in the Mirror* (*La vida en el espejo*, Argos-TV Azteca). Since then she has been scriptwriter and/or co-author in various national and international productions for TV Azteca, such as *All for Love* (*Todo por amor*), *Water and Oil* (*Agua y aceite*), *While There is Life* (*Mientras haya vida*), among others; and for Telemundo, such as *The Wounded Soul* (*El alma herida*), *Broken Heart* (*Corazón partido*), *Merry Christmas* (*Feliz Navidad*), *Zapata* and *Silverado* (*Los Plateados*). She is also co-creator and writer of the series *Cappadocia* (HBO-LA/Argos TV, 2008), which was nominated for an International Emmy for Best Series, now in its second season. She is co-author of the TV series *The Aparicio Women* (*Las Aparicio*, Argos Television/Cadena 3, 2010), which was winner of five awards at the Festival FyMTI 2010 in Mar del Plata, Argentina, including Best Original Screenwriting and Best Telenovela.

What was your training like as a screenwriter and what was your first project?

Actually I studied for a BA in History and diplomas in Journalism and Publishing . . . and that was the direction of my career until a happy accident happened: a friend, a literary consultant to Argos, signed me up for an 'audition' of writers set up by Bernardo Romero (author of *A Woman's Look* [*Mirada de mujer*]) to find scriptwriters for his project at that time, *Life in the Mirror*. Interestingly, the writers selected from twenty contestants were the only two who had never written for television. The explanation Bernardo gave us at the time was that we were precisely the ones who did not have the vices typical of telenovela writers in Mexico. *Life in the Mirror* was therefore my first project, a very important and controversial telenovela, as it was the first to tackle seriously a gay subplot in Mexico. My training as a writer is, therefore, the result of my work on more than ten telenovelas, series and mini-series in which I have participated since then, and three film screenplays, one of which, *Stone Age Man* (*Hombre de piedra*, co-written with Guillermo Ríos), is currently shooting under the direction of Eugenio Derbez.

You have collaborated for many years with the independent production company Argos and Epigmenio Ibarra. How has your experience with them compared with your work with the dominant duopoly of Televisa and Azteca?

First of all, it's only fair to mention that three of the most important projects in which I participated with Argos were actually broadcast by TV Azteca: the telenovelas *Life in the Mirror*, *All for Love* (*Todo por amor*) and *While There is Life*. As for differences, since it began Argos was characterized by a novel objective in both the language and content of its telenovelas: treating controversial issues and breaking with the past in terms of politics, love and sex; the use of colloquial language in dialogues; the break with some traditional paradigms of the telenovela . . . If there is something I admire in how Epigmenio Ibarra decided to approach the telenovela, it is precisely that he took advantage of a genre that was very well known and very close to Mexican viewers to propagate a more critical vision of our country in social, political and human relations. I feel very fortunate to be part of that group of writers who had the unique opportunity of saying different things with a reasonable degree of commercial success on TV in my country, in Latin America and in other countries that have welcomed the Argos television initiative.

How do you view the Mexican press in the context of television? Is there any serious commentary on television fiction?

I must confess that I'm not well enough aware of television criticism at home to make a serious comment about it. I do know the work of Álvaro Cueva, one of the most important TV critics both in print and on television, who has generally been very complimentary about our work. But I would not make an overall judgement about the issue.

Do you see much Mexican cinema? Do the worlds of cinema and television have some contact or there is a gulf between them? Is there a convergence between aesthetics and narrative in the two media?

I love this question because it illustrates a paradox that, for me, is one of my favourite topics of discussion: are there points of convergence . . . or unbridgeable chasms between Mexican film and television? And the answer, in both cases, is yes. Mexico has traditionally equated film scriptwriting as 'serious' work, while television is seen as a 'minor genre'. However, I think both genres would be greatly enriched if they took advantage of each other's experience. At least in my experience in Argos, I think the television that we make has benefited from the resources of film narrative and aesthetics, while remaining television.

Much the same thing, in my opinion, should occur in the other direction: namely, that Mexican cinema should benefit from the experience developed by television writers in terms of closeness to the public, not to mention the thousands of hours of 'airtime' they tend to have under their belt. I can say without false modesty that the dialogues employed in many television productions by Argos (and I speak not only of mine, but also those of peers such as Guillermo Ríos, Laura Sosa, Luis Zelkowicz, Alberto Barrera, Carmen Madrid, Natassja Ybarra, Humberto Robles, Verónica Bellver, Luis Miguel Martínez and many other colleagues) are at the level of the best international drama. When both segments of the audiovisual industry recognize and appreciate each other equally, the industry as a whole could flourish as it deserves to in our country.

Unlike in the case of film, television audiences in Mexico are mostly female. Do you see special opportunities for women and even for feminism in television fiction?

I don't agree completely with the above statement, but I have no statistics at hand to refute it. I limit myself, therefore, to answering the question of whether I see special opportunities for women and feminism in television fiction. For starters, I don't think that should be a goal in itself. We didn't write *Las Aparicio* according to any feminist agenda, or even a 'female' agenda. Rather, we wrote a story attempting to be honest from our own experience about human relationships, family and love. From that experience was born, within the fictional world, a metaphor: that of a family of women on their own (in this case, widows), who have to deal with a world in which the ideal, 'what ought to be', is still the couple and the family headed by a man. But, once more, this metaphor wasn't conceived from an ideal source in some feminist agenda, but from the personal experience of the writers who undertook the project. If the result has any significance in the public or private world of our viewers (male or female), it will depend solely on them and their reality.

You created the original story of *Las Aparicio* with Verónica Bellver and you were chief co-writer with her. What was the process of writing *Las Aparicio* like and how did the coordination between the team of writers work on a daily basis?

It was delicious . . . and terrifying at the same time. *Las Aparicio* was the result of an almost magical combination between creative restlessness and historical momentum: an emerging television channel in the Mexican media scene (Cadena Tres), an independent producer (Epigmenio Ibarra) recognized for his revolutionary expertise in Mexican television . . . and two writers eager to tell a different story about women, life, family and sex. The goal: to create a new 'hybrid' format between the Latin American telenovela and the US series, which by its subject and content would constitute a television product that was different and novel.

From this unique combination, *Las Aparicio* was born first on a paper tablecloth in a café in south Mexico City, between Verónica and me; and afterwards over many sessions with the very active participation of Epigmenio himself and his wife Verónica Velasco; a consultant on issues of sexuality and psychiatry, Esther Grindberg; our literary editor, Marcela Mejía; and five more talented scriptwriters: Natassja Ybarra, Tanya Ángeles, Carmen Madrid, Laura Sosa and Luis Miguel Martínez (the only man on the team and, curiously enough, the only writer with long hair).

After the first three episodes, which Verónica Bellver and I wrote together, there followed another 117 episodes written jointly by the team described above. The dynamic was something like this: we met weekly to discuss the topic of the week and make a broad outline of what would happen in the next five episodes. Then we went to our homes, I wrote the breakdown of each chapter (i.e. the detailed description of what would happen in each of the 35–40 scenes that made up every episode), and based on that breakdown the dialogues and actions of every scene were written, finally revised and completed by Verónica and edited by Marcela Mejía. And here, I must give special recognition to a team that took upon itself a task that in the United States is done by a team of writers who usually write thirteen episodes per season . . . but in our case it was 120 episodes.

You won an award from the Women's Institute of Mexico City, and *Las Aparicio* was recognized for its innovative and daring treatment of sex and politics. How do you view the relationship between this innovation and the traditional elements of the telenovela (e.g. romance and glamour) that the series still preserves to some extent?

I don't think there is a contradiction between the two things: women can be revolutionary in terms of our view of politics, sex, family etc. and yet still be 'romantic' and 'glamorous'. It is true that *Las Aparicio* broke with the 'Cinderella' or 'female victim' paradigms of the traditional telenovela, but, at the same time, the characters were still women with all that that entails: believing in love, in relationships, allowing ourselves to be sentimental or even 'tacky' and 'glamorous' . . . without that becoming the central goal of our life, just one more element in it. And I repeat something I said when I went to accept, on behalf of the entire team of writers and producers, the Omecíhuatl Medal of the Women's Institute of Mexico City: '*Las Aparicio* is not a "feminist" story . . . Rather, it is a story about reconciliation between the sexes, the mutual recognition of our strengths and weaknesses, of the possibility of equality in relationships, love, family, sex and also in politics.'

The lesbian and anti-homophobic theme was very striking in *Las Aparicio*. Do you think it was a positive or negative element in the reception of the series?

For me, as a writer and as a member of a team that knew we were taking a risk, it is certainly a positive element. That this may have diminished the marketability and screening of the series in other countries and/or on other television networks, that's another matter. I'll speak, therefore, of what affects and concerns me: I am deeply proud to have contributed to some extent to the nurturing of a culture of equality and tolerance in a country (my country) which unfortunately is second worldwide in the rate of homophobic crimes.

Again, it is not a matter of an 'agenda': it is a vital issue (an issue of love, I'd say), of recognizing the validity of love in all its manifestations. Quite simply I don't think it's possible not to talk honestly about the theme of love and the couple without addressing homosexual or bisexual love, even so-called 'polyamory' [relationships with several partners]. And that's what we did in *Las Aparicio*, I think, in an intelligent and respectful manner. Of course, the reception of this issue varies according to the viewer: there were those who hated it and those who loved it. Personally, I prefer the response of a mass of guys and girls to the question: 'What effect did *Las Aparicio* have on you?' They responded with hundreds of pictures of themselves that were broadcast in the final episode: photos that spoke of pride, acceptance, self-love. These testimonies, for me, can only be positive.

In developing the series through its 120 chapters, you incorporated suggestions from the public made on the internet. How did that process work?

This was another of the beautiful things brought to me and to the team of writers by the public: for the first time, at least in my experience, we had online interaction through social networks with the audience that was watching us. And it was an extraordinarily active public. While watching the transmission of each episode on the air, we were connected with Facebook and Twitter, reading the comments posted second by second by our followers (including comments on the commercials). I have not seen a more active audience since then. Today, nearly two years after the end of the broadcast, the Facebook page is more or less active. And this, at the time of writing, naturally influenced the route followed by the story and its characters. Of course it was impossible to provide an immediate response to each of the concerns expressed there, since, at the end of the day, we were writing thirty to forty chapters ahead of what was shown on the air, but it was critically important for the final course of the story.

Las Aparicio **was something like a combination of a series in the US style and a Latin American serial (telenovela). How do you view the differences between these two formats?**

When we pitched the series to the television executives, interestingly, a sentence was included saying something like: 'The up-to-date-ness of the US series, the irreverence of the Brazilian TV series and the intimacy of Mexican melodrama are found in . . .' etc. That was the initial challenge of *Las Aparicio* in creating this kind of 'hybrid format' that began with our show: drawing on the narrative resources and contemporary discourse of the US series, with the humour and sexual freedom of the Brazilians, in a format that was well known and close to the sensibilities of not only Mexico but also Latin America in general: the telenovela. The enormous difficulty of meeting this challenge, of course, lay in the difference in formats: how to incorporate the kind of narrative designed for a series of thirteen stand-alone episodes per season into a serialized format of 120 episodes? How to address issues in a contemporary way without ignoring that tradition of Mexican melodrama which is so much our own?

As to whether we did or did not meet those goals, I leave that to the judgement of the people who followed us . . . but that was what we intended and I think it was enriching for our TV. And at this point I think that we could talk about a kind of syncretism between US and Latin American television: in my opinion, shows like *Desperate Housewives* and *Grey's Anatomy* are incorporating resources from the Latin American telenovela into the fabric of their stories, giving prominence to the continuing love stories of their characters (or 'romances'), at the same time as they develop the action of stand-alone episodes. I do not know if this trend is real or I'm imagining it, whether it's intentional or not (perhaps in response to the growing presence of Latinos among the US audience), but that's my perception.

What is the most serious problem facing Mexican television?

Its lack of confidence in itself. Its fear of venturing into new formats or revolutionary themes, for fear of losing its audience. In this sense, Mexican television currently leans mightily on adaptations of proven formulas (from the US or from other countries in Latin America), forgetting that at one time the original productions of our country were spearheading those of the whole continent. The small number of original products, compared with the adaptations of telenovelas made in Brazil, Chile and Argentina, demonstrates this. The paradox is that Mexican producers complain that there are not enough competent writers in our country. But how can anyone know if there are or not if writers are not given the opportunity to develop original stories?

And what is Mexican television's greatest strength?

And here's another paradox: its strongest point is tradition. This know-how that comes from the fifty years of tradition that turned it into the most important Spanish-speaking television of its time. If that tradition were combined with innovation and a willingness to take risks, Mexican television could occupy a vital place at a global level.

(All the interviews took place in 2012 and were translated from the original Spanish by the author.)

Bibliography

20 minutos (2006) 'El laberinto del fauno', http://www.20minutos.es/cine/
cartelera/pelicula/28455/el-laberinto-del-fauno/; accessed 19 August 2010
20 minutos (2010) 'Serie mexicana favorita', http://listas.20minutos.es/lista/
serie-mexicana-favorita-257741/; accessed 8 May 2012
AfterEllen (2010) 'Interview with Eréndira Ibarra of *Las Aparicio*', http://
www.afterellen.com/people/2010/4/erendira-ibarra-interview; accessed 7
May 2012
Aguilar, Carlos (1999) *Cine fantástico y de terror español: 1900–1983* (San
Sebastián, Donostia Kultura)
Aguilar, Carlos (2005) *Cine fantástico y de terror español: 1984–2004* (San
Sebastián, Donostia Kultura)
AM [staff] (2011) 'Terminan *Mujeres asesinas* su ciclo', http://www.am.com
.mx/Nota.aspx?ID=503528; accessed 6 May 2012
Amoroso, Sebastián (2010) 'Detrás de cámaras de *Las Aparicio*', http://
www.todotvnews.com/scripts/templates/estilo_nota.asp?tipo=ultima%20
seccion&nota=nuevo/Producci%F3n/Contenidos/2010/04_abril/26
_novela_las_aparicio_argos_telemundo; accessed 7 May 2012
Las Aparicio (2012) Official website: http://www.lasaparicio.com/; accessed
7 May 2012
Arellano M., J. Fabián (2011a) 'Con el sello mexicano las series rosas tras-
pasan las fronteras', http://www.eluniversal.com.mx/espectaculos/104573
.html; accessed 8 May 2012
Arellano M., J. Fabián (2011b) 'Destacará *La teniente* labor de la marina',
http://www.eluniversal.com.mx/notas/788219.html; accessed 8 May 2012
Argos (2011) http://argostv.com/; accessed 10 April 2011
Arroyo Quiroz, Claudia, James Ramey and Michael Schussler (2011)
'Introducción: Una coherencia imaginaria: reflexiones desde México sobre
el concepto de *cine nacional*', in *México imaginado: nuevos enfoques*

sobre el cine (trans)nacional (Mexico City, Universidad Autónoma Metropolitana), pp. 9–28

Artes de Mexico (2001) Special issue: 'Revisión del cine mexicano'

Arvizu, Juan (2007) 'Mataba a una viejita cada mes', http://www.eluniversal.com.mx/ciudad/82080.html; accessed 6 May 2012

Ayala Blanco, Jorge (2001) *La fugacidad del cine mexicano* (Mexico City, Océano)

Azaola, Elena (1996) *El delito de ser mujer* (Mexico City, Plaza y Valdés)

Azteca (2010) *Drenaje profundo* (official site), http://www.tvazteca.com/drenaje-profundo; accessed 8 May 2012

Baños, Sugher (2011) 'Laura fomenta la violencia contra las mujeres', http://www.eluniversal.com.mx/espectaculos/109248.html; accessed 6 May 2012

Becerra Pino, Hernán de Jesús (1986) 'La imagen del cine mexicano sobre las bandas juveniles en la ciudad de México' [thesis]. Cineteca classmark: TE F45(72) B43

Benavides, O. Hugo (2008) *Drugs, Thugs, and Divas: Telenovelas and Narco-Dramas in Latin America* (Austin, University of Texas Press)

Berthier, Nancy (2007) 'Crítica cinematográfica y nacionalidad', in Nancy Berthier and Jean Claude Seguin (eds), *Cine, nación, y nacionalidades en España* (Madrid, Casa de Velásquez), pp. 11–24

Bonfil, Carlos (2010a) 'Convivio: el estado de las artes: cine', http://www.letraslibres.com/revista/convivio/cine?page=0,0; accessed 7 May 2012

Bonfil, Carlos (2010b) 'El infierno', http://www.jornada.unam.mx/2010/09/05/espectaculos/a08a1esp; accessed 7 May 2012

Bourdieu, Pierre (1996) *The Rules of Art* (Cambridge, Polity)

Braham, Persephone (2004) *Crimes against the State, Crimes against Persons: Detective Fiction in Cuba and Mexico* (Minneapolis, University of Minnesota)

Buonanno, Milly (2008) *The Age of Television* (London, Intellect)

Caballero, Jorge (2010) '*Gritos de muerte y libertad* muestra a los héroes "como realmente eran"', http://www.jornada.unam.mx/2010/08/18/espectaculos/a08n1esp; accessed 8 May 2012

Cabañas, Miguel A. (2008) 'El narcocorrido global y los identidades transnacionales', in Lander (2008), pp. 519–42

Cahiers du Cinéma (2011) 'Supplément: cinéma mexicain', Charles Tesson (ed.), 664 (February)

Cano, Natalia (2006) 'Hoy se gradúan Los Rebeldes', http://www.eluniversal.com.mx/espectaculos/70134.html; accessed 2 May 2012

Cano, Natalia (2007) 'Christian Chávez, una rebelde confesión', http://www.eluniversal.com.mx/nacion/149159.htm; accessed 2 May 2012

Castañeda, Roberto G. (2011) 'Facebook es un pésimo cupido', http://candidman.blogspot.com/2011/03/facebook-es-un-pesimo-cupido.html#.T6fWglG5M_s; accessed 7 May 2012

Cerrilla Noriega, Mariana (2011) 'La opción de elegir', *CineToma*, 14, pp. 38–41; http://issuu.com/josebernechea/docs/cine_toma_17a; accessed 2 May 2012

Cervera, Antonio (1968) *Índice analítico del cine fantástico* (Sitges, Semana Internacional de Cine)

Chilango (2011) 'Manual del buen chilango' [special supplement] (September)

christianchaveztv (2011) 'Libertad' [pop promo], http://www.youtube.com/watch?v=_pj1s79M3PE; accessed 2 May 2012

Cinencuentro (2009) ' "Hago las películas que quiero hacer": una entrevista con Julián Hernández', http://www.cinencuentro.com/2009/08/31/hago-las-peliculas-que-quiero-hacer-entrevista-julian-hernandez/; accessed 30 May 2012

Clover, Carol (1993) *Men, Women, and Chainsaws: Gender in the Modern Horror Film* (Princeton, Princeton University Press)

Clubcultura (2006) 'El laberinto del fauno: sinopsis', www.clubcultura.com/clubcine/clubcineastas/guillermodeltoro/ellaberintodelfauno/sinopsis.htm; accessed 19 August 2010

Cómo Hacer Cine (2004) 'Mil nubes de paz . . . de Julián Hernández', 26 February, http://www.comohacercine.com/articulo.php?id_art=582&id_cat=3; accessed 19 October 2008

Cook, Beverley Richard (2010) 'Jungian Archetypes in Guillermo del Toro's *El laberinto del fauno*', http://congreso.cgjung.cl/pdf/cursos/mesas_redondas_congreso/C12%20Cook,%20B.%20R..pdf; accessed 19 August 2010

Cortázar, Julio (2012) 'Casa tomada', http://www.literatura.us/cortazar/tomada.html; accessed 12 May 2012

Cruz, Ángel (2005) 'RBD impone su estilo de moda', http://www2.eluniversal.com.mx/pls/impreso/noticia.html?id_nota=23624&tabla=primera; accessed 2 May 2012

Cueva, Álvaro (2011) 'Crítica a *Drenaje profundo*: el pozo de los deseos reprimidos', http://www.alvarocueva.com/alvaro_cueva2011/articulo_detalle.php?IdArticulo=3155; accessed 8 May 2012

Curiel Ochoa, Sara Eny (2003) 'Algunas recomendaciones para fomentar el consumo de cine de arte en los jóvenes' [thesis]. Cineteca classmark: TE F33-053.672 C87

Dargis, Manohla (2004) Review of *A Thousand Clouds*, http://www.calendarlive.com/movies/dargis/cl-et-clouds16apr16,0,4358774.story; accessed 19 October 2008

de Valck, Marijke (2008) *Film Festivals: From European Geopolitics to Global Cinephilia* (Amsterdam: University of Amsterdam)

Derrida, Jacques (1998) *Of Grammatology* (Baltimore: Johns Hopkins University Press)

Díaz Moreno, Eva (2011) 'Telenovelas en México cavan su tumba', http://www.excelsior.com.mx/index.php?m=nota&buscado=1&id_nota=731618; accessed 7 May 2012

Directorio Producción (2010–11) http://issuu.com/todotvnews/docs/d_pro_2011; accessed 6 May 2012

DRAE (2012) *Diccionario de la Real Academia Española* s.v. revisionismo. Online at: http://buscon.rae.es/drael/. Accessed 30 May 2012.

Durand, Nayeli (2010) 'Paty Garza trabaja en serie policiaca', http://www.eluniversal.com.mx/espectaculos/100261.html; accessed 8 May 2012

Economist (2011) 'The Cartel Problem', http://www.economist.com/ node/21526896; accessed 12 May 2012

Economist (2012) 'Poverty, Inequality, and Redistribution', http://www .economist.com/blogs/graphicdetail/2012/01/focus-2; accessed 12 May 2012

Edwards, Kim (2008) 'Alice's Little Sister: Exploring *Pan's Labyrinth*', *Screen Education*, 49, pp. 141–6

EFE (2011) 'Telenovelas, ante el reto de llegar a público joven', http://www .eluniversal.com.mx/notas/806894.html; accessed 2 May 2012

El efecto tequila (2011) http://www.elefectotequila.com.mx/; accessed 10 April 2011

Evans, Peter W. (1982) 'The Monster, the Place of the Father, and Growing Up in the Dictatorship', *Vida Hispánica*, 31.3, pp. 13–17

Excelsior [staff] (2010) 'Las Aparicio: listas para el cine', http://www .excelsior.com.mx/index.php?m=nota&seccion=funcion&cat=3&id_nota =794700&photo=3; accessed 7 May 2012

Excelsior [staff] (2011) 'De la Garza dará taller de sexualidad', http://www .excelsior.com.mx/index.php?m=nota&buscado=1&id_nota=714902; accessed 7 May 2012

Fernández Fernández, José Antonio (2000) 'Entrevista con Epigmenio Ibarra', http://www.canal100.com.mx/telemundo/entrevistas/?id_nota=1199; accessed 7 May 2012

Franco Reyes, Salvador (2009) 'Gerardo Naranjo desafía a todos', *Excelsior*, 19 June, Función, p. 8

Fundación Televisa (2012) 'Si yo puedo, tú también', http://www .fundaciontelevisa.org/salud/anahi-contra-la-bulimia-y-anorexia.html; accessed 3 May 2012

Gant, Charles (2009) 'Do the "Right" Thing: European Horror at UK Box Office', *Sight & Sound* (June), p. 9

García Tsao, Leonardo (2011) 'Reír para no llorar' [review of *Saving Private Pérez*], http://www.jornada.unam.mx/2011/04/08/espectaculos/a11a1esp; accessed 7 May 2012

Garrido, Luis Javier (2010) 'La deshonra', http://www.jornada.unam .mx/2010/09/10/opinion/022a2pol; accessed 8 May 2012

Golem (no date [2004]) 'Mil nubes de paz cercan el cielo, amor, jamás acabarás de ser amor: Entrevista con el director Julián Hernández', http://www.golemproducciones.com/prod/milnubes.htm; accessed 30 May 2012

González Vargas, Carla (2006) *Rutas del cine mexicano 1990–2006* (Mexico City, CONACULTA IMCINE/Landucci)

Grabe, Maria Elizabeth (1999) 'Television News Magazine Crime Stories', *Critical Studies in Mass Communication*, 16.2, pp. 155–71

Guider, Elizabeth (2010) 'Telemundo Bowing Novela on Digital Platforms', http://www.hollywoodreporter.com/news/telemundo-bowing-novela -digital-platforms-25110; accessed 7 May 2012

Gutiérrez, Natalia (2010) 'Rosa Clará llega, por fin, a Masaryk', http://www .eluniversal.com.mx/estilos/67242.html; accessed 7 May 2012

260   *Bibliography*

Guzmán, Alejandro (2010) 'El éxito de *Mujeres asesinas 2* no conoce fronteras', http://televisa.esmas.com/entretenimiento/programastv/mujeres-asesinas/noticias/137335/mujeres-asesinas-2-rompe-record-televidentes-estados-unidos; accessed 6 May 2012

Hecht, John (2011) '*Post Mortem*, *The Prize* Take Home Top Honours at Guadalajara Film Fest', http://www.hollywoodreporter.com/news/post-mortem-prize-take-top-174022 1 April; accessed 10 April 2011

Hinojosa Córdova, Lucila (2003) *El cine mexicano: de lo global a lo local* (Mexico City, Trillas)

Holden, Stephen (2004) Review of *A Thousand Clouds*, http://query.nytimes.com/gst/fullpage.html?res=9C05E6DE153BF935A25757C0A9629C8B63; accessed 19 October 2008

Holden, Stephen (2009) Review of *I'm Gonna Explode*, http://movies.nytimes.com/2009/08/14/movies/14gonna.html; accessed 3 May 2012

Ibarra, Epigmenio (2010) 'Carta a Felipe Calderón', http://www.milenio.com/cdb/doc/impreso/9076304; accessed 7 May 2012

IBOPE (2009) *Anuario Media Performance 2009*, https://www.ibopeagb.com.mx/biblioteca/anuario.php; accessed 8 May 2012

IBOPE (2010) 'Highlights del Media Performance 2010', https://www.ibopeagb.com.mx/biblioteca/anuario.php; accessed 8 May 2012

IMCINE (2010) *Anuario estadístico de cine mexicano* (Mexico City, IMCINE)

IMCINE (2011a) *Anuario estadístico de cine mexicano* (Mexico City, IMCINE)

IMCINE (2011b) 'Películas', http://www.imcine.gob.mx/peliculas/84.html; accessed 19 August 2011

I'm Gonna Explode (2009) *Pressbook* (London, Artificial Eye)

El Imparcial [staff] (2010) 'Asesina a su novio por seguro', http://www.elimparcial.com/EdicionEnLinea/Notas/Nacional/06012010/422556.aspx; accessed 6 May 2012

Informador [staff] (2010) 'María Rojo será "asesina" de nuevo', http://www.informador.com.mx/entretenimiento/2010/206244/6/maria-rojo-sera-asesina-de-nuevo.htm; accessed 6 May 2012

Informador (2011) 'Billy Rovzar confía en Internet para difundir *Salvando al soldado Pérez*', http://www.informador.com.mx/entretenimiento/2011/278275/6/billy-rovzar-confia-en-internet-para-difundir-Saving-al-soldado-perez.htm; accessed 7 May 2012

Internet Movie Database (IMDb) (2010) 'Pan's Labyrinth', http://www.imdb.com/title/tt0457430/; accessed 19 August 2010

Jamieson, Patrick E. and Daniel Romer (eds) (2008) *The Changing Portrayal of Adolescents in the Media since 1950* (Oxford, New York, Oxford University Press)

Johnson, G. Allen (2004) Review of *A Thousand Clouds*, http://www.sfgate.com/cgi-bin/article.cgi?f=/c/a/2004/04/02/DDGNQ5UN8U1.DTL#clouds; accessed 19 October 2008

La Jornada [staff] (2004) 'En México se teme reconocer la homosexualidad: Julián Hernández', http://www.jornada.unam.mx/2004/10/

17/20an1esp.php?origen=espectaculos.php&fly=1; accessed 19 October 2008

JuárezDialoga [staff] (2011) 'Justicia para Canelita, que no quede impune su muerte', http://juarezdialoga.org/noticias/justicia-para-canelita-que-no -quede-impune-su-muerte/; accessed 7 May 2012

Kermode, Mark (2006) 'Girl Interrupted', *Sight & Sound* (December), www .bfi.org.uk/sightandsound/feature/49337/; accessed 19 August 2010

Koehler, Robert (2011), Review of *Moon Rain/Lluvia de luna* at Guadalajara Film Fest 30 March, http://www.variety.com/review/VE1117944929? refcatid=31; accessed 10 April 2011

Labanyi, Jo (2010) 'Coming to Terms with Ghosts and Spectrality in Contemporary Spanish Culture', http://arachne.rutgers.edu/vol1_1labanyi .htm; accessed 19 August 2010

Lander, María Fernanda (ed.) (2008) 'Narcogeografías', Special Issue of *Revista de Estudios Hispánicos*, 42

Letras Libres (2008) October issue

López Martínez, María Teresa (2001) 'Los jóvenes vistos por el cine mexicano en la actualidad' [thesis]. Cineteca classmark TE F45-053 6(72) L66

Lozano, Jesús Mario (2011) '*Mexican cinema vs. cinéma mexicain*: notas en torno a lo posible del cine y lo mexicano en el imposible cine mexicano actual', in Claudia Arroyo Quiroz et al. (eds), *México imaginado: nuevos enfoques sobre el cine (trans)nacional* (Mexico City, Universidad Autónoma Metropolitana), pp. 265–82

Luna, José Luis (2006) 'Jesús Mario Lozano: porqué *Así* lo dice él', http:// cineralia.blogspot.com/2006/09/jess-mario-lozano-por-que-as-lo-dice-l .html; accessed 30 May 2012

Madrigal, Álex (2010a) '*Las Aparicio* hablarán sin tapujos', http://www .eluniversal.com.mx/espectaculos/97898.html; accessed 7 May 2012

Madrigal, Álex (2010b) 'Libre y sin miedo', http://www.eluniversal.com.mx/ espectaculos/100097.html; accessed 7 May 2012

Madrigal, Álex (2010c) 'TV Azteca busca el éxito en el *Drenaje profundo*', http://www.eluniversal.com.mx/espectaculos/100650.html; accessed 8 May 2012

Madrigal, Álex (2010d) 'El lado bueno de la policía', http://www.eluniversal .com.mx/espectaculos/100817.html; accessed 8 May 2012

Martín Barbero, Jesús (1992) *Televisión y melodrama* (Bogotá, Tercer Mundo)

Martín Barbero, Jesús (2012) 'La telenovela en Colombia: televisión, melo-drama, y vida cotidiana', http://www.dialogosfelafacs.net/wp-content/ uploads/2012/01/17-revista-dialogos-la-telenovela-en-colombia.pdf; accessed 6 May 2012

Matellano, Víctor (2009) *Spanish Horror* (Madrid, T&B)

Milenio [staff] (2008) 'Gerardo Naranjo se estrena en Venecia', http://www .milenio.com/cdb/doc/impreso/8100103; accessed 3 May 2012

Milenio [staff] (2010) 'El amor es su preferencia', http://www.milenio.com/ edicion-impresa?page=30300&%253F=lhxvjujoyipx; accessed 7 May 2012

Millán, Francisco Javier (2006) *Entre la inocencia y la rebeldía: infancia y juventud en el cine latinoamericano* (León, Guanajuato, Fundación Expresión en Corto)

Miller, Toby et al. (2001) *Global Hollywood* (London, BFI)

Ministerio de Cultura (2010) 'Base de datos', www.mcu.es/cine/CE/BBDD Peliculas/BBDDPeliculas_Index.html; accessed 19 August 2010

Miranda Duarte, Héctor (1999) 'La imagen del cine industrial mexicano sobre la juventud de 1960–69' [thesis]. Cineteca classmark: TE F46"1060-69" M57

Miranda López, Raúl (2006) *Del quinto poder al séptimo arte: la producción fílmica de Televisa* (Mexico City, Conaculta)

Miss Bala (2011) *Pressbook* (London, Metrodome)

Molina Ramírez, Tania (2008) 'En *Voy a explotar* hablo sobre qué es la rebeldía en la actualidad: Gerardo Naranjo', http://www.jornada.unam .mx/2008/09/01/index.php?section=espectaculos&article=a17n1esp; accessed 2 May 2012

Mujeresaseinas [fan forum] (2012) http://mujeresasesinasmex.mejorforo .net/; accessed 6 May 2012

Mun2 (2011a) '*Las Aparicio*: Press Release', http://www.nbcumv.com/ mediavillage/networks/mun2/lasaparicio/pressreleases?pr=contents/press -releases/2011/03/31/mun2announcesus1301617142343.xml; accessed 7 May 2012

Mun2 (2011b) *Las Aparicio*: Synopsis, http://www.mun2.tv/shows/las -aparicio/las-aparicio-catemaco-curse-episode-1; accessed 7 May 2012

Mun2 (2011c) *Las Aparicio*: Synopsis, http://www.mun2.tv/shows/las -aparicio/las-aparicio-labels-episode-26; accessed 7 May 2012

Network 54 (2010) Fan forums on *Drenaje profundo*, http://www.network54 .com/Search/?term=drenaje+profundo&page=10; accessed 8 May 2012

Newman, Kim (2009) 'Horror will Eat Itself', *Sight & Sound* (May), pp. 36–8

Noble, Andrea (2005) *Mexican National Cinema* (London, Routledge)

OBITEL (2011) *Quality in Television Fiction and Audiences' Transmedia Interactions*, http://obitel.net/; accessed 8 May 2012

O'Donnell, Hugh (1996a) 'People's Home to Home and Away: The Growth and Development of Soap Opera in Sweden', http://dit.ie/icr/media/diticr/ documents/7%20O%20Donnell%20ICR%20Vol%206.pdf; accessed 6 May 2012

O'Donnell, Hugh (1996b) 'From a Manichean World View to the Kitchen Sink', *International Journal of Iberian Studies*, 9, pp. 7–18

O'Donnell, Hugh (2007) 'High Drama, Low Key: Visual Aesthetics and Subject Positions in the Domestic Spanish Television Serial', *Journal of Spanish Cultural Studies*, 8, pp. 37–54

Olivares, Juan José (2009) '*Voy a explotar* se exhibirá en la Berlinale', http:// www.jornada.unam.mx/2009/01/15/index.php?section=espectaculos&art icle=a08n2esp; accessed 2 May 2012

Olivares, Juan José y Agencias (2008) 'Conciliar el cine de festivales y el público, lo ideal: Gerardo Naranjo', *La Jornada*, 30 July, Espectáculos, p. 8

Olivares Alonso, Emir (2010) 'Plagada de inconsistencias, la serie *Gritos de muerte y libertad*: experto', http://www.jornada.unam.mx/2010/09/15/politica/009n2pol; accessed 8 May 2012

Oren, Tasha and Sharon Shahaf (eds) (2012) *Global Television Formats: Understanding Television Across Borders* (London and New York, Routledge)

Orozco Gómez, Guillermo (1996) *Televisión y audiencias: un enfoque cualitativo* (Madrid, De la Torre)

Orozco Gómez, Guillermo (2001a) 'Audiencias, televisión, y educación: una deconstrucción pedagógica de la "televidencia" y sus mediaciones', http://www.rieoei.org/rie27a07.PDF; accessed 2 May 2012

Orozco Gómez, Guillermo (2001b) *Televisión, audiencias, y educación* (Buenos Aires, Norma)

Orozco Gómez, Guillermo (2006) 'La telenovela en México: ¿de una expresión cultural a un simple producto para la mercadotecnia?', http://publicaciones.cucsh.udg.mx/pperiod/comsoc/pdf/2006_6/11-35.pdf; accessed 2 May 2012

Orozco, Guillermo et al. (2011) 'Mexico: "Mexicanos al grito de guerra . . ." also in fiction [*sic*]', in OBITEL (2011), pp. 279–307

Polit-Dueñas, Gabriela (2008) 'On Reading about Violence, Drug Dealers and Interpreting a Field of Literary Production Amidst the Din of Gunfire: Culiacán – Sinaloa, 2007', in Lander (2008), pp. 559–82

Potter, W. James (2008) 'Adolescents and Television Violence', in Jamieson and Romer (2008), pp. 221–49

Premiere [staff] (2010) 'Veto a actores de *Las Aparicio*', http://www.cinepremiere.com.mx/node/11535; accessed 7 May 2010

Ramírez, Andrés (2010) 'Telenoveleando la Independencia', http://www.eluniversal.com.mx/espectaculos/100728.html; accessed 8 May 2012

Ramos, Pablo (2010) '*Las Aparicio*, ¿una apuesta perdida?, http://www.eluniversal.com.mx/columnas/83538.html; accessed 7 May 2012

RBD Sitio Oficial (2011) http://www2.esmas.com/rbd/index.php; accessed 2 May 2012

Reguillo, Rossana (2008) 'Las múltiples fronteras de la violencia: jóvenes latinoamericanos frente a la precarización y del desencanto', http://www.pensamientoiberoamericano.org/articulos/3/84/0/las-m-ltiples-fronteras-de-la-violencia-j-venes-latinoamericanos-entre-la-precarizaci-n-y-el-desencanto.html; accessed 8 May 2012

Rodríquez, Martín Diego (2007) '*Voy a explotar*, denuncia sobre la doble moral de los políticos', *La Jornada*, 18 August, Espectáculos, p. 8

Rodríguez González, Adriana (2004) '*Rebelde* presentará la vida de niñas bien', http://www2.eluniversal.com.mx/pls/impreso/noticia.html?id_nota=56333&tabla=espectaculos; accessed 2 May 2012

Rodríguez Pardo, José Manuel (2007) 'El inverosímil *Laberinto del fauno*', www.nodulo.org/ec/2007/n067p14.htm; accessed 19 August 2010

Rohde-Brown, Juliet (2007) Review of *Pan's Labyrinth*, *Psychological Perspectives*, 50.1 (January), pp. 167–9

Rosenberg, Tina (2011) 'To Beat Back Poverty, Pay the Poor', http://opinionator.blogs.nytimes.com/2011/01/03/to-beat-back-poverty-pay-the-poor/; accessed 7 May 2012

Segal, Timothy (2009) '*Pan's Labyrinth*: A Subjective View on Childhood Fantasies and the Nature of Evil', *International Review of Psychiatry*, 21.3 (June), pp. 269–70

Shaw, Deborah (2011) '*Babel* and the Global Hollywood Gaze', *Situations* 4.1, http://ojs.gc.cuny.edu/index.php/situations/article/view/742/1203; accessed 30 April 2012

Silva G., Gustavo (2009) 'Pedro Torres llevará *Mujeres asesinas* a EU', http://www.eluniversal.com.mx/espectaculos/93551.html; accessed 6 May 2012

Silva G., Gustavo (2010) 'El Iturbide de Giménez Cacho no está esculpido en bronce', http://www.eluniversal.com.mx/espectaculos/100420.html; accessed 8 May 2012

Smith, Paul Julian (2003) *Amores perros* (London, British Film Institute)

Smith, Paul Julian (2007) '*Pan's Labyrinth (El laberinto del fauno)*', *Film Quarterly*, 60.4, pp. 4–9

Smith, Paul Julian (2009a) Review of *I'm Gonna Explode*, http://sites.google.com/site/pauljuliansmithfilmreviews/Home/voy-a-explotar-i-m-gonna-explode-july-2009; accessed 2 May 2012

Smith, Paul Julian (2009b) *Spanish Screen Fiction: Between Cinema and Television* (Liverpool, Liverpool University Press)

Smith, Paul Julian (2012) 'Transnational Cinemas: The Cases of Mexico, Argentina, and Brazil', in Lúcia Nagib et al. (eds), *Theorizing World Cinema* (London, New York, I. B. Tauris), pp. 63–76

Solís, Ricardo (2011) 'No se puede negociar con la imagen de mi padre' [interview with El Hijo del Santo], *Días de Cine: Suplemento de la Jornada Jalisco*, 29 March, p. 4

Solórzano, Fernanda (2010) 'El infierno, de Luis Estrada', http://www.letraslibres.com/revista/artes-y-medios/el-infierno-de-luis-estrada; accessed 7 May 2012

Stern, Susannah and Jane D. Brown (2008) 'From Twin Beds to Sex at Your Fingertips: Teen Sex in Movies, Music, Television, and the Internet', in Jamieson and Romer (2008), pp. 313–46

Tavira, Alberto (2009) '*Mujeres asesinas* arrasa rating y ventas', http://www.cnnexpansion.com/expansion/2009/10/28/La-muerte-le-sienta-bien; accessed 6 May 2012

Tolosa, Víctor M. (2011) 'Aciertos y errores de la TV', http://www.excelsior.com.mx/index.php?m=nota&buscado=1&id_nota=700534; accessed 7 May 2012

Torres San Martín, Patricia (2011) *Cine, género, y jóvenes: el cine mexicano contemporáneo y su audiencia tapatía* (Guadalajara, Universidad de Guadalajara)

Triana Toribio, Nuria (2003) *Spanish National Cinema* (London, Routledge)

Tuckman, Jo (2006) 'The Lady Killer', http://www.guardian.co.uk/world/2006/may/19/gender.mexico; accessed 6 May 2012

Tuñón, Julia (1998) *Mujeres de luz y sombra en el cine mexicano: la construcción de una imagen (1939–52)* (Mexico City, Colegio de México and IMCINE)

Tuñón, Julia (2008) *Enjaular los cuerpos: normativas decimonónicas y feminidad en México* (Mexico City, Colegio de México)

Ulloa, Aída (2006) 'Rebelde resultó un fenómeno muy redituable', http://www.eluniversal.com.mx/guiaocio/8842.html; accessed 2 May 2012

El Universal [staff] (2006) 'Mueren fans de RBD en Brasil', http://www2.eluniversal.com.mx/pls/impreso/noticia.html?id_nota=68139&tabla=espectaculos_h; accessed 2 May 2012

El Universal [staff] (2010a) 'Julio Bracho quiere ser Zapata', http://www.eluniversal.com.mx/notas/705545.html; accessed 8 May 2012

El Universal [staff] (2010b) 'El Pípila es un mito fundacional', http://www.eluniversal.com.mx/notas/707581.html; accessed 8 May 2012

Vanguardia [staff] (2009) 'Mujeres asesinas hace versión libre', http://www.vanguardia.com.mx/mujeres_asesinas_hace_version_libre-344208.html; accessed 6 May 2012

Vanguardia [staff] (2010a) 'Las Aparicio será uno de varios proyectos', http://www.vanguardia.com.mx/lasaparicioseraunodevariosproyectos-467283.html; accessed 7 May 2012

Vanguardia [staff] (2010b) 'Las Aparicio, mujeres a la conquista', http://www.vanguardia.com.mx/lasapariciomujeresalaconquista-489824.html; accessed 7 May 2012

Vargas, Juan Carlos (ed.) (2011) *Tendencias del cine iberoamericano en el nuevo milenio* (Guadalajara, Universidad de Guadalajara)

Vargas Cervantes, Susana (2010) 'Performing *Mexicanidad*: Criminality and *Lucha Libre*', *Crime, Media, Culture*, 6.2, pp. 185–203

Vázquez, Luis Bernardo Jaime (2004) 'Hernández y la prisión del deseo', http://www.elojoquepiensa.udg.mx/espanol/numero01/cinejournal/02_hernandez.html; accessed 19 October 2008

Vega Montiel, Aimée (2012) 'Las Aparicio y El sexo débil, ¿una apuesta por la igualdad de género?', http://rotativo.com.mx/reginacantu/las-aparicio-y-el-sexo-debil-una-apuesta-por-la-igualdad-de-genero/52001/print/; accessed 7 May 2012

Weissberg, Jay (2008) Review of *I'm Gonna Explode*, http://www.variety.com/review/VE1117938195/; accessed 2 May 2012

Wikipedia (2012) Episode guide to *Rebelde*, http://es.wikipedia.org/wiki/Anexo:Episodios_de_Rebel; accessed 28 January 2012

Wood, Jason (2006) *The Faber Book of Mexican Cinema* (London, Faber and Faber)

Yahoo (2010) 'El tango de *Las Aparicio*', http://mx.answers.yahoo.com/question/index?qid=20100605170602AAxrWG2; accessed 7 May 2012

Zonadiversa (2012) 'Julián Hernández: homoerotismo en la gran pantalla', http://www.zonadiversa.com/entrevistas/23-julian-hernandez-homoerotismo-en-la-gran-pantalla; accessed 30 April 2012

Index

Note: page numbers in *bold* refer to illustrations.